Albrecht Dürer (German, 1471-1528), Philipp Melanchthon, 1526, engraving, Rosenwald Collection.

The Honeycomb Scroll

The Honeycomb Scroll

Philipp Melanchthon at the Dawn of the Reformation

Gregory B. Graybill

Fortress Press
Minneapolis

THE HONEYCOMB SCROLL

Philipp Melanchthon at the Dawn of the Reformation

Copyright © 2015 Fortress Press. All rights reserved. Except for brief quotations in critical articles or reviews, no part of this book may be reproduced in any manner without prior written permission from the publisher. Visit http://www.augsburgfortress.org/copyrights/ or write to Permissions, Augsburg Fortress, Box 1209, Minneapolis, MN 55440.

Cover image: Philipp Melanchthon/World History/Super Stock

Cover design: Laurie Ingram

Library of Congress Cataloging-in-Publication Data

Print ISBN: 978-1-4514-9704-5

eBook ISBN: 978-1-5064-0045-7

The paper used in this publication meets the minimum requirements of American National Standard for Information Sciences — Permanence of Paper for Printed Library Materials, ANSI Z329.48-1984.

Manufactured in the U.S.A.

This book was produced using PressBooks.com, and PDF rendering was done by PrinceXML.

Contents

	Acknowledgments	ix
	Abbreviations	xi
	Maps	xiii
	Introduction	1
1.	Wars and Rumors of Wars	7
2.	The Armorer 1459–1493	27
3.	A Bride from Bretten 1493–1508	35
4.	The Passing of the Age 1493–1508	49
5.	A Time to Mourn 1493–1508	61
6.	Pforzheim 1508–1509	77
7.	Heidelberg 1509–1512	95

8.	Tübingen 1512–1518	115
9.	Wittenberg 1518–1519	145
10.	All In. The Wittenberg Movement 1519–1520	179
11.	Wedding Bells and Papal Bulls 1520–1521	201
12.	Taking a Stand 1521	229
13.	Bounding the Fire 1521–1522	249
14.	Old Testament Dreams 1522	265
15.	Homecoming 1522–1524	289
16.	Epilogue	321
	Bibliography	339
	Index of Names and Subjects	355
	Index of Biblical References	369

Acknowledgments

I give thanks to God, to whom all praise is ever due.

I am grateful also to everyone at Global Scholars (especially Margaret Nichols), and to the Fulbright Commission, which funded me during the academic year 2012-13 to conduct research for this book at the European Melanchthon Academy in Bretten, Germany (Melanchthon's birthplace). Thank you to Carolin Weingart-Ridoutt at the German Fulbright Commission for much practical help. Thanks also go to the director of the Melanchthon Academy, Günter Frank, and to Gerda Bauder, Claudia Martin, Hendrik Stössel, Andreas Klein, and Axel Lange. I am grateful to F. Dale Bruner, Diarmaid MacCulloch, and Graham Tomlin for supporting my Fulbright application. Thank you, too, to Richard Hunt, for giving me feedback on it. In Ruit, we are very grateful to the extended Ehrismann family (especially Carmen and Christoph), who helped us in countless ways.

Cathryn and I would like to recognize our families for their support, both moral and practical: Torrence and M. C. Hunt, Shirley Graybill Mozena, Caroline and Chris Zaw Mon, Jonathan Graybill, Tod and Kate Hunt, and Bonnie and Brad Pierson.

Thanks especially go to my wife, Cathryn, who lived in a foreign land with an infant daughter for a year to help make this book possible.

Apologies to anyone I have inadvertently left out.

To God be the glory.

At the Peter and Paul Festival
European Melanchthon Academy,
Bretten, 2013

◆ ◆ ◆

In the nearly two years since first writing these acknowledgements, I now have a few more people to add. Thank you to Jeffrey Mathison for the wonderful maps and bird's eye views. At Fortress Press, I must recognize Michael Gibson for his support for this project. Lisa Gruenisen and Esther Diley have been invaluable in shaping and presenting the final form of this text. Thanks are due also to Matt Forster for his careful copyediting of the manuscript. Numerous libraries and institutions have kindly granted permission to publish images. Finally, I am glad of the encouragement of the congregation at the First United Presbyterian Church, in Moline, Illinois.

Many deserve credit. The errors are all my own.

Blue Grass, Iowa
May 12, 2015

Abbreviations

ARG   *Archiv für Reformationsgeschichte*

BSLK   *Die Bekenntnisschriften der evangelisch-lutherischen Kirche /herausgegeben im Gedenkjahr der Augsburgischen Konfession 1930* (Göttingen: Vandenhoeck & Ruprecht, 1952).

Cam., *Vita*   Camerarius, Joachim, *De vita Philippi Melanchthonis narratio*, ed. Theodore Strobelius (Halle: Ioannis Iac. Gebaveri, 1777).

Cam., *Das Leben*   Camerarius, Joachim, *Das Leben Philipp Melanchthons*, trans. Volker Werner (Leipzig: Evangelische Verlagsanstalt, 2010).

CR   Melanchthon, Philipp, *Corpus Reformatorum: Philippi Melanthonis opera quae supersunt omnia*, ed. K. Bretschneider and H. Bindseil, 28 vols. (Halle: Schwetschke, 1834–60).

EE   Erasmus, Desiderius, *Opus epistolarum Des. Erasmi Roterodami*, ed. P. S. Allen et al, 12 vols. (Oxonii: Typographeo Clarendoniano, 1906–58).

Hill   *Melanchthon: Selected Writings*, trans. Charles Leander Hill, eds. Elmer Ellsworth Flack and Lowell J. Satre (Minneapolis: Augsburg Publishing House, 1962).

Keen   *A Melanchthon Reader*, trans. and ed. Ralph Keen. Vol. 41 in *American University Studies, Series VII, Theology and Religion* (New York: Peter Lang, 1988).

LCC   *Library of Christian Classics*, ed. John Baillie et al, 26 vols. (Philadelphia: Westminster, 1950–1969).

LW	Luther, Martin, *Luther's Works: American Edition*, ed. Jaroslav Pelikan and Helmut Lehmann, 55 vols. (Saint Louis/Philadelphia: Concordia/Fortress, 1955–86).
MBW	Melanchthon, Philipp, *Melanchthons Briefwechsel: Kritische und kommentierte Gesamtausgabe,* ed. Heinz Scheible, 12+ vols. (Stuttgart: Frommann-Holzboog, 1977–). MBW *Regesten* volumes give summaries of Melanchthon's letters, while the *Texte* volumes provide the actual text.
MBWT	The *Texte* volumes of MBW (see above).
Melanchthonhaus, Wittenberg	Museum placards and explanatory texts at the Melanchthonhaus, Wittenberg.
MSA	Melanchthon, Philipp, *Melanchthons Werke in Auswahl [Studiensausgabe]*, ed. R. Stupperich, 7 vols. (Gütersloh: Gerd Mohn, 1951–75).
OER	Hans J. Hillerbrand, ed., *The Oxford Encyclopedia of the Reformation*, 4 vols. (New York: Oxford University Press, 1996).
Suppl. Mel.	Melanchthon, Philipp, *Supplementa Melanchthoniana. Werke Philipp Melanchthons die im Corpus Reformatorum vermisst werden,* ed. O. Clemen (Leipzig: 1910–29).
WA	Luther, Martin, *D. Martin Luthers Werke: Kritische Gesamtausgabe* (Weimar: H. Bölau, 1883–).
WABR	Luther, Martin, *D. Martin Luthers Werke: Kritische Gesamtausgabe. Briefwechsel* (Weimar: H Böhlaus Nachfolger, 1930–).
WATR	Luther, Martin, *D. Martin Luthers Werke: Kritische Gesamtausgabe. Tischreden,* 6 vols. (Weimar: H. Bölaus Nachfolger, 1912–21).

Maps

Maps illustrated by Jeffrey Mathison.

MAPS

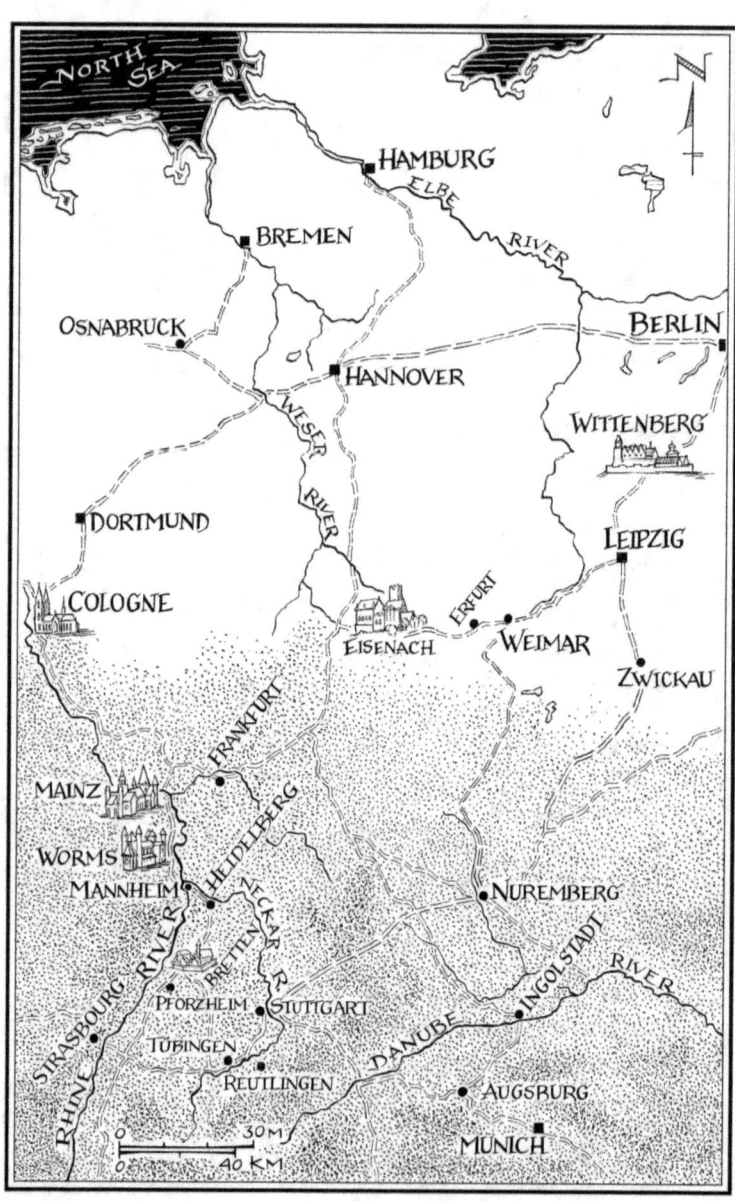

Central German lands.

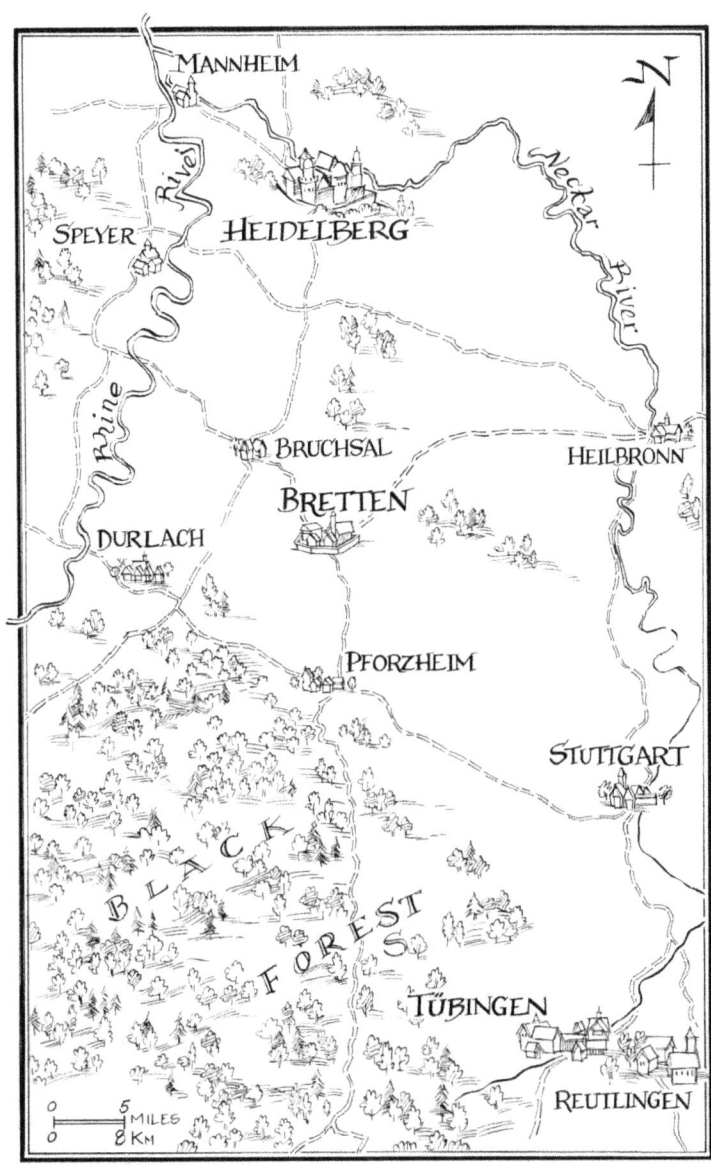

Southwestern German lands.

Introduction

> As for man, his days are like grass;
> As a flower of the field, so he flourishes.
> For the wind passes over it, and it is gone,
> And its place remembers it no more.
> —Psalm 103:15-16[1]

Central Europe five hundred years ago was an entirely different place. Imperial Rome had faded a thousand years earlier in the West. German-speaking lands were divided into a patchwork of principalities—and those ostensibly under the unifying headship of the Holy Roman Emperor rarely saw much change in their daily existence. Life was short and extremely difficult in this era of dwindling feudalism and growing cities. Suffering and death were not so easily hidden as today. Infants routinely did not survive childhood. The nauseating memory of the Black Death still hung like a miasma over a continent where one in three was consumed by pestilence.

How could a society *not* have a heightened spirituality in such a context? With few economic or technological means of comfort, God becomes a very attractive option. Luther would later argue that such hard times are often God's veiled grace (or alien work), where

---

1. Unless otherwise noted, all scripture quotations come from the NKJV.

he strips people of earthly attachments so that they might turn to him in genuine faith. Of course, not every individual at this time was a pious God-fearer. Observers of the age often complained about the crassness and worldliness of their contemporaries. But as a whole, European civilization held a distinctly Christian ethos at this time, combined with the ancient memory of a Roman Empire ostensibly unified under the lordship of Christ.

The present-day reader quick to dismiss the concerns of those from the sixteenth century would be well-served to try to get inside their worldview. The main solution on offer to suffering and death was a better life to come. The abundant physical perils of life were mirrored by assumed abundant spiritual perils. Passing safely through the crisis of death and onwards to heaven, therefore, was a very serious matter. This is part of the reason why theological disputes were so heated in the early sixteenth century. Additionally, most people assumed that Christendom could and should be *one*—united around a single institution with a single agreed-upon doctrine. The theological disputes of the early Reformation were not about obscure disagreements on matters of personal spiritual preference. The participants in these struggles believed that they were either seeking a return to pure Christian doctrine (the Protestants), or were struggling to maintain it (the Roman Catholics). They thought that Christendom could be one. They thought their entire civilization, and indeed all civilizations, should embrace a unified Christian doctrine in a unified Christian church. They had in mind matters of eternal life and death, as well as what world society as a whole should look like. These are high matters.

> *And though this world, with devils filled, should threaten to undo us,*
> *We will not fear, for God hath willed His truth to triumph through us:*
> *The Prince of Darkness grim, we tremble not for him;*

INTRODUCTION

His rage we can endure, for lo, his doom is sure,
One little word shall fell him.[2]

To truly understand the Reformation era, the contemporary reader must see it through the eyes of the early modern denizen. The present book is just such an exercise—an attempt to see the early Reformation through the eyes of Philipp Melanchthon.

Historians in recent decades have begun to dispute the use of such a monolithic title as "*the* Reformation." The definite article implies a single, distinct event—when the reality is that this era held a multiplicity of interconnected theological, political, economic, technological, artistic, and ecclesiastical developments. It has become popular to speak of Reformation*s*, rather than *a* Reformation. However, I shall maintain the traditional nomenclature here, with the tacit understanding that life at any level is always more complicated than one first expected. A great movement of peoples and ideas is no different.

In its most simplistic form, the Reformation was an attempt by certain individuals to promote a reformation of the Roman Catholic Church where it had drifted from its founding principles in both theology and ethics. Martin Luther's is always the first name mentioned on this list. However, not as well known in the English-speaking world is the name of Philipp Melanchthon. This younger colleague of Luther's at Wittenberg was a prodigy. A tireless and talented scholar, he systematized evangelical theology while Luther polemicized. This puts it a bit too simply (for Melanchthon indeed engaged in polemic as well), but his theological textbooks, biblical commentaries, ecumenical work, and authorship of key confessions were vital in solidifying the intellectual rigor and rational consistency

---

2. A verse from Luther's hymn, "A Mighty Fortress."

of the new (or old, depending on one's perspective) evangelical theology. This alone makes Melanchthon well-worth attention.

The purpose of this book, then, is to tell something of the story of the dawn of the Reformation, chiefly from the perspective of one of its central players—Philipp Melanchthon. By tracing his family origins, childhood, education, and early career at Wittenberg, I hope to convey something of the ethos and significance of the times. By combining a sharp biographical focus with occasional broad glances at much wider geopolitical considerations, my goal is to narrate a story both rich in detail and panoramic in scope. So many accounts keep the spotlight on Luther, and relegate Melanchthon to a supporting role. This one, by contrast, keeps the spotlight on Melanchthon, and in so doing, provides a unique perspective on the dawn of the Reformation.

Of course, any study of the life of Melanchthon immediately runs into the problem of the vastness of his literary output (thousands upon thousands of letters and works) and the complexity of his thought. This book is not intended to do justice to Melanchthon's thought—neither his theology nor his philosophy. To attempt this, one usually either writes a lengthy monograph on a single doctrine (as I did in my previous work on Melanchthon[3]), or else one must give brief snippets on a variety of topics (as in Nicole Kuropka's slim volume[4]). Instead, the focus of the present book is more on the man himself. It is about Melanchthon's faith, professional development, work, and family in the midst of a world undergoing radical change. This is a personal framework which can complement the specialized studies of the Melanchthon monographs.

---

3. Gregory B. Graybill, *Evangelical Free Will: Philipp Melanchthon's Doctrinal Journey on the Origins of Faith* (Oxford: Oxford University Press, 2010).
4. Nicole Kuropka, *Melanchthon* (Tübingen: Mohr Siebeck, 2010). (This book is in German.)

INTRODUCTION

I have been fortunate to spend the past year living and researching this book in Melanchthon's hometown of Bretten, Germany. This book has been written almost entirely at the exact location of Melanchthon's birth—at the European Melanchthon Academy and the Melanchthon House in Bretten. While his teaching career took him to Wittenberg, much of his heart remained in Bretten. Now the spires, woods, and fruitful green hills of Bretten are part of my life as well, and for this I am grateful to God.

1

Wars and Rumors of Wars

You will hear of wars and rumors of wars. See that you are not troubled; for all these things must come to pass, but the end is not yet. For nation will rise against nation, and kingdom against kingdom. And there will be famines, pestilences, and earthquakes in various places. All these are the beginning of sorrows.
—Matthew 24:6-8

On the evening of May 28, 1453, Constantine XI, the last of the ancient line of Roman Emperors, stood in the lamplight of the mighty Hagia Sofia, giving a funeral oration for the Roman Empire. Mehmed, of the lineage of Osman, and his vast force seethed outside, ready to storm the ancestral seat of the Christian empire in the East. After an artillery bombardment, the janissaries advanced on the gates. A crescent moon gave feeble illumination on this night when Byzantium, that glittering jewel of Medieval Europe, fell. "Animals may run from animals," said Constantine in the church, "but you are men, and worthy heirs of the great heroes of ancient Greece and Rome."[1]

Osman

That heritage would not die in the slaughter of May 29. Hearing of the Ottoman approach, a remnant fled before the encircling forces cut off all escape. They brought manuscripts with them—the literary treasures of Greek antiquity. The refugees made their way to the Latin West, even to Rome. There, some began to support themselves by teaching the Greek language. Others shared their venerable documents with local scholars, who were entranced by this high culture of a lost age. With Roman ruins as daily reminders, they yearned for past glories. What wisdom, what shining eloquence, might that old world have to pass on to the modern age? In this way, a new intellectual movement—humanism—flourished, with its focus on returning to the original sources (*ad fontes*).

Further west, Christians slowly pushed the Moors south out of the Iberian Peninsula—though at great cost. In the siege of Moorish Grenada in 1489, three thousand Spanish war casualties were dwarfed by seventeen thousand struck down by a new pestilence. Typhus had just made its European landfall. In the course of the *Reconquista*, Spanish forces discovered many classical Greek texts that had been preserved in the Arab world. News of ancient texts therefore came to the Italian Peninsula from both Spain in the west and dead Byzantium in the east, providing rich materials for a rebirth of classical studies.

Meanwhile, the Ottoman Empire did not sleep. Further east, it expanded into Persian lands. Christian enthusiasm for crusading had been waning for centuries, and when Pope Leo X preached a crusade in 1518 against the Turks, almost no one responded. But the Knights of St. John (the Hospitallers) remained at their posts—they still held

---

1. Donald M. Nicol, *The Immortal Emperor* (Cambridge: Cambridge University Press, 1992), 67. See also Lars Brownworth, *Lost to the West: The Forgotten Byzantine Empire That Rescued Western Civilization* (New York: Crown, 2009), chap. 25.

a fortress on the island of Rhodes, and from there they conducted sea raids against Ottoman shipments so successfully that the price of grain rose 50 percent in Istanbul in 1512. Suleiman steeled himself to root them out, but the Hospitallers were more stubborn than expected. With Barbary pirates trolling for plunder and Christian captives for the North African slave markets, Ottoman power surged in the Mediterranean. They expanded and consolidated their control of North Africa. Barbarossa even captured the port of Tunis, a bare hundred miles from Sicily. This was not good news for the papacy, in light of Suleiman's goal of conquering Rome in order to show the superiority of Islam over Christianity.

Back in southeastern Europe, the armies of the Prophet advanced into Hungarian and Balkan regions, absorbing large numbers of southern Slavs, Greeks, Albanians, and Magyars. Ottoman forces pressed forward into Moldavia, Wallachia, and Transylvania. In 1526, at the Battle of Mohács, the Turks won a grisly victory over Hungarian forces. Of a force of twenty-five thousand Hungarian soldiers, as many as twenty-three thousand died in the battle. About two thousand survivors were captured, paraded before the sultan, and then decapitated. Three years later, the armies of Sultan Suleiman stood before the very gates of Vienna. On this occasion, he was repulsed, but he promised to return (which he did, in 1532). Considering himself a new Alexander the Great, Suleiman pledged to create a single Islamic empire stretching from the Rhine to the Indus. These Ottoman desires to subjugate the German-speaking lands of central Europe provided a potent geopolitical and even apocalyptic backdrop to much of the drama of the Reformation age. The mortal enemies of Christendom, the expansionist Muslim threat could never entirely be put out of mind, no matter how much European powers might war among themselves.[2] This "scourge of God" was viewed as a divine chastisement of Christendom for its sins, like the Babylonians in Judea. Suleiman may have styled himself a new Solomon, but for the West, a more fitting analogy was Nebuchadnezzar—or perhaps even Shalmaneser.

Ottoman Emperor Suleiman (1494-1566, r. 1520-66).

Papa

In Western Europe, the spiritual and administrative hub of Christendom lay in Rome, with the papacy. The pope ("*Papa*" in Italian) represented Christ on earth as the personal successor of St. Peter, and so exercised vast spiritual authority.

In the late fifteenth and early sixteenth centuries, however, that spiritual authority diminished. While many popes displayed genuine piety and integrity, others did not do so consistently, such that the very term "Renaissance Papacy" carries strongly negative

---

2. Francis I, however, found it convenient to ally himself with Suleiman, seeing that he would only be attacking the territories of the pope and Charles V anyway.

connotations still today. Thus, Pius II (1458–64) often favored family members for coveted ecclesiastical positions. Paul II (1464–71) was vain and relished costly spectacles. He was an enthusiastic backer of carnivals and built himself a magnificent personal residence, the Palazzo S. Marco. He had the historian Bartolomeo Platina imprisoned and tortured.[3] Sixtus IV (1471–84) established the Spanish Inquisition and appointed Torquemada as Grand Inquisitor (although he did, admittedly, seek to rein in the abuses). Meanwhile, he also sought to aggrandize his own family by giving a multitude of lucrative ecclesiastical appointments to relatives. Active in northern Italian political intrigues, Sixtus even played a significant role in the notorious Pazzi affair, where a rival Florentine banking family sought to replace the Medicis as the official papal bankers. The affair resulted in the murder Giuliano de Medici and the wounding of Lorenzo de Medici. An extravagant spender, Sixtus left a large deficit for his successor, despite a vigorous expansion of revenues from indulgences.

That successor was Innocent VIII (1484–92)—a relaxed character surrounded by cardinals of princely ambition. To battle the financial crisis he inherited from Sixtus, Innocent simply created large numbers of new clerical offices and sold them off to the highest bidders. In German lands, he ramped up the Inquisition against witchcraft. In the Papal States, his political governance was calamitous, resulting in anarchy and violence upon his death—which then led to the accession of the Borgia family.

As a youth, Rodrigo Borgia found himself the beneficiary of numerous benefices, bestowed on him courtesy of his uncle (Pope Calixtus III). As a cardinal, Rodrigo became extremely wealthy from these various ecclesiastical income streams. Unabashedly promiscuous, he fathered seven children before becoming Pope

---

3. Platina, outlived Paul II. As Vatican librarian, he had the opportunity to write the papal biography of his persecutor. One may easily imagine the tenor of his tome.

Alexander VI (1492–1503)—and then fathered two more for good measure. Alexander vigorously promoted his progeny (especially his son Cesare) from his perch on the chair of St. Peter. Striving for Italian political dominance for the Borgia family, Alexander was accomplice to assassinations, property seizures, and the steady creation of new church offices for auction. Indulgences continued to provide useful income. He died in 1503, possibly due to poisoning.

Next, a man of culture and integrity, Pius III, followed, but only reigned for a few weeks before dying. Bribes were then of great assistance to Julius II (1503–13) in his election as pope. Once installed, he strove to increase papal power, particularly in the expansion of the Papal States on the Italian Peninsula. Ruthless and violent, some of his methods fit better with the teachings of his contemporary, Niccolo Machiavelli, than with the Nazarene carpenter. The word of God was not Julius's only sword.

In 1513, the cardinals met to elect the next pope and decided on Giovanni de Medici, the son of Lorenzo the Magnificent (whom Sixtus IV may have tried to assassinate in the Pazzi affair). With refinement and cunning, he was a clever politician with a penchant for nepotism. Like Julius II, he was a successful military leader who had no qualms about engaging in war. He borrowed extensively, enjoyed a lavish style, once pawned the palace furniture, and revived the practice of simony on a grand scale. As the scion of the Florentine banking family of the Medicis, it was not surprising that he also hit on the idea of radically expanding fundraising through the sale of indulgences. This, especially, would cause some difficulties north of the Alps.

Apart from their failings, all these popes also had noble and pious achievements. For example, Julius II, despite his military adventures, commissioned Michelangelo to paint the Sistine Chapel. He also banned simony.[4] However, in the minds of the public (especially north of the Alps), the abuses were what stood out.⁵ These provocations provided part of the moral basis for a call to reform.

In the early sixteenth century, the language of reform was commonplace in the church. Prior to the Reformation, the most significant attempt at reform took place in 1512–17, at the Fifth Lateran Council, called by Pope Julius II (though mainly, it must be said, to condemn the schismatic Pisan council of his enemies, as well as to attempt to rein in the Pragmatic Sanction of Bourges, which was serving as a check on papal power in France⁶). Some of the reform proposals at the Fifth Lateran Council included the appointment of only qualified (that is, pious and well-educated) candidates to church office, ending the practice of purchasing ecclesiastical office (especially in papal elections), reforming the morals of the clergy, enforcing current church law, and seeking peace among Christian princes. However, Leo X let practical enforcement of the reforms drift. After all, the primary reason for calling the council in the first place was political gain, rather than ecclesiastical reform. Simony, too, helped pay the bills. It did not hearten reform-minded individuals that when Pope Leo X ascended the throne, he reportedly said, "We have been given the papacy. Now let us enjoy it."

Financial reforms were an especially touchy topic. The Medici popes (Leo X and Clement VII), after all, rose to power through the influence of their family's papal banking services. Additionally, many offices in the church were, in fact, purchased. These offices were supposed to be exclusively administrative roles, and not ecclesiastical

---

4. Leo X, however, rather flamboyantly undid that decree.
5. Nepotism, simony, sexual immorality, and occasional unscrupulous geopolitical maneuvering did not always play well with the masses—especially those who took their faith seriously. While older Reformation scholarship overemphasized this fact and its role in the tumults that followed, current scholarship has swung too far in the other direction of *under*-emphasizing it. Abuses in the church and by the popes did strengthen cries for reform.
6. Cajetan, Luther's interrogator at Augsburg in 1518, also helped mobilize opposition to the Council of Pisa.

appointments. In practice, however, the simony overlapped into all areas. Additionally, when an ecclesiastical office became vacant, the income for the position reverted to the pope, which made him somewhat disinclined to fill that vacancy expeditiously. The popes were heavily dependent on the funds raised in these ways, in order to maintain their political standing in relation to other European princes. Further, the papacy also borrowed on credit, and needed to make interest payments. So while some revenue did derive from church offerings, the fees for purchased offices combined with the taxes from the Papal States to provide the bulk of papal revenue. Indulgences also proved quite helpful.

In the meantime, papal authority did not extend merely to matters of faith, for the papacy claimed not only spiritual authority, but also political. This was not an era where ecclesiastical and temporal matters were held to be distinct. The *pope* was the one who crowned kings, and *he* was the one who had the right to chastise the crowned heads of Europe. The image comes to mind of Henry IV, King of the Romans, standing in the snow outside of the castle of Canossa in repentance, begging Pope Gregory VII to lift a sentence of excommunication in 1077. The power of the Keys meant power over kings—or, at least some in the papal line sought to make it so. Thus the pope was effectively a prince among princes, with expansive lands, military forces, and all the trappings of state as well.

Pope Leo X (1475-1521, r. 1513-21). Left is Giulio de Medici—Pope Clement VII (r. 1523-25).

The direct political rule of Christ's vicar extended to the Papal States—a vast swath of land in the central and northern regions of the Italian Peninsula, which gradually expanded from the time of Alexander VI in 1492 onward. Popes frequently named nephews or other family members lords (or at least senior military and administrative officials) of these Papal States in order to exert better control. Some have referred to these creations as nepotal principalities.[7] The papacy justified these temporal holdings as necessary to preserve the genuine independence of the pope. Otherwise, local temporal authorities might seek to exercise undue influence through the threat of force.[8] However, noticing the

---

7. This phrase occurs in the *Oxford Encyclopedia of the Reformation* article, "Papal States."
8. With the same reasoning, the federal government of the United States is not located within the jurisdiction of any of the fifty states.

gradually expanding borders of the Papal States in the early sixteenth century, others wondered if the popes really wanted to establish a double-monarchy—with all of Christendom under the absolute authority of the pope in both spiritual and temporal affairs.[9] Hence, the papacy in this age is better symbolized by Julius II in full armor at the head of an army, rather than Francis's gentle demeanor in the present age.

This papal assertion of temporal authority, however, had the unintended consequence of making the papacy subject to earthly calculations of power politics. Hence, despite papal claims of preeminence, various popes often, in fact, found themselves in positions of relative political weakness. Gazing out upon the world from under a papal tiara, every pope felt strong pressure from the expansionist imperial Islamic Ottoman Empire looming in the east. More pious popes took this seriously. Less pious popes (such as Alexander VI) sought lucrative deals with the sultan. To the west and north of Rome, the ever-networking Habsburgs of the Holy Roman Empire seemed to be forever expanding their reach in Spain, the Netherlands, and in numerous German-speaking territories. Hence, Christ's vicar often found himself making common cause with the Valois of France to act as a counterbalance to burgeoning Habsburg hegemony. For example, after Francis I won a decisive victory over Swiss Confederation forces at the Battle of Marignano in 1515, Pope Leo X quickly concluded the Concordat of Bologna with him. This agreement allowed the papacy to continue collecting monies from the French church, but also gave the King of France significant leeway in selecting ecclesiastical officials within the boundaries of French territory. This strengthened both parties in relation to the Holy Roman Empire, and the idea was swiftly confirmed at the Fifth Lateran Council in 1516. Further, in 1519, when it was time for the

---

9. Maximilian I, Holy Roman Emperor actually endorsed this idea in 1511—at least in theory.

election of a new Holy Roman Emperor, Leo X lobbied the select group of princely electors to choose Francis. One of those electors was Friedrich[10] of Saxony, with whom Leo was stepping softly on the issue of a certain outspoken monk at Friedrich's new university in Wittenberg. Nevertheless, the electors unanimously selected the Habsburg scion Charles V.

In return for these machinations, both Habsburgs and Valois took an active interest in the election of the next pope in the College of Cardinals in 1521 and beyond. Here, several large factions developed—Habsburg, Valois, and those with connections to previous popes. If the popes sought to bring spiritual authority to temporal rulers, then the earthly princes sought to bring temporal authority to the spiritual ruler. Nevertheless, at the end of the fifteenth century, Sixtus IV had already packed the College of Cardinals with Italians, so little danger remained of the election of anyone from either Habsburg or Valois patrimony. By this point, the papacy and the Curia was an exclusive club for a few north-central Italian aristocratic families.

Electoral insularity only goes so far, though. When in 1527, Clement VII's political machinations became too transparently anti-Habsburg, Charles V decided to treat the pontiff as just another contentious worldly prince. He invaded Italy, and sacked Rome. It was the worst looting Rome had seen since its fall more than a thousand years earlier to the Visigoths. Much of Europe was horrified, and the political influence of the pope was radically diminished.

---

10. This name is often rendered "Frederick" in English-language literature.

Valois

To the west and north of the Papal States lay France. At the beginning of the sixteenth century, the French domains held approximately sixteen million people—twice the population of Spain, and four times that of England. They were ruled with strongly centralized powers by the House of Valois, a cadet branch of the Capetian line, which had claimed the throne in the fourteenth century. The English disputed the right of Philip of Valois's accession in 1328, however, and the Hundred Years' War ensued. Though it was often a close-run contest, the Valois finally succeeded in pushing the English back across the Channel by 1453—the same year as the fall of Constantinople. The Valois now pivoted to contest with the Burgundian kings for preeminence. The Burgundians, however, ended up marrying into the Habsburg family, thus becoming the direct ancestors of Charles V, Habsburg Holy Roman Emperor from 1519 onward. Valois tensions with the Habsburgs had deep roots.

Meanwhile, Valois forces pursued dynastic claims on the Italian Peninsula in both Naples and Milan. The pope, effectively king of his own Papal States in the area, intensely opposed these actions. In 1508, Pope Julius II organized a Holy League, and in 1509 attempted to use it to expel the French from Italy. Louis XII cordially responded by organizing the Council of Pisa in an effort to depose Pope Julius. By 1515, the French forces had indeed been removed from the Italian Peninsula. In this year, upon the death of Louis XII, Francis I ascended the throne. He went right back across the Alps to Milan, crushing the Swiss armies who thought to protect that city at the Battle of Marignano. It was at this point that Pope Leo X made his peace with Francis I at Bologna. From here on, papal and French interests often made common cause against the largest player on the western European stage at this time—the Holy Roman Empire. For instance, Pope Leo X supported Francis's failed attempt to be elected Holy Roman Emperor himself, and then, in 1533, Francis I had his son, Henry, marry the niece of Pope Clement VII, Catherine de Médicis. Not only did this tie France to papal power, it also fostered a helpful blood bond with the powerful Medici family, who had a legacy of dominating both the papacy and the city of Florence. The Habsburgs were famous for using marriage as a diplomatic tool for self-advancement, but Francis I was not ignorant of these wiles, either.

In 1521, Francis I employed more direct means of conflict and went to war against Charles V. Driven out of Milan in 1522, Francis was defeated on the field of battle at Pavia, and taken prisoner by Charles in 1525. Released in the next year, he held no affection for Charles, who continued to hold his two sons for ransom in Spain until 1530.[11] Francis therefore felt few qualms about engaging in an alliance with Sultan Suleiman of the Ottoman Empire. Suleiman was, after all, set on attacking Habsburg lands, and was actively pursuing the goal of conquering Habsburg and other German principalities all the way across central Europe and right up to the Rhine River (well short of Francis's territory). Seeing that Suleiman had no immediate plans to attack French territory, Francis pragmatically decided that the enemy of his enemy was his friend.

---

11. The eventual ransom paid was rather steep: two million crowns, and the French renunciation of all rights to Naples, Milan, and Flanders.

King Francis I (1494–1547, r. 1515–47).

His antagonism to the Habsburg ruler outweighed the long history of Frankish leadership in anti-Muslim crusades, as well as the painful lessons learned in the eighth century that imperial Islamic armies do not always make for benign neighbors. Charles Martel had no easy day when he turned back the Umayyad invaders at Tours in 732. Regional politics took pride of place over the greater clash of civilizations—especially when regional Christian powers were too ponderous to handle alone. Likewise, the Catholic Francis was not averse to building bridges to evangelical princes in German-speaking lands if it would damage Charles V. For decades, these connections helped prevent the Catholic Charles from exercising the full might of his forces against German Protestants—thus giving the evangelical movement time to grow.

Habsburg

From the mid-fifteenth century onward, the Holy Roman Empire of the German Nation was ruled by a steady stream of members of the Austrian Habsburg family. Seeking to be the successor-entity to the ancient Roman Empire and the medieval might of Charlemagne, the Holy Roman Empire encompassed territories extending from the Iberian Peninsula to Hungary, and from the Baltic to the Alps. Additional Habsburg claims to Burgundian lands put them at odds with France, with whom they were repeatedly in armed conflict. Although frayed into a patchwork collection of territories in the German-speaking lands, the Holy Roman Empire dominated early-modern Europe. Challenged by both the papacy and France, the Empire nonetheless remained the most significant force to be reckoned with in Europe, outside of the Ottoman Empire in the east.

The emperor was elected by a group of seven princely "electors" (*Kurfürsten*)—the margrave of Brandenburg, the duke of electoral Saxony, the count Palatine of the Rhine, the king of Bohemia, and the archbishops of Cologne, Mainz, and Trier. Because candidates had to make certain promises and concessions in order to get elected (or have their progeny elected), this system served as a check on absolute power. It also provided shelter for Luther and the evangelical movement, in the form of the favor of Saxon electoral princes. Under their explicit protection, Charles V did not have the free hand he desired to crush the nascent movement.[12] He needed financial and military support from the Saxon *Kurfürsten* for ongoing wars against both France and the Ottoman Empire.

Charles V stands preeminent among the Habsburg emperors of the Reformation period. Probably the most significant political figure of the age, Charles V reigned as Holy Roman Emperor from 1519 until

---

12. In 1546, however, he would get his chance.

1556. Born in 1500, he received the unprecedented inheritance of the Netherlands, Burgundy, and the Austrian Habsburg possessions through his father, along with Aragon, Castile, Naples, and Sicily through his mother. Later Spanish explorations in the New World would further enlarge his empire. He was tutored by the humanist Adrian of Utrecht, who served as pope in 1522–23. Possessed of a mild underbite, hunting and chivalry occupied much of his attention as a youth—as did eating and drinking to excess. Devout, given to contemplation, and a diligent father, he also loved his wife (though he did sire illegitimate children both before his marriage, and after Isabella's death). He considered the preservation of true religion to be his main duty as sovereign.

Only nineteen when he was elected emperor, Charles V consistently sought to promote Roman Catholicism, halt Protestantism, and protect the West from Ottoman advance. He supported and expanded the role of the Inquisition in his territories, he attacked the Protestant princes when he had the chance in 1546, and he battled the Ottomans on land and by sea.

Holy Roman Emperor Charles V (1500-58, r. 1519-56).

Most of all, he expended much time, blood, and treasure in sustaining the long Habsburg-Valois conflict that extended essentially from 1521 until 1559. All these activities left him chronically in debt. He was hard-pressed, with active enemies in the Turks, French, and Protestants (and occasionally the pope). More than any other figure, the movements and decisions of Charles V provided the political backdrop for the development of the Protestant Reformation. Without Charles V's concerns to combat Francis I, oppose Muslim forces bombarding Vienna, and stay in the good graces of the Saxon princely electors, the German Reformation never could have flourished to the extent that it did.

Immediately preceding Charles as Holy Roman Emperor, however, was his grandfather, Maximilian I, who reigned from 1493 until his death in 1519. As a youth, Maximilian was highly energetic, and had trouble concentrating on anything for long. He was devout, and promoted moral reform in the church. In 1477, he married Mary, the sole heir of Duke Charles of Burgundy. Upon the death of Duke Charles, King Louis XI sought to recover Burgundy for France, and Maximilian took up arms to defend his wife's inheritance. Thus began the long history of Valois-Habsburg bad blood.

At a *Reichstag* in Worms in 1495, Maximilian sought to bring greater administrative unity to the empire by establishing a standing imperial court. The court was established, but its funding was not—which led to its eventual demise. Meanwhile, in the days leading up to the diet, a curious character arrived on the scene. Some sources name him Fandius Mandari,[13] others call him Claude de Vauldrey.[14] Mandari was a bellicose Burgundian knight originally from Welschland (Romandy—the French-speaking area of Switzerland[15]). He arrived in Worms hot-blooded and calling out for the bravest German to step forward to take him on in single combat. Nobody, however, was coming forward. Maximilian, somewhat impulsive, bold, and enamored of chivalrous traditions of knighthood, decided to rise to the challenge himself. For actions such as these, he has been called "the Last Knight." After confirming Mandari's rank and valor, the Emperor himself agreed to take on the challenger in single combat.

In preparation, Maximilian summoned his master armorers and weaponsmiths. He wanted truly superior kit for this confrontation. He needed armor that was both strong and light—impenetrable, yet

---

13. CR 10:257. Richard, 5.
14. Scheible, *Melanchthon*, 13. Cam., *Das Leben*, 297 (cf. 40). Ed. Werner seems to follow Scheible's lead in a number of places.
15. German-speaking Swiss refer to the Suisse romande as Welsches (this word is related to Walloon and Welsh—it refers in German to a foreigner of Celtic or especially Gallic origin). The etymology of *Welscher* goes back to a word the ancient Germans used to refer to the Romans ("foreigners").

flexible. It also needed to be beautiful. A master armorer, a craftsman from Heidelberg, went to work.

On the day of battle, Maximilian rode out in glittering helmet and armor. The confrontation was a swift and spectacular affair. Maximilian thoroughly routed the boastful Welscher—due in no small measure to his superior armor. The emperor was so pleased with his exquisite equipment that he bestowed on his armorer a family coat of arms—a lion holding a hammer and tongs in his paws. The craftsman went away pleased. His name was Georg Schwartzerdt, meaning "dark earth," and his son would know greater fame than this.

Schwartzerdt coat of arms, on the Melanchthonhaus, Bretten. Photo by Gregory Graybill.

2

The Armorer

1459–1493

> Take up the whole armor of God, that you may be able to withstand in the evil day, and having done all, to stand.
> —Ephesians 6:13

Georg Schwartzerdt began his life in relative obscurity. He was born in 1459 in Heidelberg, where Philipp the Upright (*Philipp der Aufrichtige*) reigned as Count Palatine (*Pfalzgraf*). Philipp also happened to be Elector on the Rhine (*Kurfürst am Rhein*). As one of the seven German princes who had the privilege of selecting the Holy Roman Emperor, Philipp held significant political clout. Georg Schwartzerdt's father, Nikolaus (or Claus) was a prominent citizen of Heidelberg. He lived below the mountain, and more than a century later, his gravestone was still visible there. With a reputation as a good and pious man, Claus was married to Elisabeth. Young Georg, his brother Iohannes (Hans), and his older sister Barbara were diligently brought up in the fear of the Lord. Barbara married a master-builder from Heidelberg and had a son. Hans went on to become a locksmith.

Holy Roman Emperor Maximilian I
(1459–1519, r. 1486–1519), in his armor.

Georg, however, showed more exceptional talents. An active and vigorous boy, Georg did all that was asked of him with both alacrity and dexterity. The excellence of the boy's work came to the attention of Elector Philipp, who brought him to court to show him the various crafts and trades available to see what might suit him best. Georg soon gravitated toward the armorers, showing a great interest in all kinds of knightly gear—both defensive and offensive. Accordingly, the elector himself sponsored Georg's training.

Elector Philipp apprenticed Georg to a master armorer in the Upper Palatinate at Amberg Castle. There, the talented young man pressed into his work with enthusiasm. In addition to making armor, Georg also began to learn about the strange new technology of firearms. Meanwhile, Georg progressed in armoring skill so swiftly that the other apprentices and junior tradesmen began to hate him. One jealous rival attacked him with molten lead, burning him so severely that he hovered on the brink of death. Despite a grim prognosis, he survived, and later attributed his unlikely recovery to painstaking medical care and the grace of God.

Upon hearing of this incident at Amberg, Elector Philipp decided to remove Georg from the situation. He sent him on to learn from another master armorer in Nuremberg. This *Rüstmeister* was exacting in even the smallest details. Georg paid close attention and replicated the exquisite minutia with a fine precision. Impressed, the master armorer began to invest more and more of his time and attention in his unusual apprentice. Georg flourished under such personal training, rapidly picking up skills and techniques without much need for explanation or repetition. Soon he began to comprehend how to make nearly anything shown to him. He could produce beautiful work right from the forge as smooth as if it had been filed. After a couple of years under the master in Nuremberg, Georg reached maturity in his craft. He could now produce the very finest armor and weapons of the highest possible level of workmanship. Consequently, Elector Philipp summoned him back to his court at Heidelberg to be his official armorer and weaponsmith.[1]

The armor Georg made for Elector Philipp was both light and secure. He took great pains with it, and with ingenuity and creativity, produced remarkable work. Georg understood the nuances and details of armor crafting for both battle and riding. His son would later demonstrate a similar eye for detail—though in language rather than metal.

---

1. *Rüstmesiter und Waffenträger.* CR 10:256. Otto Beuttenmüller, in *Nachfahren Philipp Melanchthons: Eine genealogische Sammlung,* uses the title *Waffenschmied* for Georg (p. 10).

THE HONEYCOMB SCROLL

With an interest in both offensive and defensive gear, and with his wide-ranging talents, it was no surprise that Georg had also come to possess prodigious skills in firearms and artillery. He proved himself an expert at making guns, firing them, and effectively deploying them in combat. Noticing this expertise, Elector Philipp promptly attached Georg to an artillery brigade. Likewise, he also set Georg in charge over his entire armor supply. Philipp the Upright felt comfortable doing this because Georg's technical talents were matched by a reliable character.

At the core of Georg's personality lay an intense devotion to God. He strove to cultivate a godly spirit and diligently practiced spiritual disciplines. Psalm 119:164 says, "Seven times a day I praise You, Because of Your righteous judgments." Earnest in prayer, Georg kept these monastic hours, despite his secular vocation. He let nothing keep him from his appointed devotions. Georg prayed earnestly and fluently, on his knees. He even rose from his bed in the middle of the night for prayer.[2] Contemporaries called him righteous, a man of faith, pious, and God-fearing.[3] He attended church services (*Gottesdienst*) without fail.

From this love of God flowed a godly character that included love of neighbor. Georg was respected not only for his intelligence and skills, but also for his integrity, seriousness, discretion, and piety. Throughout his life, he was never heard to curse, nor was he observed drunk. Likewise, he ate in moderation in an age when many did not.[4] Always proper in speech, he was reserved, serious, loyal, and peaceful. Perhaps in the spirit of 1 Corinthians 6:1–7, he never went to court. Likewise, he sometimes refused payment from poor customers.[5] He

---

2. Later, his son, Philipp, would routinely rise at 2 a.m. to start his workday.
3. CR 10:256.
4. Later, Georg's son, Philipp, once exclaimed, "We Germans still eat poorly, and it is making us sick and destroying us!" Mühlhaupt, 5. CR 24:529.
5. Deane, 16.

showed contentment without avarice, diligence in his work, faithfulness to God, and care for others. These character traits, in combination with his uniquely high-quality armor, put Georg Schwartzerdt in high demand among some of the most powerful and prominent figures of the age.

As his fame spread, Georg became known simply as "the Heidelberg armorer." By this point, he owned his father's house, and had his main workshop there. From this location he fulfilled orders from electors and kings, who became aware of his work through Elector Philipp. Duke (*Herzog*) Ulrich from nearby Württemberg (of whom we shall hear more shortly) placed orders. Duke Hans Friedrich, elector of Saxony did as well, along with Margrave[6] Christoph von Baden. Among other prominent men could even be found the King of Poland. Most preeminent among all Georg's foreign patrons, however, was the Holy Roman Emperor Maximilian I.

Maximilian was not quite ready to let the age of knightly chivalry slip into history. A lover of jousting and medieval tournaments, Maximilian cut a fine figure in the helmet and armor of Georg's making. He loved the lightness, strength, and elegance of Georg's work. After his successful duel at Worms in 1495, he was only too pleased to award Georg a family coat of arms. Elector Philipp, delighted with the reflected glory he received from his gifted armorer, made sure he remained richly rewarded. It would not do for Schwartzerdt to disappear *permanently* into the services of the Holy Roman Emperor.

Still single at age 34, it appeared that Georg was married to his work. However, to entice him to stay in the region, Elector Philipp hit on the idea of arranging a marriage for his armorer to a

---

6. "Margrave" refers to a military governor of a German mark (province).

distinguished local girl. Perhaps this stratagem would tie Georg to the land and prevent him from moving away to serve more influential courts.

Philipp accordingly approached Iohannes (Hans) Reuter, the well-respected mayor of Brettheim (today called Bretten), a small town about a day's ride south of Heidelberg. Reuter had an attractive sixteen year-old daughter named Barbara, who was known as a virtuous and well-put-together child.[7] The elector asked Reuter for Barbara's hand in marriage for Georg, and, after some negotiations, he accepted (presumably, Barbara did, too). Philipp Melanchthon's later colleagues in Wittenberg eulogized that this marriage was due to the providence of God.

Freydal, Maximilian I's Tournament Book, 1515.
Copyright Kunsthistorisches Museum Wien.

---

7. . . . *die ein tugendsam und wohlgezogen Kind war.* CR 10:256.

The wedding took place in 1493 at a location between Heidelberg and Bretten—at the church in Speyer.[8] The service was packed with knights, who turned out in force to support the renowned armorer of Heidelberg. Afterward, perhaps in deference to his wife's youth, Georg moved into the Reuter house in the Bretten town center. Nevertheless, he kept his workshop in Heidelberg, and was frequently traveling for work. The couple would not start a family for another four years.

---

8. The Wittenberg professors in CR 10:256 claim that Georg was 30 at the time of the marriage. Some biographers (such as Stupperich and Greschat) claim 35 instead. However, assuming the fixed dates of his birth in 1459, marriage in 1493, and death in 1508 at the age of 49, then we may assume that Georg was about 34 at the time of the wedding. Scheible uses 34 as well in his biography (p. 13).

3

A Bride from Bretten

1493–1508

Ceres and Bacchus have both bestowed their gifts on Bretten.
—Jacob Micyllus[1]

Born in 1476 or 1477, Barbara Reuter was about sixteen when she married Georg Schwartzerdt. She came from a distinguished family—her father was the mayor of Bretten, and her mother, Elisabeth, was related to the famous humanist Johannes Reuchlin of Pforzheim (1455–1522).[2] Her lifestyle was more comfortable than

---

1. *Sylvarum Libri* V (1564), 141. Micyllus was a student of Melanchthon's in 1522. A Latin poet, humanist, and teacher, Micyllus went on to found a Latin school in Frankfurt, under Melanchthon's recommendation.
2. The exact relationship between Elisabeth Reuter and Johannes Reuchlin is a matter of some controversy. Was she Reuchlin's sister, or a more distant relative? Many, going back even to the sixteenth century, believed that Melanchthon's grandmother was the sister of Reuchlin. David Chytraeus indicated this in 1574 with the phrase *ex sorore nepotem*. *Oratio in scholae provincialium inclyti ducatus Stiriae introduction habita* (Graz: 1574), p. C4b. Further, some of Luther and Melanchthon's opponents at the Leipzig Disputation in 1519 derided Philipp as the nephew of Reuchlin. Accordingly, most biographers since then have taken this line, including Stump, Manschreck, Mühlhaupt, Maurer, and Wilhelm Pauck (in LCC 19). However, more recently, Scheible has argued for a greater degree of separation between Melanchthon and Reuchlin, and

many of her contemporaries, but it was by no means luxurious. Effectively an only child, she apparently had no siblings until a brother, Iohannes (Hans) Philipp Reuter was born around 1500—three years after the birth of her own son![3]

Barbara Schwartzerdt was known to be pious, intelligent, and gentle. She made for a good match with Georg. Occasionally, however, she could show a lively temper.[4] Her son, Philipp would inherit this trait, and from his childhood strove to keep it under control.

Barbara was prudent and thrifty, but not miserly. She kept an orderly household, and she argued for self-discipline and living within one's means. She often said,[5] "Whoever wishes to consume more than his plow can support will at last come to ruin and perhaps die upon the gallows" (it rhymes in German):[6]

---

the majority of Melanchthon scholars have followed suit (e.g., Werner [see esp. p. 43, n. 23], Greschat, Jung, and Birnstein—though not Peter Bahn). Scheible's evidence is indeed strong: on May 7, 1518, Reuchlin wrote a letter of recommendation for Melanchthon to the Elector Friedrich the Wise of Saxony. In it, he referred to Melanchthon as his *cousin* (*Vetter*), rather than nephew. CR 1:29. Similarly, on May 1, 1559, Melanchthon wrote a letter of recommendation for Wendelin Gürrich, in which he discussed his time in Pforzheim. There, he said that he lived with "the sister of Reuchlin, a sweet lady" (*ibi adolescens apud sororem Capnionis suavissime vixi*). If she was actually his grandmother, wouldn't he have said so? MBW 8942. For the Latin text, see Hannemann, Kurt, "Wendelin Gürrich der Ältere und der Jüngere (um 1495-1561): Lebenswege und Schicksale" in *Zeitschrift für die Geschichte des Oberrheins* 126 (1978): 145–46. Hence, Scheible is most likely correct that Melanchthon's grandmother was *not* Reuchlin's sister, though still related somehow. See his detailed discussion in "Melanchthons Pforzheimer Schulzeit. Studien zur humanistischen Bildungselite," in ed. Hans-Peter Becht, *Pforzheim in der frühen Neuzeit: Beiträge zur Stadtgeschichte des 16. bis 18. Jahrhunderts* (Sigmaringen, Germany: Jan Thorbecke Verlag, 1989), 21–27.

3. Scheible insists that Hans Reuter was the *uncle* of Philipp Schwartzerdt, even though they were almost the same age. "Melanchthons Pforzheimer Schulzeit," 28. This comes from Camerarius's account. See Cam., *Das Leben*, 43. However, Pauli (p. 29) and Manschreck (p. 31) employ the title of *cousin* instead. This would suggest that Barbara had other siblings. Some sources (such as CR 10:258) suggest that Barbara may have had a brother who died, leaving a child (Iohannes) behind. One cannot say with complete certainty. Our two earliest biographical sources, the *Brief Report* of CR 10, and Camerarius's biography, conflict.
4. For example, she was irritated to receive the news of her son Philipp's marriage in 1520, and upon hearing it, immediately remarried herself.
5. CR 10:469. Cf. Mühlhaupt, 4.
6. Trans. Manschreck, 30.

Germanici rythmi matris Philippi.

Wer mehr will verzehren
Denn sein Pflug kann ereren,
Der wird zuletzt verderben,
Und vielleicht am Galgen sterben.

Fiscal prudence did not exclude charity, however. Barbara showed deliberate benevolence, giving generously to both the church and the poor, even though the family was not wealthy. As a boy, young Philipp often heard his mother say,[7] "Farmers should divide their produce into three: one for planting; one for taxes, tithes, and alms; and one for self-support":

Ego saepe audivi a matre mea puer, Es muß ein Ackerman die frücht, die im jherlich wachsen, in 3 theil theilen, den erste theil müß er haben den Acker widerum anzubauen, den Andern theil müß er der Oberkeit vnd armen leuten geben, der 3. theil kompt aller erst im zu nüß.

Likewise, even decades later, Melanchthon still recalled an adage his mother taught him from a prayer book: "Giving alms will not impoverish you. Going to church will not delay you. Injustice will not enrich you."[8] These words held a personal application for the family, for some Bretteners became critical of Barbara for her

---

7. CR 20:549.
8. *Almosengeben armet nicht, Kirchengehen säumet nicht, unrecht Gut gedeihet nicht.* CR 24:263, 528, 539. CR 25:268. Cf. Mühlhaupt, 5.

generosity when the family began to grow in size. She insisted, nonetheless, that alms do not impoverish.

Bretteners had ample opportunity to observe the Reuter and Schwartzerdt households due to the central location of the family home. The house sat directly on the main thoroughfare at the town center, across from the marketplace, a large fountain, and the Krone ("Crown") guesthouse. The town hall (*Rathaus*) stood right next door (it is now a pleasant restaurant called, fittingly enough, the *Altes Rathaus*). Travelers often stopped to water their horses at this prominent fountain, which can still be seen today in the *Fußgänger* Zone of the *Stadtzentrum*. Likewise, one may still overnight in the comfortable surroundings of the Krone Hotel. Out the backdoor of the Reuter house and down the hill, one could reach the town church in just a minute or two.

Though it lasted for generations, unfortunately the Reuter/Schwartzerdt house was burned by a French invasion force on August 13, 1689. All that remains of the original house is the plaque that once hung there commemorating its historical significance.

Photo by Gregory Graybill, at the Melanchthonhaus.

On the site currently stands the brainchild of Professor Nikolaus Müller—a beautiful museum built in 1903 called the Melanchthon House,[9] with an attached international research facility called the European Melanchthon Academy. With their indulgence, and funding from the Fulbright Commission, the present writer sits on the third floor of that very site as he types these words.

Bretten lies in southwestern modern Germany, in Baden-Württemberg. At the close of the fifteenth century, this area lay under the rule of the Elector Palatine. At this time, the town consisted of around three hundred families, with a total population of about 2,000. Pforzheim lay twelve miles to the south, Stuttgart thirty-five miles to the southeast, and Heidelberg could be reached in a day's ride, thirty-two miles to the north. The town was situated in the southern edge of Baden, with Württemberg immediately to the south, and Swabia further east. However, these regional distinctions were not always clear-cut, and Melanchthon later sometimes referred to himself as Swabian.

Bretten provided a convenient stop on regional and international trading routes. Italian and French traders bringing their wares to German lands often passed through. Traffic going to and from the Rhine River, with its connections to the Netherlands and the sea, also brought merchants through Bretten. It is no accident that the Krone Hotel has been in business for more than five hundred years.

Situated in the Kraichgau Valley, Bretten lies in a beautiful, fertile area. Hilly and green, with rolling fields and shaded woods, it is a plentiful land. The present writer, walking in the fields of nearby Ruit and Knittlingen, observed apple trees bursting with heavy fruit, and thick vines packed with beautiful ripe red grapes draped over the

---

9. Another private building stood on the site for about two hundred years following the French conflagration and before the new construction at the turn of the nineteenth century. The foundation stone for the present *Gedächtnishall* was laid on Melanchthon's 400th birthday in 1897.

gates of village houses. Neighbors gave us crates of apples—so many that we used them to decorate our house. The region was famous for its wine at the turn of the sixteenth century, and it remains so today.

Melanchthonhaus, 2012. With Cathryn Graybill (and Lucy). Photograph by Gregory Graybill.

Bretten still has a *Weinfest* in late September in the town center. We had excellent wines in Bretten, costing no more than four euros per bottle. Riding the train from Rechberg to Ruit outside of Bretten, watching the hills and woods stream by, it is easy to see why Melanchthon held a special affection for this place.

Woodcut of Bretten, 1645.

At the dawn of the sixteenth century, the town boasted a stone watch-tower (which is still present) and a serviceable wall. Its defenses were adequate, but not especially robust. The houses were narrow, and the buildings generally unremarkable, though of solid construction. In keeping with the age, the town had no paved streets or organized means of sanitation. Public fountains provided relatively convenient access to water in this rainy region. Nutrition was generally poor, but through farming, trade, weaving, and tanning, the people earned a living, and even set aside enough to build a church.

Although the occasional priest wearing gold rings earned the scorn of some parishioners, the Schwartzerdts and Reuters nevertheless attended the church down the hill from their back door faithfully. A few years later, Georg and Barbara's young son sat for many a worship service pondering the two prominent symbols in the church. One was a pelican, which had used its beak to open up its chest to feed its young with its own blood (it was thought at the time that pelicans would indeed go to such lengths to nurture their young). The pelican was therefore meant to be a symbol of Christ's passion and life-giving self-sacrifice. Popular in medieval Europe, it also pointed towards the Eucharist. Later, Elizabeth I of England would adopt this symbol for herself as "the mother of the church of England." Nicholas Hilliard's *Pelican Portrait* of 1573 displays the symbol prominently.

The second symbol in the church was that of the phoenix, rising from its own ashes. The classical myth held that this bird would live for hundreds of years, and then, finally, build itself a nest of twigs, climb in, and ignite the whole thing. After a furious inferno, a new phoenix would arise out of the ashes. In this vein, the symbol was thought to point to resurrection and immortality. For Philipp Melanchthon, this symbol always spoke more of Christian themes, rather than pagan antiquity.

The inhabitants of Bretten were neither rich nor poor. They had a reputation for being humanitarian, polite, friendly, and good. Contemporaries described them as courteous, proficient, refined, and with a positive natural disposition. Despite this sunny reputation, however, human cruelty exists in every age, including this one.[10] We shall hear more below about men and women burned alive in the *Marktplatz* in front of the Reuter residence in 1504.

Georg and Barbara loved and honored each other. Georg still maintained his primary workshop in Heidelberg, but made the Reuter house his permanent residence. Unfortunately, with his line of work, he had to be away traveling frequently. With this consideration, and in light of Barbara's youth at age sixteen, it made sense that she continued to live in her parents' home in Bretten. Considering Georg's character, he probably wanted his wife to feel

---

10. Melanchthon later gave a horrifying report of the torture and murder of an adulterer in the area at about this time. WATR 5:549, Nr. 6224. Cf. CR 24:616; 20:542. Mühlhaupt, 7.

comfortable, and he knew that it would have been harder for her to move to Heidelberg at this stage.

Nicholas Hilliard's Pelican Portrait of Elizabeth. Notice the small pelican in the center of the corset.

Georg and Barbara waited four years before having children, with their first arriving on the Thursday after Invocavit, on February 16, 1497.[11] The baby boy was born in the Reuter house in Bretten at 12:06 p.m. His parents named him in honor of the man who brought them together—Elector Philipp the Upright of the Palatinate (*Philipp der Aufrichtige, Kurfürst der Pfalz*).[12] Barbara was twenty years old.

---

11. For more on Melanchthon's family of origin and his years in Bretten, see Peter Bahn, "Das Haus am Brettener Marktplatz—Biographische Notizen zu Herkunft und Familie Melanchthons," in ed. Peter Bahn, *Als ich ein Kind war… Bretten 1497—Alltag im Spätmittelalter* (Ubstadt-Weiher: Verl. Regionalkultur, 1997), 9-28.
12. In speaking of Melanchthon's birth in their extended eulogy in 1560, the Wittenberg professors spoke of him as "our beloved lord and preceptor" (*unser lieber Herr und Praeceptor*). CR 10:256.

Looking back on this event from the vantage point of 1560, the Wittenberg colleagues of Philipp Melanchthon saw God's providence at work. They commended the piety of Philipp's father, Georg Schwartzerdt, and ventured that perhaps the birth of such a son was God's blessing on the life of his devoted servant, Georg: "God blessed this pious and God-fearing man [Georg] with the gift of such a child, who, later, would be enjoyed by not just one land, or even many lands, but indeed by all of Christendom. He will without doubt be appreciated until the end of the world."[13] It is an interesting theory—that in the divine economy, in the spirit of the first being last and the last being first, that perhaps Philipp will be a footnote to the life of Georg, rather than Georg being a footnote to the life of Philipp.[14]

Nevertheless, despite Georg and Barbara's serious Christian faith, they both held to some superstitions characteristic of the age.[15] Upon Philipp's birth, Georg solicited a horoscope for the boy from his friend the mathematician and astrologer Iohannes Vierdung of Hassfurt. Vierdung warned that if Philipp ever travelled to the north, he would be shipwrecked in the Baltic Sea. This made a strong impression on Melanchthon for his entire life. The boy learned a serious piety from his father, but also fell prey to Georg's earnest embrace of astrology. Throughout his life Philipp considered it to be somehow grounded in reality—even to the extent of refusing tempting invitations to go to Britain or Denmark. At the age of 60, he wrote, "Even though I wanted to accept calls to Britain and

---

13. *Also segnet Gott diesen frommen und gottfürchtigen Mann mit der Gabe eines solchen Kindes, dessen hernach nicht ein Land sondern viel Länder, ja die ganze Christenheit groß genossen hat, und ohne Zweifel bis ans Ende der Welt genießen wird.* CR 10:257.
14. God seems to find these reversals somewhat humorous.
15. Deane, p. 16, makes this claim about Barbara, though without compelling evidence to substantiate it. Perhaps it can be sustained through assuming her tacit approval of Georg's astrological predilections. It should also be noted that astrology was generally considered to be a science at this time.

Denmark, I fear the fates, even though I am not a stoic."[16] Despite only a few years together, Georg made a deep impression on his son.

Just over two years after the birth of Philipp, little Anna Schwartzerdt came into the world on April 5, 1499. She would grow up in Bretten, marry Chilian Grumbach, have two children, and spend the rest of her life in Heilbronn, where she died sometime before 1560. Next came Georg the Younger, born in 1501. Philipp wrote him at least twice a year for his whole life (though few of these letters are extant[17]). Georg grew up in Bretten, studied at the Latin school in Pforzheim, and attended Tübingen University from 1514 until 1518, after which he returned to his hometown. There, the manager of the Krone guesthouse, Melchior Hechel, had an attractive daughter named Anna, whom Georg the Younger married in that same year. Interestingly, later on when Georg's mother, Barbara, was a widow, she ended up marrying Melchior Hechel himself. Mother and son ended up married to father and daughter.

Eventually, Georg the Younger became the manager of the Krone guesthouse, the author of a history of the 1504 siege of Bretten, and the town mayor for seventeen years, beginning in 1546. He continued to live in the Reuter house for the duration of his life, marrying twice more after the death of his wife Anna sometime after 1542.[18]

Georg and Barbara Schwartzerdt contented themselves with three children for several years, but in 1504, Georg became terminally ill. As death inexorably crept closer, he and Barbara decided to create

---

16. July 30, 1557. Letter to Matthesium, recorded in CR 1:CXLV, "Anno 1497." CR 9:188-9, Nr. 6291. MBW 8288.
17. See Nikolaus Müller, *Georg Schwartzerdt, der Bruder Melanchthons und Schultheiß zu Bretten* (Leipzig: Verein für Reformationsgeschichte, 1908), 200–11. MBW has the letters, though they do not all show up when one searches by name in the online MBW.
18. For a full biography of Georg Schwartzerdt the Younger, see Müller, *Georg Schwartzerdt, der Bruder Melanchthons und Schultheiß zu Bretten* (Leipzig: Verein für Reformationsgeschichte, 1908).

new life. Margarethe Schwartzerdt soon arrived, born on March 17, 1506. She would have no memories of her father, who passed in 1508. Margarethe married at the tender age of 14. Her betrothed was Andreas Stuchs (an administrator for the Elector Palatine), with whom she had almost ten years of marriage. However, Andreas died in Heidelberg before his wife's twenty-fourth birthday. Margarethe then married another electoral court secretary, Peter Harrer, in 1530. After another ten years of marriage, Margarethe herself died in Heidelberg on January 17, 1540, at the age of 34.[19]

Finally, as Georg's strength began to give out in his forty-ninth year, little Barbara was born. Her birth and her father's death happened almost simultaneously. She grew up in Bretten, had an unhappy marriage to a knight named Peter Kechel, and died on October 26, 1542, at the age of 34.[20] Both of Philipp's youngest sisters, Margarethe and Barbara, died at the age of 34. Both married honest, upright men, and left a lasting legacy of many children and grandchildren, all brought up well, with God's grace.

Philipp, the firstborn of the five Schwartzerdt children, grew up in relatively comfortable, orderly circumstances. He was the son of a religious, loyal, civic-minded family. He loved both his father and his mother. We have no evidence of domestic dysfunction in his home life, nor did he consider the piety of his parents smothering or controlling. Far from rebelling against his parents' faith, young Philipp embraced it with all the earnestness and seriousness he saw modeled in his father, along with a touch of his mother's lively temperament.[21]

---

19. Margarete's second husband, Peter Harrer, remained a widower for up to twelve years, before marrying a widow named Barbara Hess in about 1551. Harrer himself died around 1555.
20. Peter Kechel, *Amtsknecht,* died in November of 1561.
21. Those who stereotype Melanchthon as solely meek and mild would be well-served to review the tenor of the *Loci communes* of 1521, where the young theologian often expresses himself heatedly.

Due to Georg's busy travel schedule, he was not home much. Philipp once accompanied him to Heidelberg,[22] and recalled vividly years later that Johann von Dalberg, the bishop of Worms and the chancellor of Heidelberg, died in an accidental fall down a flight of stairs while the six year-old boy was in town. Georg did not tell his son all the details about that fall—the boy would come to an have an even more distinct impression of the event once he returned to Heidelberg as a university student a mere six years later.

Nevertheless, despite Georg's frequent absences, Philipp always expressed a positive view of his childhood. While his father's pious example deeply affected the boy, so did his mother's deliberate teaching. The family read in the Bible every day. Philipp recalled that a favorite family verse was 1 John 4:16: "God is love, and he who abides in love abides in God, and God in him." Philipp held fond memories of reciting this verse thankfully with his siblings.[23] As a professor later on, he often spoke of such verses learned from his mother.

Frequent church attendance exposed Philipp to many dramatic stories of saints. Philipp later reminisced, "I remember how much we liked stories about the saints. The preacher told them in the church. Then we children would imitate them at home."[24] His parents, too, would tell stories of martyrs and holy men. Indeed, they kept the children busier than other kids with pious training. Likely this proclivity flowed primarily from Georg, who demonstrated such views so clearly in his own life. The Schwartzerdt family thought it frivolous for children just to run around being noisy in the streets all day. Instead, Philipp remembered his parents frequently remarking, "There is nothing greater, better, or more holy than to meditate

---

22. On July 27, 1503.
23. CR 24:502. Mühlhaupt, 4.
24. CR 24:786. Mühlhaupt, 4.

on the passion of Christ."[25] As an adult, Philipp expressed gratitude for this godly training—and also sorrow at how few parents were currently supplying it: "When I was a child, I knew the biblical texts, and I read in them more than today's children. These days nothing is considered to be beautiful and good, but what is wild and rough![26] And they call it Gospel freedom!"[27] Indeed, those who thought it foolish to provide a thorough education for their children were themselves fools.[28] Philipp thus came to see his parent's strong commitment to his education as God's grace.

---

25. CR 24:652. Mühlhaupt, 4.
26. Literally, "cyclopean"—a reference to Homer's destructive cyclops in *The Odyssey*.
27. CR 24:718. Mühlhaupt 4.
28. CR 24:786. Mühlhaupt, 4.

4

The Passing of the Age

1493–1508

Train up a child in the way he should go, and when he is old he will not depart from it.
  —Proverbs 22:6

The start of the sixteenth century saw the turning of the age. The medieval era was fading away, while a new early modern era gathered strength. While it would take endless volumes to tell the tale of this transition properly, we must content ourselves here with a few issues so broad that they impacted even little Bretten, where a small precocious boy was just beginning to learn about God and the world.

Cities throughout Europe were growing, and people were living longer. Life expectancy at birth was ticking up well over the grand old age of 30. Feudalism was gradually giving way to new capitalistic practices. Technological innovation brought new efficiencies, and the printing press opened up a whole world of possibility. With moveable type and the ability to mass-produce books (rather than copy them by hand), the chance to spread knowledge and ideas increased dramatically. Some saw this as God's providence. Martin Luther once said, "Printing is the latest of God's gifts and the greatest. Through printing God wills to make the cause of true religion known to the whole world even to the ends of the earth."[1] However, technology is but a tool that can be turned either for good or ill. The printing press allowed for the diffusion of Bibles and godly writings. But it also allowed for the widespread distribution of erroneous or harmful writings. Arguments in print flourished ("pamphlet warfare" might put it more accurately), with the attendant phenomena of insults, indexes of forbidden books, and even the burning of offensive writings. Religious controversy became popularized, often tying into underlying social, national, regional, and economic forces. The printing press was an attack on obscurity—information became available to great numbers of people, and ideas deemed by some to be unacceptable could no longer easily be hidden or suppressed. The stakes were raised—affirmations of authority had to be backed up by documentary proof and with reason. Learning to read became a vital skill, and European levels of literacy began to rise.

The invention of the printing press allowed for the dissemination of ancient texts. This bolstered the growing movement of humanism,[2] which emphasized renewed study of ancient sources, with the understanding that much had been corrupted or obscured during the medieval period. Ancient sources, such as the Bible, Plato, Aristotle, and Cicero, could provide purer knowledge and better rhetorical techniques than the often muddled writings of the previous ten centuries.

---

1. Quoted in OER, "Printing."
2. Sixteenth century humanism, with its emphasis on eloquence and original sources (often in service of the Christian faith) must be distinguished from twenty-first century "humanism," which is an affirmation of the individual so extreme that it either ignores or denies God.

THE PASSING OF THE AGE

An early printing press.

While humanism in Italy focused primarily on studying ancient sources as a means to improving the effectiveness of contemporary communication, humanism in its northern European form emphasized the study of ancient sources not just for written and spoken eloquence, but also in order to bring new life and vigor to the Christian faith. These scholars believed that the careful study and explication of the Scriptures and the early church fathers would lead to a spiritual renewal.

Northern European humanism, empowered by a growing number of texts made available due to the wonders of the printing press, placed a high value on a rigorous education for the promotion of the glory of God. Georg Schwartzerdt, with his personal piety and court connections in Heidelberg, was well placed to be receptive to this movement. Likewise, Barbara would have been familiar with these ideas through her relative, Johannes Reuchlin of Pforzheim, the most famous humanist in the southern German lands at that time. Thus, from both sides of his family, the bright young Schwartzerdt boy of Bretten was poised to receive the scholarly and spiritual heritage of this dawning age—intellectual rigor, an emphasis on original sources rightly interpreted, and a fierce determination to put it all to work for the revival of a Christian church in need of reformation.

As a young child, Philipp Schwartzerdt experienced relatively peaceful and comfortable circumstances.[3] He was compliant and diligent with a remarkable memory. Philipp was a small boy with large eyes and a head full of Latin. He was bright, loving to study. He was friendly, cordial, well-spoken, and kind—though he did have a moderate temper that he strove to keep in check. With two families under one roof in the center of town, Philipp had to get along with the adults, his siblings, and his younger uncle Iohannes. The

---

3. For more on Philipp's years in Bretten, see also Heinz Scheible, "Melanchthons Werdegang," in Heinz Scheible, ed., *Aufsätze zu Melanchthon* (Tübingen: Mohr Siebeck, 2010), 29–30.

importance of peaceful coexistence was impressed upon him from an early age.

Although Philipp's parents highly valued his education, Georg was away on business so often that he could not properly oversee the training of the children. As a result, he asked his father-in-law, Hans Reuter, to do it. Reuter gladly did so, and continued in this capacity after 1504, when Georg remained home, but was too ill to look after the children properly.

Barbara's father, Hans Reuter, was not a native of Bretten, but moved there for marriage. He likely came from Speyer, where he still had family. His trade in textiles was fruitful, and he was also the well-respected mayor of Bretten. Widely considered a man of understanding, he had been a diligent student himself. A conscientious, pious, and civic-minded public servant, he loved the children and sought their best. He made sure they attended church regularly and he even bought them a Missal so they could learn the hymns and chants used for worship.[4] When the three young boys (Philipp Schwartzerdt, Iohannes Reuter, and Georg Schwartzerdt the Younger) reached the appropriate age, Reuter made sure they regularly attended school in Bretten. It was under Reuter's supervision that Philipp first began to encounter the northern European humanist breezes of culture and scholarship.

Bretten only had one school at this point, and Reuter carefully oversaw the boys' studies to make sure they made good progress. All seemed to be going well—until the school teacher suddenly developed a cough. He became feverish and sensitive to light, with a rash spreading over his body. Headaches and muscle pain followed. His thinking became hazy, and as the rash culminated in foul-smelling open sores, he became delirious.[5] Rumors of this condition sprouting up in the region had already reached Bretten, with

---

4. CR 10:258.

contemporaries calling it "a loathsome disease from France."[6] Others referred to it as the Spanish plague. It apparently arrived in the Kraichgau Valley courtesy of mercenary soldiers from further west—and it was highly contagious.

This wasting pestilence now afflicting people throughout Germany was most likely *epidemic typhus*, transmitted by bacteria on human lice.[7] Both excruciating and often mutilating, this was a horrible disease introduced to Europe in the Spanish siege of Moorish Grenada in 1489, where 3,000 Spanish war casualties were dwarfed by 17,000 struck down by the disease.[8] On a continent once traumatized by a contagion so deadly that the word "decimated" is three-fold too small,[9] any new plague would have been greeted with great trepidation. Reuter certainly wasted no time and promptly withdrew all three boys from the school. He decided to hire a private tutor to teach in his home instead.

The Reuters consulted with their Pforzheim relative, Johannes Reuchlin, for a recommendation. He suggested a young man of twenty years named Iohannes Hungaris (or Unger). This *Paedagogum* turned out to be both respectable and excellent. He moved to Bretten and began instructing the boys on a daily basis. Unger proved to be a meticulous tutor. He focused on Latin from the beginning, making sure his charges mastered the grammar. They had to know all the rules, without leaving any out. He held them to high standards,

---

5. *U. S. National Library of Medicine.* www.ncbi.nlm.nih.gov/pubmedhealth/PMH0002339. Accessed on October 16, 2012.
6. *Die abscheuliche Krankheit der Franzosen.* CR 10:258
7. "Typhus" comes from a Greek word meaning "smoky" or "hazy," referring to the later mental states of those afflicted.
8. Later, in 1528, the French would lose 18,000 troops to typhus in Italy.
9. The word "decimate" has its roots in a grievous ancient Roman military practice where a general or emperor wishing to severely punish a legion (perhaps for military failure) would order the soldiers to draw lots, and every one in ten (hence *dec*-imate) was to be beaten to death with clubs by his fellow soldiers. "Decimate" technically, therefore would refer to a one-in-ten reduction of a force, whereas the bubonic plague brought a three-in-ten to six-in-ten reduction in population to the regions of Europe.

assigning ample homework—twenty to thirty lines of Latin verse to translate daily), and applying the rod or strap for slipshod work. Translations needed to be both precise and concise. Although Unger introduced the children to Virgil, Horace, and Ovid, the primary text he employed for homework and disputation came from the contemporary Latin author Baptista Mantuanus. This work made an impression on Philipp, and later on as a professor, he would often employ cutting quips from Mantuan.

Despite Unger's severity, he also held genuine affection for his students and sought to inspire them. One bit of practical advice he offered stuck with Philipp throughout his life: *Cave et cede* ("Be cautious, and yield.") Later in life, in high-stakes international diplomacy, this approach sometimes brought progress, and at other times infuriated Philipp's allies (who thought he yielded too much).

In the meantime, Philipp flourished under Unger's instruction. The Pforzheim native noticed right away that his student was quick to perceive, comprehend, make connections, and memorize information accurately. The boy could explain what he had learned smoothly. His excellence was swiftly on display. Soon Philipp was reading and writing fluently in Latin, and he learned the grammar so well that he reached the end of it.

Philipp showed enthusiasm for his studies, and could not keep quiet among other (even older) children. He was always inquiring and disputing about everything. He launched into lively discussions with other schoolboys, even on the rules of Latin grammar. Tireless in disputation, Philipp routinely dispatched other students in debate. Grandfather Reuter was proud and moved by this speedy progress, and he did everything in his power to encourage it. With the family home located just across the street from the Krone guest house, Reuter stayed vigilant for news of educated travelers stopping over for the night.

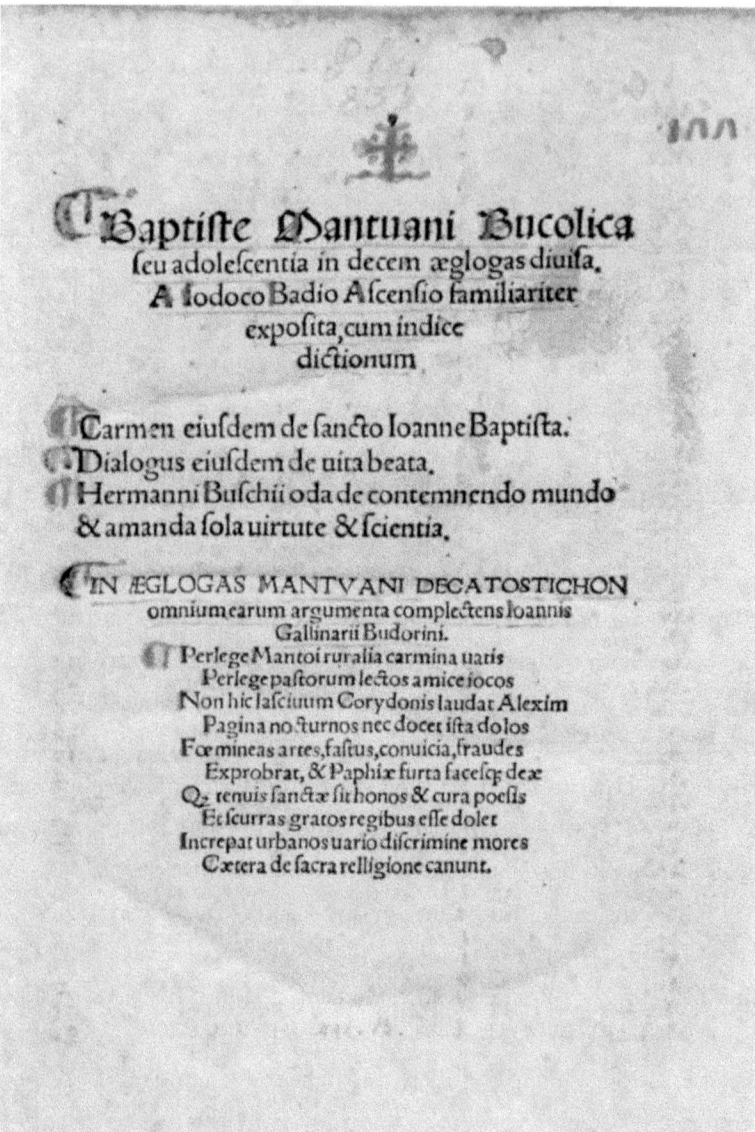

The first page of an edition of one of Philipp's likely childhood textbooks. Baptiste Mantuani Bucolica seu adolescentia in decem aeglogas diuisa. (Straßburg: 1502). Bayerische Staatsbibliothek München. VD16 S 7165. Bildnr. 7 (title page). URN:nbn:de:bvb:12-bsb00004187-9.

He sought to engage them in debate with his precocious grandson, sometimes at the fountain just outside the guest house where travelers watered their horses.

The boy Philipp, with his mother (to the left) and Hans Reuter (to the right) debating with learned travelers at the fountain across from his house in the center of Bretten. This painting is on the wall of the Gedächtnishalle in the Melanchthonhaus in Bretten. Photo by Gregory Graybill.

Though it was seldom that someone was willing to engage him, Philipp had success even in debating educated adult travelers. They were amazed by his knowledge and ability. Pleased, Reuter kept his grandson well supplied with books and whatever learning materials he could find. Encouraged by his triumphs and the praise he received, Philipp pursued his studies with interest and attention. It became clear to Reuter, as well as to Georg, Barbara, and all other observers, that this boy would do well with further education. As a family, they committed themselves to seeing this happen, and, in due course, carried it our successfully.

After his years in Bretten, Iohannes Unger became a teacher in Pforzheim. Later, he became an effective and influential pastor, serving as court chaplain for the Margrave of Baden. Many years later, Melanchthon's friend Joachim Camerarius heard Unger preaching in Pforzheim for an audience of Margrave Ernst von Baden and his son Karl II, along with a large crowd. Camerarius reported that Unger spoke passionately and persuasively, clearly explaining the gospel of Jesus Christ. He further added that Unger was a good man (*virum optimum*).[10] Upon his death in 1553, Melanchthon referred to him as "an old friend of the family,"[11] and wrote, "He was an honest man who taught the Gospel and suffered much for the Gospel's sake. He was a pastor at Pforzheim. He drove me to grammar and made me do twenty or thirty verses from Mantuan each day. He would not allow me to omit anything. Whenever I would make a mistake, he applied the rod to me, and yet with the moderation that was proper. Thus he made me a linguist. He was a good man; he loved me as a son, and I him as a father; and in short time we shall meet, I hope, in eternal life. I loved him notwithstanding that he used such severity; although it was not

---

10. See Cam., *Das Leben*, 41. Cf. Cam., *Vita*, 7.
11. May 8, 1553. MBW 6825. CR 8:83. Cf. Mühlhaupt 6.

severity, but parental correction which prompted me to diligence. At evening I had to hunt the rules in order to recite. You see, discipline was stricter then than now!"[12]

The happy memory of a good teacher, however, could not obscure the memory that Bretten was the scene of both joys and sorrows for Philipp. The pleasures of the home fires would give way to a pyre in the street, and a military conflagration outside the city walls that would injure the young boy's heart forever.

---

12. CR 25:448–49. Trans. in Manschreck, 31. See also Richard, 7.

5

A Time to Mourn

1493–1508

> I saw many changes in public matters—but even greater ones loom. I pray that God will guide you in the midst of them. I am warning you ahead of time, son, to fear God, and to live an upright life.
> —Georg Schwartzerdt the Elder

The bucolic nature of Philipp Schwartzerdt's early childhood came to an abrupt end in 1504. He was seven years old when fire and blood came to the city. Executions took place outside his front door. Siege cannons were set up on the hills of Gölshausen just north of the city walls. A murder suspect fled through the Reuter family home, with a vengeful mob in pursuit. What effect might these events have on a precocious, sensitive child?

Maleficium

In 1504, a huge hailstorm destroyed much of the crops standing in the fields surrounding Bretten. While today such an event would be

61

lamented as a natural disaster, in 1504 it sparked outraged accusations of supernatural intervention by diabolical forces, instigated by spiteful human beings. In 1487, an inquisitor named Jakob Sprenger[1] wrote a book called *Malleus maleficarum (The Hammer of Witches)*. Published fourteen times between 1487 and 1520, it enjoyed wide popularity. It included as an introduction a papal bull[2] from Innocent VIII establishing witch hunting (especially in the Rhineland) as an official task of the Inquisition.

Primed by such official attention to the issue, citizens of Bretten blamed the unexpected destructiveness of the hailstorm on *maleficium*—the demonic intercessions of witches. A witch-hunt ensued, and four suspected culprits were seized, tried, and found guilty. The people of Bretten built a great pyre in the city center, just outside the front door of the Reuter house, next to the fountain, across from the Krone guesthouse. A great crowd gathered, and the four accused were burned to death, the smoke rising to the heavens from the usual playground of the Schwartzerdt children.[3]

The Siege of Bretten

Meanwhile, conflict smoldered outside the city walls as young Philipp worked through his lines of Mantuan. In 1474, Elector Philipp the Upright of the Palatinate had married Margaret of Bavaria-Landshut, daughter of Louis IX, Duke of Bavaria. By 1503, it was clear that no male heir would appear for the somewhat distant but attractive duchy of Bavaria-Landshut (it had productive mining operations and efficient administration). A disagreement about how rule of that duchy would move forward touched off a conflict.

---

1. Some think the real author was Heinrich Kramer, who used Sprenger's name as a pseudonym.
2. *Summis desiderantes affectibus*, 1484.
3. Georg Schwartzerdt (Melanchthon's younger brother) wrote about this incident, as well as the siege of Bretten, in 1561. See Leo Vogt's modern edition of the text in *1504: Die Chronik des Georg Schwarzerdt. Eine Stadt lebt ihre Geschichte* (Verlag Regionalkultur, 2000).

A TIME TO MOURN

Woodcut from Jackob Sprenger's Malleus maleficarum (Colonia: 1511). Bayerische Staatsbibliothek München. VD16 S 8380. Bildnr. 8 (title page). URN:nbn:de:bvb:12-bsb00014933-4.

Bretten. Illustration by Jeffrey Mathison.

During 1503 and 1504, the villages of Landshut were ravaged. An extended network of alliances and family connections brought the fight to the Palatinate and the Kraichgau Valley as well. Elector Philipp, through his wife's family, ended up in the middle of the conflict, with Emperor Maximilian eventually getting involved (who thought domains without an heir should revert to the empire), as well as the hot-headed Duke Ulrich of Württemberg, who found himself conveniently allied with forces on the opposite side as Elector Philipp. Ulrich jumped at the opportunity to scoop up some new possessions for himself at the expense of Philipp's holdings in Baden. This Landshut War, or the Bavarian-Palatinate War of Succession of 1504–07, would come to make an impact so strong on Bretten that its memory is kept alive in the annual Peter and Paul Festival held in June, which is attended by around eighty thousand people yearly.

In June, 1504, Ulrich first bore down on the nearby twelfth-century Cistercian monastery at Maulbronn, just six miles southeast of Bretten. He arrived with a force of twenty to thirty thousand men.[4] Ulrich brought with him as many of his male subjects of military age as possible without leaving his own lands defenseless. They traveled by foot and by horse, armed with guns, and laden with provisions. His force also included a large number of mercenary knights. The monks at Maulbronn cleared out before this army arrived, and Elector Philipp was unable to mount a defense, due to the simultaneous attack on his domains from several directions at once. Maulbronn surrendered, but that did not prevent Ulrich's forces from pillaging the area. The duke had no trouble adding Maulbronn to his domains.

---

4. Although it ceased functioning as a monastery in 1537, it still stands today, and remains an attractive tourist destination.

Pfeifferturm: A defense tower in Bretten. Built in the fifteenth century, it was in place during the siege of 1504. Photograph by Gregory Graybill.

Meanwhile, although Elector Philipp had been unable to send aid to Maulbronn, he did manage to send large stocks of guns, powder, lead, and provisions to Bretten. Additionally, he ordered the people of the surrounding villages of Rinklingen, Diedelsheim, Gölshausen, Sprantal, and Ölbronn to provide manpower and supplies for the defense of Bretten, which was now definitely feeling the heat—both of the summer weather, and of the impending assault.

Under pressure, tempers in Bretten began to grow short. In one public meeting at the *Rathaus*, Friedrich Hack and several dozen followers began to show disdain and impatience with the citizens of Bretten. Hack and his crew had come from the village of Weingarten *before* Elector Philipp had ordered such groups into the town, and he took this to mean that they should receive special consideration. A fiery argument broke out at the *Rathaus*, and Hans Lott, town mayor at the time, sent everyone home. However, a few individuals from both sides continued to yell at each other in the town center, just in front of young Philipp Schwartzerdt's house. Lott forced his way between the two groups, and sent them packing, narrowly avoiding violence. The dispute would simmer, however.

Duke Ulrich now pushed several miles to the northwest from Maulbronn to Knittlingen, where he set up camp to prepare for the assault on Bretten. At this time, a furious storm broke, with a gale so great that it carried away tents and set the entire camp into an uproar. Some blamed it on the recent witch burning in Bretten, taking it as evidence of the practice of *maleficium* in the area, and that the whole town of Bretten must be full of witches to kick up so great a shrieking tempest. Once the storm finally ended on June 11, 1504, the army prepared to march on the citizens of Bretten, whom many of the Württembergers now considered to be diabolically deserving of destruction. The people of the town retreated behind their walls and prepared to endure a siege. They began manning the walls night and day.

Ulrich and his forces moved past Knittlingen and advanced on Bretten from the north, through the little village of Gölshausen.

There, on the high ground facing the walls of Bretten, Ulrich began to erect earthwork counter-fortifications, mostly by night. When it was complete, he mounted his artillery atop the fortifications, and began a dawn barrage of Bretten's guard tower, walls, and houses. The town shook with the thunderous cannon fire. Dust, smoke, and steam soon obscured everything. While the barrage damaged the walls markedly, the town held out, day after day.

June 15, day three of the siege, however, brought matters to a head between the men of Weingarten and some of the other defenders, trapped together in the bombarded city. During an altercation near the market fountain in front of the Reuter house, Carius Einhart from Weingarten used a boar spear to stab a man from the Oberes Reich—a region on the Rhine just south of Strasbourg. Many witnesses were on hand. Seeing an open door, Einhart dashed inside the house of Hans Reuter, young Philipp Schwartzerdt's home.[5] The men of the Oberes Reich put up a cry, rallying to the Reuter house to demand the surrender of Einhart, whom they now branded murderer for the lifeblood of their compatriot. What they did not realize, however, was that Einhart had already run out the back door just as swiftly as he ran in the front door. Before the outcry had a chance to spread, he immediately and calmly made his way to the Salzhof Gate, which was normally guarded but left open, and made his escape out of the town and away.

Meanwhile, the men of the Oberes Reich encircled the Reuter house, believing the fugitive to be hiding inside. This created a certain difficulty for the Reuter and Schwartzerdt families. The men of the Oberes Reich insisted on their right to justice for the criminal, and the citizens of Bretten likewise gathered together to see what the commotion was about and to try to hold together the ranks for their all-important defense of the city. The citizens and the men of

---

5. As an adult, Georg Schwartzerdt the Younger would take over ownership of the Reuter house.

the Oberes Reich quickly antagonized each other, with the men even threatening Hans Reuter by holding spears and halberds to his chest. Eventually, it was agreed that a thorough but respectful search of the house would be made. A number of cool-headed men were selected, who went with Reuter and searched every room, every cupboard, every door, nook, and cranny of the entire house. When they did not find the culprit, someone finally reported that they had seen a man run out the lower downhill backdoor of the Reuter house right after the incident. The men of the Oberes Reich investigated the report, deemed it to be true, and grudgingly left. The Schwartzerdt children were allowed back in at this point. Seven years old, Philipp had just seen his grandfather threatened with death, and his home overturned.

Six days later, on June 21, the unity of the defenders again frayed. The hired knights under Albrecht Schedel had served honorably and well—and just that day they had taken four casualties in the fighting. However, they had not been paid in over a month, and so they gathered in the Bretten marketplace at the house where Schedel was staying to demand their pay. They were being slaughtered like sheep in the bombardment, and they would not keep it up without their pay. Soon, all the mercenary knights were gathered around their leader, making the same case. Because the defense of the city hinged on these knights, the situation was tense. Schedel explained that he had no gold available in this besieged town, but that the knights would have to trust to the promise of the Elector Philipp to pay. Unimpressed, they continued threatening to leave the city. When Schedel tried to remonstrate with them, they shouted him down and used their drummers to drown him out.

Seeing the fate of the town at stake, the leaders of Bretten called a meeting and sought to find a way to keep the knights in the city. Hans Reuter and Jacob Schmeltzle organized (and were the main contributors toward) a town-wide funds drive. The citizens donated gold and valuables, until they had about half of what the knights were owed. Reuter comforted the people that the Elector Philipp would make good these temporary losses. The alternative, of course, was to lose everything—perhaps even life and limb. Schedel offered the funds along with promises to help with necessities to the rebellious knights. He also reproved them for their lack of faithfulness. While some were willing to accept the offer, others continued to shout that they would either have full payment, or go serve someone else.

The town bailiff then mustered the fighting men of Bretten, armed and in full armor, telling the scoffers among the knights either to get out, or to accept the current offer of half pay, provisions, and a promise to pay the rest when possible. They decided to take the offer.

On the next day, June 22, the arrival of 1,500 knights sent by Elector Philipp from the regions of Sundgau, Elsaß, and Breisgau made the issue moot. The incoming knights brought with them adequate gold to pay all the knights, so that the citizens of Bretten could be paid back. This solidified the defense of the city, and even led the defenders to consider taking the offensive.

Accordingly, early in the morning of June 28, the defenders successfully sallied forth, inflicting hundreds of casualties on the Württembergers and taking some forty-one enemies prisoner. Ulrich then renewed the artillery bombardment, firing over three hundred cannonballs into the city, by the Brettener's count. Most ominously, the attackers successfully fired three incendiary rounds into the city. One fortunately landed in the fountain in front of the Reuter house and was immediately extinguished by the water. Another landed in an alley, and the third lodged in the outer fortifications. Due to the summer heat, the dryness, and the lack of surplus water in the town, these attacks represented a serious threat. However, Ulrich was not equipped to sustain an incendiary bombardment, much to the relief of the Bretteners.

Actual cannon balls from the siege of Bretten in 1504, stored today in the Simmelturm in Bretten. Photo by Gregory Graybill.

After several weeks of the siege, the Württembergers did not seem to be much closer to taking the town. Could they starve them out? At this point, mention must be made of what can only be termed "the chubby pug gambit." Although Georg Schwartzerdt the Younger made no mention of it in his official history of the siege written within living memory of the event, it is celebrated in modern Bretten with a prominent fountain on the Melanchthonstraße, several stone monuments, a restaurant (the Brettener Hundle), and a number of books at the tourist center. The legend is that as the siege dragged on and food supplies became low, the citizens of Bretten wanted to fool the attackers into thinking they were well-stocked. So, despite the limited food, they made sure to feed (indeed, *over*-feed) a certain pet pug in the town until he was of a noticeably corpulent stature.

Then they allowed him to "escape" the city toward the attacking forces. The Württembergers purportedly fell for the gambit, thinking Bretten to be well-provisioned if even their dogs were this fat. So they cut off the little pug's tail and sent him back (the modern fountain in the town dutifully depicts the pug with his tail sliced off).

Sign in the Goldener Schwan im Schweizerhof Restaurant, Bretten. Photograph by Gregory Graybill.

Whether or not the legend of the pug is true,[6] Duke Ulrich tired of the siege after about three weeks and made peace. The sides sealed the agreement on July 4, 1504. Ulrich then withdrew to his own territories, though retaining Maulbronn, and adding the villages of Besigheim, Weinsberg, and Möckmühl as a sop so that he

---

6. Pauli, 15, for example, makes the case for this incident. On the other hand Peter Bahn argues that it did not occur (at least in 1504): *Das Brettener Hundle: Eine Spurensuch* (Karlsruhe: Lindemanns Bibliothek, 2011), 42–48.

could declare victory. The Bretteners were angered by these further conquests, seeing it as a violation of their agreement—but they were not in a position to do anything about it.

Wooden toy Hundles in the Bretten Stadtzentrum, 2013. Photograph by Gregory Graybill.

The war moved on from Bretten, flaming out after another few years in 1507. The Elector Philipp permanently lost the monastery of Maulbronn and the village of Knittlingen to Württemberg.[7] But the memories of the siege, the mutiny of the knights, and the flight of the murderer through his home must surely have stuck with young Philipp. Likewise, Philipp's brother, Georg the Younger, in his *Chronik* tells of a monk from a preaching order who was in Bretten during the siege. He took confession and spoke words of

---

7. Located near Knittlingen and Bretten, the village of Ruit (the present writer's home for a year), served as the boundary between Baden and Württemberg until modern times. This reflects the furthest extent of Ulrich's advance in 1504.

trust to the wounded and dying. But he did not forget himself. He asked for money for absolutions, and forcibly took it from those unwilling to give. He collected nearly a hundred gulden like this.⁸ Such behavior may have contributed to Melanchthon's later negative attitudes toward monasticism. He himself, however, never discussed the siege, or how it impacted him.⁹ It is interesting, though, that one who experienced war so closely as a boy, should become so dedicated to peacemaking as an adult.

The top of the Hundle Fountain, on Melanchthonstraße, Bretten. Photograph by Gregory Graybill.

---

8. "Der Feldpater," in Schwartzerdt, Georg, *Die Chronik*, chapter 32, pp. 54–55.
9. At least, as far as I know. Perhaps there is some thus-far undiscovered mention of this time in his thousands of letters and works.

A TIME TO MOURN

A Casualty of War

Although I have found no record of Melanchthon discussing the siege of Bretten, he did speak with some emotion about the effect of the Landshut War on his father—and through him, on himself.

At the outbreak of the Landshut War in 1504, Georg the Elder found himself in the service of Emperor Maximilian, who it seemed was going to come into conflict with Elector Philipp. Seeing the threat to his prince, however, Georg took a leave of absence from Maximilian and secretly returned to Heidelberg for service to Elector Philipp. Philipp promptly attached Georg to a small artillery company of fourteen men. While camped near Mannheim, the men drank from a poisoned well. Over the course of four days, all died, except for Georg, who lingered in a state of desperate illness.[10] The elector's personal doctor ministered to Georg and stabilized him—though he saw very little improvement.

Georg returned home to Bretten, where his family cared for him during his continuing illness. During this time, Georg's personal piety became even more pronounced, as he continued to seek the Lord, even in this state of suffering. His faith set a powerful example for young Philipp, who was overcome with grief when his mother explained to him how serious his father's illness was.

Although he lived for four more years, and indeed had additional children during that time, Georg the Elder remained incapacitated, and neared his end in the autumn of 1508. Later in life, Melanchthon wrote, "Often today I think about my father's peaceful death, and about the dread events that followed. I remember that he prophesied two days before his death, when I was ten years old. He commended

---

10. Some suggest that Georg's illness may have sprung from working with lead as an armorer. However, the earliest accounts from contemporaries (CR and Camerarius) claim that he drank poisoned well water during the war. The nearly immediate deaths of his companions who also drank from the well supports this theory.

me to God, and exhorted me to fear of the Lord. 'I saw,' he said, 'many changes in public matters—but even greater ones loom. I pray that God will guide you in the midst of them. I am warning you ahead of time, son, to fear God, and to live an upright life.'"[11]

After this last charge and blessing, the distraught young Philipp and his siblings were sent off to relatives in Speyer so they would not be present for the death itself. Two days later,[12] Georg the Elder died at the age of 49. At about the same time (within a week and a half), his father-in-law Hans Reuter also died, bringing a double-grief to the Reuter and Schwartzerdt household. All told, in the year 1508, Barbara Schwartzerdt saw the death of her husband, the death of her father, and the birth of a daughter, also named Barbara.

The pressures of taking care of at least six children (five of her own plus her much younger brother) would be too much for Barbara, even with her mother's help. Something would have to give, and what this meant for a certain grieving boy of eleven was that his childhood in Bretten was now over.

---

11. October 27, 1554, letter to Georg Fabricius. CR 8:367, Nr. 5680. MBW 7315.
12. Some sources say it was September 29 (e.g., CR 10:258), and others (e.g., Stupperich and Scheible) claim October 27, based on a letter Melanchthon wrote to Georg Fabricius on October 27, 1554. MBW 7315. CR 8:367, Nr. 5680. A few sources, such as the CR and Richard, also claim that the death happened in 1507, rather than 1508.

6

Pforzheim

1508–1509

And an inscription also was written over Him in letters of Greek, Latin, and Hebrew:

> THIS IS THE KING OF THE JEWS.
> —Luke 23:38

Strained by the momentous events of the near-simultaneous birth of her daughter, the death of her husband, and the death of her father, Barbara Schwartzerdt had some difficult decisions to make in the fall of 1508. How would she and her mother, Elisabeth, move forward in managing their household of at least six young children? Most sources suggest that Barbara remarried within a year.[1] But the question remained: how would the education of the boys proceed, now that Georg the Elder and Hans Reuter were both gone? Here Elisabeth took matters into her own hands and consulted with her

---

1. E.g., Scheible, Greschat, and Peter Bahn. If she did, then Christoph Kolb is named as the new husband, with perhaps a son and two daughters following before his death in 1519 or 1520. A few sources (e.g., Cox, 7) suggest she remained a widow for twelve years.

THE HONEYCOMB SCROLL

famous relative, Johannes Reuchlin of Pforzheim (though he now lived in Stuttgart where he served as a counselor to the very Duke Ulrich of Württemberg who so recently had besieged Bretten). Reuchlin recommended that the boys attend the excellent Latin school in Pforzheim run by Georg Simler. Elisabeth and Barbara acted promptly, and sent the three boys to Pforzheim—Philipp (age eleven), Georg the Younger (age seven), and Johannes (Hans) Reuter the Younger (also somewhere around age eleven).

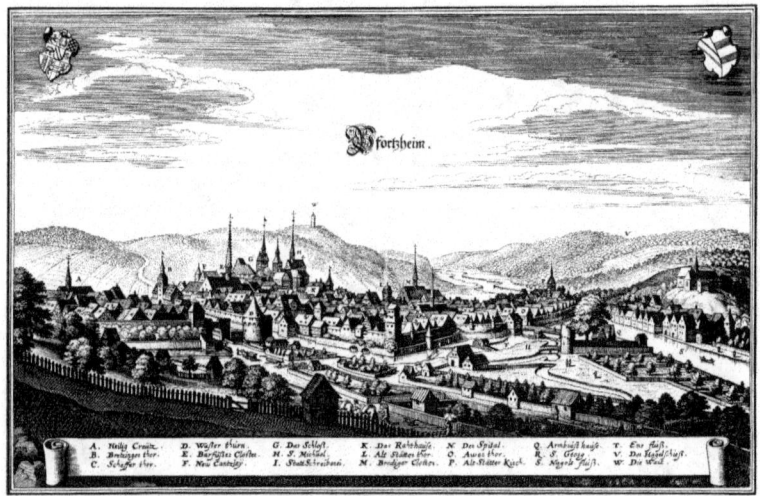

Woodcut of Pforzheim from 1643, by Mattäus Merian.

Town and Country

A full day's hike for the boys, Pforzheim lay twelve miles south of Bretten. The Enz, Nagold, and Würm rivers came together at this city, sometimes called the Three Valleys Town. In Roman times, the settlement was called Portus, or the Gateway to the Black Forest. The streams held abundant fish, and for the four thousand inhabitants of the city, timber-rafting lumber downriver to the regions of the

Netherlands provided an important economic foundation. Besides the timber raftsmen, fraternities of tailors, bakers, weavers, and wine growers were also significant. The Margraves of Baden viewed Pforzheim as an important administrative center. It held both Dominican and Franciscan monasteries. A land of natural beauty, the forests, fields, meadows and streams made a lasting impression on young Philipp.

Soon the boys arrived at their new home for the next year—the house of Elisabeth Reuchlin, Johannes Reuchlin's sister. Philipp remembered her as a sweet lady; and Reuchlin himself, though living in Stuttgart, visited often.

The Latin School

Philipp, Georg, and their young uncle Hans arrived in Pforzheim sometime in October or November, 1508. From their new home with Reuchlin's sister, they made their way each day to the Pforzheim Latin School. In sending the boys here, the Schwartzerdt/Reuter family was providing them with the best possible education. Famed for its emphasis on integrity, virtue, zeal, and reliably excellent teaching, the Latin school at Pforzheim was widely considered to be the best school of humanist learning in the entire southwestern region of the German-speaking lands. Likely founded by the Dominicans in their monastery in the 1460s, several notable contemporaries of Melanchthon also attended this Latin school. He came to know some of them during his time in Pforzheim, and corresponded with them later in his career.

Twelve years older than Philipp, Nicholas Gerbel (or Göbel) (1485–1560) came from Pforzheim, and so did not have far to come for the Latin school. A well-known scholar of the classics, Gerbel was an expert in Greek culture. He became a lawyer in ecclesiastical administration in Strasbourg, as well as a history teacher in the

Strasbourg Gymnasium. Gerbel became an intimate friend of Luther (whom he supported over Bucer and Hedio—though with no hard feelings). He also maintained a lifelong friendship with Melanchthon,[2] as well as with Erasmus. He aided Erasmus in preparing his Greek and Latin editions of the New Testament. Erasmus once remarked of Gerbel that "No man's society has given me the same pleasure."[3]

Notable contemporary graduates of the Pforzheim Latin School

Nicholas Gerbel (1485–1560).

---

2. See, for example, MBW 93 and 104.
3. *Collected Works of Erasmus*, Ep 366B.

Berchtold Haller (1492–1536).

Simon Grynaeus (1493–1541).

Caspar Hedio (1494–1552).

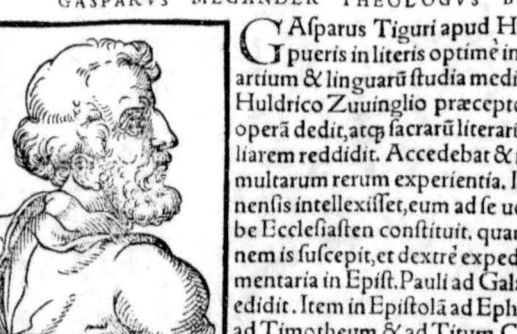

GASPARVS MEGANDER THEOLOGVS BERNENSIS.

GAsparus Tiguri apud Heluetios natus, & à pueris in literis optimè institutus est. Cum is artium & linguarū studia mediocriter percepisset, Huldrico Zuuinglio præceptore usus Theologię operā dedit,atcȝ sacrarū literarū lectionē sibi familiarem reddidit. Accedebat & naturalis facūdia,& multarum rerum experientia. Id cum respub.Bernensis intellexisset,eum ad se uocauit atcȝ in sua urbe Ecclesiasten constituit. quam quidem uocationem is suscepit,et dextrè expediuit.Scripsit is commentaria in Epist.Pauli ad Galatas,atcȝ Tiguri 1533 edidit. Item in Epistolā ad Ephesios, atcȝ in utrācȝ ad Timotheum,& ad Titum. Collegit etiam farraginem annotationum in Genesim & Exodum, ex ore Zuuinglij. pari ratione in epistolam ad Hæbræos, & priorem Ioannis Canonicam, cum annotationibus in Euangelia & in aliquot Pauli Epistolas, quæ quidem omnia Tiguri publicauit.Tandem etiam Gasparus in Acta Apostolorum commentaria cōposuit,& in gratiam iuuentutis Bernensis Catechismum collegit.Cum hoc modo suis uigilijs omnibus innotuisset, tādem immatura morte apud suos obijt, & honestè terræ mandatus fuit.Con.Gesl.in Bib.

Kaspar Megander (1495–1545). Courtesy of the Digital Image Archive, Pitts Theology Library, Candler School of Theology, Emory University.

Berchtold Haller (1492–1560) of Alldingen was a student at the Pforzheim school when Philipp arrived. The two established a lasting friendship here. Haller went on to study theology in Cologne, and then became a teacher first in Rottweil, and then in Bern, where he also soon took on an ecclesiastical role and began preaching. In 1521, he began to preach reform, and soon established a strong epistolary friendship with Huldrych Zwingli. Haller became the Reformer of Bern, and had ties in the early 1530s with both Heinrich Bullinger and Guillaume Farel (Calvin's coworker in Geneva).

Three years younger than Haller, Kaspar Megander (1495–1545) of Zürich also had a key role to play in Bern. After Pforzheim, he studied in Basel, and then returned to Zürich as a priest. He became a proponent and confidant of Zwingli as he advocated his Reformed theology from 1519 onwards. In 1528, he moved to Bern, where he advocated for Zwinglian theology, and strenuously opposed Bucer's attempts at reconciliation with the Lutherans in the Wittenberg Concord of 1536. Initially Haller had greater prominence in Bern, and Megander did not seek to eclipse him. But with Haller's passing in 1536, Megander necessarily rose to the fore for the next decade.

Perhaps Philipp's closest friend from his Pforzheim days was Simon Grynaeus (1493–1541). A native of the Swabian village of Veringen, Grynaeus was a farmer's son who became one of the greatest Greek scholars of the age. Philipp and Simon studied Greek together at Pforzheim. Grynaeus went on to study in Vienna, and then led a grammar school in Buda—though his Lutheran views soon got him into trouble. From there he went to Wittenberg in 1523, and then onward to teach Greek at the University of Heidelberg. He departed from Luther by embracing Zwingli's eucharistic theology, and moved to Basel in 1529, where he continued teaching. There his classical learning and knack for locating rare manuscripts (he once discovered five previously lost books of Livy) were put to good use by the circle around Erasmus and the Froben Press. Grynaeus translated Chrysostom's homilies on 1 Corinthians at Erasmus's request, and Erasmus wrote a preface for Grynaeus's Greek edition of Aristotle. Grynaeus traveled to England in 1531, and there met Henry VIII, as well as Thomas Cranmer, Thomas More, and Cardinal Reginald Pole. He was allowed some very fruitful manuscript hunting in the libraries of Oxford. A few years later, he successfully spent a year reorganizing the University of Tübingen, after Duke Ulrich was restored to power in Württemberg following his years in the wilderness. Grynaeus also helped draft the first Helvetic Confession, and maintained cordial relations with John Calvin. Grynaeus strove to build bridges between the Lutheran and Reformed camps, though he was not known to be as deft a mediator as was Melanchthon. He died of the plague in 1541.

Three other boys at the Pforzheim school, all from Ettlingen, went on to notable public careers. Caspar Hedio (1494–1552), became a renowned historian and theologian. After Pforzheim, he went on to the universities of Freiburg and Basel, where he also became a vicar, and studied theology under Wolfgang Capito. There he became familiar with other local humanist scholars, including Erasmus and Oecolampadius. Hedio went to Mainz as Capito's assistant, but then accepted a position as the cathedral preacher in Strasbourg. He began promoting the theology of the Reformation, much to Erasmus's displeasure. At the same time, Hedio pursued scholarly work as a historian, translating Eusebius into German, for example. He also wrote detailed accounts of the councils of Constance and Basel.

Matthias Erb (1495–1571), also from Ettlingen, became a notable theologian and reformer in Württemberg. Likewise notable was Franciscus Irenicus (or Franz Friedlieb) (1495–1553), who went on from Pforzheim to become a famous German humanist and historian. His history of Germany extended to twelve volumes.[4] He studied at Heidelberg and Tübingen, became canon and court preacher of Baden, and finally became a pastor and Latin school rector at Gemmingen, near Heidelberg.

Statue of Johannes Reuchlin, on Schloßberg
Straße, Pforzheim. Photo by Gregory Graybill.

Finally, Reuchlin himself may have attended the Pforzheim school as a child. He promoted it actively, helping to build and sustain its level of excellence. In this, he was successful, even to the extent that a school favoring classical learning in the tradition of this original Latin school can still be found in Pforzheim today. The Reuchlin Gymnasium greatly values this connection.

---

4. *Germaniae exegeseos volumina duodecim a Francisco Irenico Ettelingiaco exerata* (Hagenua, 1518).

Georg Simler

Young Philipp's intellectual horizons began to expand rapidly during his time in Pforzheim. His own passion for his studies made this possible, but it was the high level of excellence at the school, rooted primarily in its rector, Georg Simler, that truly allowed him to flourish. In an era when many Latin school teachers had no university education and were not necessarily moral people, Simler stood head and shoulders above his peers.

Born around 1477, Simler came from Wimpfen am Neckar, about forty miles northeast of Pforzheim, near Heilbronn (today it is known as Bad Wimpfen).[5] Raised in a relatively prosperous family, he matriculated at the University of Leipzig in the winter of 1490–91. There he received a good deal of exposure to humanist scholarship, with its emphasis on ancient languages and returning to the original sources. Konrad Wimpina (sometimes called Konrad Koch) proved to be an influential teacher for him.[6] In 1493, Simler went on to the University of Cologne, where he became familiar with Reuchlin through his scholarly Latin and Greek publications—likely his Latin dictionary, and his Greek *Micropædia*.[7] Cologne continued Simler's immersion in humanist scholarship, and when he began attending the University of Heidelberg in 1495, he received more of the same—although this time his studies included theology. At this point, Simler developed a great appreciation for Reuchlin's comedies, even to the extent of writing a commentary on Reuchlin's *Sergius*. The two met and became lifelong friends in 1496.[8] Each was impressed

---

5. Hence he is sometimes known as Georg Simler Wimpmensis.
6. Though, ironically, Wimpina was an early opponent of Luther's and a defender of Catholic theology. He even wrote theses for Johannes Tetzel to use in debate.
7. *Vocabularius breviloquus*, Basel, 1478. The Greek *Micropædia* is no longer extant.
8. Simler was an advocate for Reuchlin in his later controversies with the Cologne Dominicans.

with the other. Upon Reuchlin's recommendation, Simler went to Pforzheim in 1498 to assume leadership of the Latin school.

Simler was an expert in classical Latin (as opposed to the medieval practice of just learning the much-adulterated *ecclesiastical* Latin of more recent centuries). He also knew Greek well, and Hebrew to a lesser extent. By all accounts, Simler was a natural-born teacher, and Melanchthon often spoke of his excellence. Hence, with his training from Unger, his new instruction from Simler, and his connections to Reuchlin and Simler's friend, the Pforzheim printer Thomas Anshelm, young Philipp was well-positioned to rise as quickly as his abilities and hard work could take him. Talent, achievement, and great networking were as important in the sixteenth century as they remain in our own.

Simler did not remain the sole teacher at the Pforzheim Latin school, though. Soon Iohannes Hiltebrandt, who was about five years younger, also began teaching there. Although he did not have the advanced degrees that Simler did, Hiltebrandt's bachelor of arts degree from Heidelberg still gave him greater qualifications than the average teacher of the day.

Simler successfully led the Pforzheim school for over ten years. By the time young Philipp arrived, Simler was nearing the end of his tenure at the school, and Hiltebrandt was well-integrated into the teaching curriculum. Simler was 31 years old, with a blend of youth and experience that made the most of his teaching talents.[9]

Pedagogy and Piety

Young Philipp was steeped in a humanist milieu from his birth. His parents highly valued his education, and so did his grandfather when he took it over. Through Reuchlin and the arrival of Unger

---

9. Admittedly, considering that the average life expectancy at this time was somewhere in the mid-30s, one may rightly challenge whether age 31 was genuinely "youthful."

in Bretten, Philipp was trained from the beginning in a rigorous study of Latin. Simler carried this forward with a vigorously humanist pedagogy. He introduced the boys to Greek and Roman classics, and sought to impart to them a mastery of Latin prose and verse, both written and spoken. Not yet dead, Latin remained in active use in the sixteenth century as the international language of scholarship and diplomacy. That is why Simler was so tough on his students. Later in life, Melanchthon remembered, "When I was a boy I had two very learned men for teachers. One was Georg Simler.[10] He first explained to me the Latin and Greek poets and introduced me to a purer philosophy. In lecturing on Aristotle, he often referred directly to the Greek"[11]—and young Philipp loved it.

Further, Simler's pedagogical approach was no barren secular method. Although he did not actively teach the boys theology, he was still influenced by the pedagogy of Jacob Wimpfeling, who believed that it was imperative to focus on the things that were good for the health of the soul, the glory of God, and the fame of the state.[12] Accordingly, Simler embraced a level of piety, but abhorred the scholastic methods of speculating about useless, abstract things.

Concurrently, young Philipp did not neglect the piety of his upbringing. He participated in public worship, and he read the Bible avidly. Strasbourg was not far away, and the boy became an admirer of a pastor there called Johann Geiler von Kaisersberg (1445–1510)—a friend of Wimpfeling and one of the most influential preachers of the fifteenth century. He was a powerful public speaker, and a serious critic of abuses in the church. Geiler once explained that the Greek etymology of "bishop" meant "shepherd." However,

---

10. The other was either Unger or Hiltebrandt—but probably Unger.
11. CR 10:259. Trans. in Manschreck, 32.
12. See Birnstein, 16.

in Germany, *Bischof* had become *Bieß di Schof* ("bite the sheep")![13] Upon Geiler's death in 1510, Philipp dedicated a poem to him.[14]

Philipp's Progress

Simler was challenging, but Philipp made tremendous progress nevertheless. He worked on his own, and loved and praised all the subjects of his studies. Reuchlin made regular inquiries to check on the boys to see how their studies were progressing. He even quizzed them and assigned them additional exercises from time to time. Philipp demonstrated a great capacity for study, and was always doing well. Reuchlin was delighted and impressed with his splendid, exacting mental ability. He became quite fond of the boy, and commended him highly for his skill and obvious promise. Young Philipp thrived on the praise, and pushed himself to study even more diligently.

Philipp was a talkative boy. Not by any means a loner, he loved to be in conversation and community. He had a quick mind, prodigious recall, and a forceful style of expression. Therefore it irritated him to find that he had a stuttering problem. His stammering was easy to understand, and some even thought it pleasant. But Philipp attached great importance both to rhetoric, and to the correct pronunciation of Latin. As a result, he became absolutely determined to overcome this mild speech impediment. He struggled to tame it, and largely succeeded. Only the slightest trace of the problem remained afterwards. Therefore, it is unfair of previous biographers to make the blanket statement that "Melanchthon stuttered," when the truth is most likely that he stuttered as a child, but hardly at all as an adult.

Likewise, for those who think of Melanchthon solely as a mild, irenic figure, it may come as some surprise to learn that he had a

---
13. In modern German it would be *Beiß die Schafe*. Mühlhaupt, 13. CR 24:85.
14. *Epicedion.* CR 10:469–70.

temper. Especially early in life, those who knew him reported that he was easily irritated. He was brilliant, but could also be sharp and bitter. One should not make too much of this, however, considering that he was a pre-adolescent tween who had just lost his father and grandfather and who was now living away from home and his mother for the first time. Moreover, Philipp was aware of his behavior, and sought to change it. He did not allow himself to give way to grief or severity, but instead made a serious effort to get along well with those around him. He embraced meekness and serenity, rather than fury and hostility. Even though he had a fiery, passionate nature (by all accounts inherited from his mother), he kept it within bounds, showing a growing self-discipline that would make him a central figure decades later as a high-stakes international mediator in matters of both faith and politics.

Greek

Although the youngest in a class full of intelligent students, Philipp was clearly one of the most gifted. Simler taught Latin primarily, but when a few students would demonstrate exceptional ability, he would invite them for private lessons in Greek as well.[15] Philipp swiftly joined this group. Here Philipp learned Hellenistic language, and Simler then immediately used it to introduce these students to Hellenistic thought. Just as they read and analyzed original Latin sources in conjunction with language study, so they read and analyzed original Greek sources in conjunction with their Greek drills. In this manner, Philipp became familiar with Greek poets, as well as Aristotle in his own words.

Simler showed an enthusiasm for Aristotle, and this early exposure had at least two lasting effects for the boy from Bretten—first, he

---

15. CR 10:259 erroneously names Hiltebrandt as Philipp's Greek teacher. It was actually Simler, as Melanchthon himself attests. CR 4:715. Camerarius, 9, says the same.

embraced a philosophical nominalism rooted in Aristotelian assumptions (we will discuss this further below, in the chapter on Melanchthon's years at the University of Tübingen). Second, Philipp developed a lasting affinity for Aristotelian logic. While later in his career he would insist on the separation of philosophy from theology, his persistent adherence to the assumptions of Aristotelian logic (particularly in its aversion to paradox, or apparent contradiction), would have an effect in shaping the evolution of his theology.

Meanwhile, Reuchlin, observing the boy's quick progress, decided to do everything in his power to encourage him. Accordingly, he sent him objects of enormous value—books. At this time in the early days of the printing press, books could be of such immense value that they were often chained up in libraries. This was a significant gift. One can only imagine Philipp's wonder and delight at receiving these treasures.

First came a small Greek grammar—the 1480 Mailand edition by Konstantin Laskaris (1434–1501), with explanations in Latin.[16] Reuchlin included a personal inscription. Nicholas Gerbel, who was passing through on his way to Mainz, witnessed the event. Reuchlin also sent along a note saying that he would be visiting in a few days, and that if Philipp would compose a number of verses in Latin, then he would present him with another book. When Reuchlin arrived, Philipp indeed had completed the verses, his *Carminibus,* and Reuchlin was pleased to present him with a small Greek lexicon, with Latin translations. Soon after he also sent a Latin Vulgate Bible, as well as a red doctor's hat, proclaiming the boy worthy of a doctorate!

Philipp treasured these books, and put them to good use. In gratitude, he organized his fellow students (including Franciscus

---

16. This volume can be found at the university library in Uppsala.

Irenicus) to perform one of Reuchlin's comedies on his next visit. No doubt Simler, a fan of Reuchlin's comedies for at least a decade, played an integral role in pulling this off. The year before (1508), Simler had just finished editing two of Reuchlin's comedies, and his friend, Thomas Anshelm, had published them at his press in Pforzheim. This explains how Philipp gained access to the text. Reuchlin, upon seeing the performance, was surprised and delighted. Philipp recited his lines from the *Comoediam* with such wonderful delicacy and emotion that everyone was pleased and impressed. Reuchlin viewed Philipp as a son and had high hopes for his future.

Dark Earth

Reuchlin's inscription in the little Greek grammar by Laskaris turned out to be very significant. Fortunately, we still have it today.

In this inscription, Reuchlin paid Philipp one of the highest compliments possible from a humanist scholar—he translated his German name into Greek. Philipp's last name was Schwartzerdt, which, in German, is *Schwartz* ("dark") and *Erdt* ("earth"). In Greek, "dark" is rendered as *melan* (as in "melancholy" or "melanin"), and "earth" is *chton*. So Reuchlin translated the German *Schwartzerdt* to the Greek *Melanchthon* in order to indicate Philipp's mastery of ancient languages. Philipp did not use this newly Hellenized last name immediately—he still registered at the Universities of Heidelberg and Tübingen as Schwartzerdt. However, his friends began to call him Melanchthon, and within a few years he adopted it fully.

Reuchlin's inscription to Melanchthon in
the Greek grammar, March, 1509.
Uppsala University Library Ink. 35b:42.
Reproduction made by Uppsala
University Library, Sweden.

Indeed, others had done the same for Reuchlin himself. "Reuchlin" is related to *Rauch*, which means "smoke" in German. A poet and politician from Venice named Ermolao Barbaro (1453–93), a leading authority on the Greek and Latin works of antiquity, had once dubbed him "Capnio," which means "smoke" or "smoky" in Latin. Hence Reuchlin was often called Capnio, although sometimes he also referred to himself as Phorcensis, to show his love of Pforzheim. While such name changes were popular in some circles for a certain time (including Oecolampadius, and Melanchthon's classmate, Franz Friedlieb/Franciscus Irenicus), family members often disapproved, seeing the practice as elevating a foreign culture above their own. It did not turn out to be a lasting practice.

A Brief Sojourn

After only one year in Pforzheim, it was clear that Melanchthon was ready to move on. He had mastered Latin, he was good at Greek, and he had a solid grasp of grammar, arithmetic, rhetoric, dialectics, history, and geography. He would be well ahead of his peers matriculating at university. Melanchthon enjoyed learning, he was talented at it, and he was now ready for the next step.

Georg Simler stayed at Pforzheim for another year before moving on to teach at the University of Tübingen in the summer of 1510. Iohannes Hiltebrandt likewise moved to Tübingen in 1511. Melanchthon would see them both again there. His brother, Georg, eventually made his way to Tübingen University as well a few years later, before moving back home to Bretten and a life of public service. Philipp's young uncle, Hans Reuter, went on to become the prior of a monastery in the city of Speyer—the home town of a number of Reuter relatives. Camerarius met him some years later, and described him as humane, dignified, and cultured. Hans Reuter the Younger served in Speyer until his death in 1551.

Meanwhile, in 1509, young Philipp Schwartzerdt/Melanchthon, only twelve years old, set out for new adventures at the University of Heidelberg.

7

Heidelberg

1509–1512

> Almost nothing was taught me except trivia compounded with more of the same.
> —Melanchthon[1]

Heidelberg University was an obvious choice for Melanchthon. His family and teachers unanimously recommended it—not so much because of its academic excellence (which was fair), or its commitment to humanistic studies (which was fading), but simply because the boy was only twelve years old. Heidelberg was his father's hometown. Georg's service to the elector was still warmly remembered, so there were people nearby who could help Philipp if necessary. Likewise, Philipp's parents had been married in Speyer, and he still had relatives there only a short journey away—just a day's walk. Even better, his mother in Bretten was only a day's ride to the south.

---

1. CR 4:715. Cf. Manschreck, 33.

Reuchlin, too, had connections in Heidelberg. When a change of power took place in Württemberg in 1496, court politics made it clear to Reuchlin that he ought to leave town. So he fled to Heidelberg, remaining there until 1498.[2] There he served as an adviser to Elector Philipp, and tutored the princes. He wrote his comedies at this time, and may even have had Simler and Hiltebrandt, Melanchthon's teachers from Pforzheim, as boarders while they studied at the university. During these years, humanistic intellectual life was still in full bloom at Heidelberg.[3] It is not difficult to see why Reuchlin, Simler, and Hiltebrandt all recommended this university to Melanchthon. Heidelberg University presented adequate intellectual rigor (or so they thought), combined with access to family networks of aid, if needed.

Leaving Pforzheim, Melanchthon headed north and stopped over at the family home in Bretten. He would have had some time to see his mother and siblings before traveling further north to Heidelberg. Meanwhile, in that summer of 1509, just over 300 miles to the west, a baby boy named Jean Calvin was born. 680 miles to the south, beyond the Alps, a new building project called St. Peter's basilica was in its third year of construction.

Due to his early rigorous education, rapid progress, hard work, and natural talent, Philipp Melanchthon was ready for university by the age of 12. He was indeed young to be heading off to university, but it was not as unusual then as it would be today. At the time, average university students ranged between 14 and 18 years of age.[4] A university education then more closely resembled a good high school education now.

---

2. See Marlis Zeus, *Johannes Reuchlin: Humanist mit Durchblick* (Karlsruhe: Helmesverlag, 2011), 79–82.
3. Scheible, *Melanchthon*, 17.
4. OER, "Universities."

Heidelberg Castle, 1620, with the town below.

Boarding with Pallas Spangel

Upon arrival in Heidelberg, Melanchthon made his way to the house of Dr. Pallas Spangel. This would be his home for the next three years. Spangel, formerly vice-chancellor and rector of the university, was now a popular and engaging professor of theology. Reuchlin knew him well from his years in Heidelberg, and no doubt helped facilitated the arrangement to take on Philipp as a boarder. Spangel very well also may have known Melanchthon's father through court connections.[5]

Spangel was kind, nurturing, inspiring, and encouraging. His contemporaries described him as wise, pious, and generous. He was quick to provide assistance when needed, he was known for giving good counsel, and he was more inclined to humanistic studies than the other professors at Heidelberg. Melanchthon remembered him fondly.

---

5. He once represented the university to Elector Philipp. CR 3:673.

Inclined to hospitality, Spangel not only housed a number of students, but also often had guests from out of town. Melanchthon met some important figures this way. For instance, when Duke Georg of Pomerania came to town in 1512 to marry Amalie, the daughter of the Elector, Melanchthon was tasked with serving wine to Spangel's distinguished Pomeranian guests.[6] More significantly, through Spangel, Melanchthon met well-known scholars visiting the area, and gained access to some of the best professors and most interesting intellectual life at the university. In fact, one may even claim that Melanchthon learned more at the house of Dr. Spangel than he did at the University of Heidelberg.

Heidelberg University

On October 14, 1509, Melanchthon matriculated at Heidelberg University. The official notation read, *Philippus Schwartzerdt de Brethenn Spir dyoc. XIIII Octobris* (Philipp Schwartzerdt of Bretten, from the diocese of Speyer, October 14.)[7] Founded in 1386, Heidelberg was already one hundred twenty-three years old at the time of Melanchthon's entry. It was the oldest university in the German lands west of Vienna and Prague. All instruction was in Latin, and although the university was celebrated in its own right[8] and significant for its ties to the Palatine electoral court, it was not then operating at an appreciably high level of excellence. While Pforzheim stood out among other Latin schools, Heidelberg did not stand out among other universities.

However, a few decades earlier, in the 1480s and 90s, Heidelberg had shone as a jewel of early German humanism. Bishop of Worms Johann von Dalberg (1455–1503), an early proponent of humanism,

---

6. CR 11:442, 1094.
7. Matr. Heidelberg 1:472. Cf. Probst, 20.
8. See Cam., *Vita*, 11–12; Cam., *Das Leben*, 45.

served as chancellor of the university. He was responsible for bringing another famous humanist, Rudolf Agricola (1444–85), to teach Greek in 1482. Agricola has been called the pioneer of classical learning in Germany, and the most important humanist prior to Erasmus.[9] Additionally, Jacob Wimpfeling (1450–1528) taught at Heidelberg at the latter end of these years. Theologian, poet, humanist, and expert in canon law, he famously advocated for a pedagogy that included an essential ethical core. He sought to add humanist learning to traditional scholastic theology. The poet Conrad Celtis (1459–1508) was also active at this time, founding an important intellectual group in 1495 called the Rhineland Literary Society (*Sodalitas litterarum Rhenana*).[10] Reuchlin reveled in all this deep humanist scholarship when he arrived in 1496, and no doubt recommended Heidelberg in part because of his experiences there. This lively group of scholars also made a deep impact on Georg Simler, who brought their spirit of restless curiosity and passionate commitment to excellence to his work as rector of the Pforzheim Latin School.

These glories of humanist learning were fading and almost gone when Melanchthon arrived. The humanist circle was no more, and only Wimpfeling and Reuchlin survived and, on occasion, still visited. Otherwise, the university had firmly retrenched into a traditional scholasticism emphasizing the teachings and methods of Thomas Aquinas.

---

9. See "Agricola, Rudolph," in *The Catholic Encyclopedia*, and Probst, 21.
10. Or, in German, the *Rheinischen Literarischen Gesellschaft*. Cf. Greschat, 17. It has also been called the *Societas Rhenana*. See Mühlhaupt, 15. Celtis founded similar groups in Hungary and Vienna. Melanchthon's friend from his days in Pforzheim, Nikolaus Gerbel, studied under Celtis in Vienna from 1501–05. So Celtis's name may have already been familiar to Melanchthon.

THE HONEYCOMB SCROLL

Epitaph of Conrad Celtis. bpk, Berlin / Kupferstichkabinett, Staatliche Museen / Photo: Jörg P. Anders. / Art Resource, NY.

The death of Bishop Dalberg in 1503 had especially brought scandal to the humanist group at Heidelberg. Young Philipp, at the age of six, was visiting the city with his father when the forty-eight-year old bishop unexpectedly died from a fall down a flight of stairs. The event made a large impression on the boy at the time. What he likely did not discover until later was that the bishop had broken his neck falling down a flight of cellar stairs *in a brothel*. Suddenly the humanist sodality was not all that attractive anymore. In a later lecture on the Sermon on the Mount, Melanchthon told this story, commenting, "You see, how many adulterers are killed in the midst of their shameful acts."[11] The event made an impact on Melanchthon—we have at least two more accounts of it in his writings,[12] and even one retelling from Luther in his *Table Talk*.[13]

By 1508, the humanist sodality was dead or departed, and its princely supporter, the Elector Philipp also died in the same year. His death followed the disastrous events of the Landshut War of Succession, which he lost. The elector's son, Ludwig V, now took control, and he had enough problems trying to deal with the unfortunate aftermath of the war to worry about promoting humanist scholarship at the university. Melanchthon tried to glean what he could of the remnants of classical humanist learning at Heidelberg. Spangel was one connection, and occasional visits from Reuchlin and Wimpfeling provided another. But humanist learning would not revive at Heidelberg until it did more generally across Germany as a whole. This happened piecemeal in the German lands between 1515 and 1535, and can be seen at Heidelberg in 1524, when the chancellor called Simon Grynaeus to a professor's chair to restore the study of Greek at the university. In the meantime, the young

---

11. CR 25:748.
12. CR 12:133; 24:279. Cf. Mülhaupt 17, Birnstein 20, and Probst, 21.
13. WATR 5:549, Nr. 6225.

Philipp could only discern echoes of the great humanist learning that had come before.

Scholarly Connections

Some of Melanchthon's closest friends at Heidelberg went on to relatively quiet lives, largely disappearing from the pages of history. Others were more well-known in their day. Irenicus, Melanchthon's friend from Pforzheim, came to Heidelberg in 1510. Iohannes Sorbil became a humanist poet, for whom Melanchthon held a lifelong appreciation. Peter Sturm, the brother of the mayor and reformer of Strasbourg, Jacob Sturm, was a fellow student. The theologian and reformer of Zweibrücken, Johannes Schwebel (1490–1541) became a lasting friend. Melanchthon also knew Theobold Billican (1493–1554), who became the reformer of Nördlingen, and later a professor at Heidelberg and Marburg. Philipp once said, "He was my schoolfellow, and in talents and eloquence he greatly surpassed me."[14] A native of Eppingen (just twelve miles northeast of Bretten), Hartmannus Hartmanni (1495–1547) went on to be a professor at Heidelberg, an advisor to the Elector Palatinate, and a proponent of the Reformation. Melanchthon met him again at the Regensburg Colloquy in 1541, and when his son of the same name visited Wittenberg, Melanchthon extended hospitality to him.[15] A native of Heilbronn (28 miles northeast of Bretten), the theologian, pastor, and Württemberg reformer Erhard Schnepf (1495–1558) also attended Heidelberg with Melanchthon. All these people were significant figures in southwestern Germany during the Reformation.

---

14. Quoted in Richard, 18 (who does not give the original source). If Billican's talents and eloquence truly did surpass Melanchthon's, then this shows how Philipp was in just the right place at just the right time when Reuchlin recommended him for the vacancy at the University of Wittenberg—again demonstrating the value of both providence and networking.
15. Scheible, *Melanchthon*, 18–19.

Still well-known today are Johannes Brenz, Martin Bucer, and Oecolampadius. Brenz (1499–1570), a native of Schwäbisch Hall, arrived at the end of Melanchthon's time in Heidelberg or just after, though most sources claim the two made their acquaintance at this time.[16] Brenz, who operated mostly in Württemberg, is widely considered to be the most influential preacher of Lutheran theology in southwestern Germany. Bucer (1491–1551), the famous reformer of Strasbourg, is often numbered among the most significant of all reformers, second only to Luther, Calvin, Zwingli, and Melanchthon. Although he did not begin his studies at the University of Heidelberg until 1517, he was living in the Dominican monastery in the city while Melanchthon was in town.[17] It is likely that the two made their acquaintance during these years, perhaps through gatherings at Spangel's house when Reuchlin or Wimpfeling came for a visit. In this fashion Melanchthon also may have come to know Johannes Oecolampadius of Weinsberg (near Heilbronn).[18] Oecolampadius (1482–1531) had attended the University of Heidelberg from 1499–1503, and tutored the sons of the Elector. He knew Reuchlin, and through him must have heard of young Philipp. Oecolampadius went on to become the reformer of Basel, second only to Zwingli in importance in the early Swiss Reformation.

---

16. See Mühlhaupt, 14–15 who argues that Brenz and Melanchthon did *not* necessarily meet at Heidelberg. By contrast, Greschat (p. 19), Kuropka (p. 19), and Maurer say that they *did*. Cf. Scheible, *Melanchthon*, 19.
17. Horst, 12. See also MBW 76a, from early 1520, when Melanchthon wrote to Bucer (unfortunately, the content is lost).
18. If Melanchthon did not come to know Oecolampadius during his time in Heidelberg, then he certainly did a few years later in Tübingen. At issue is a passage in CR 4:715, where Melanchthon spoke of receiving a copy of Agricola's *Dialectics* from Oecolampadius during his days in the Academy. Manschreck (pp. 34–35) takes this to mean during the Heidelberg years, whereas Scheible attributes it to the Tübingen years (p. 22).

Johannes Brenz.

Martin Bucer.

If Oecolampadius visited Heidelberg during Melanchthon's student days, he probably would have visited the house of Spangel, especially when his mentor, the former Heidelberg professor Jacob Wimpfeling was in town—which he often was. Wimpfeling came frequently to check on the educational progress of several boys from Strasbourg, where he now lived. He almost always stayed with Spangel when he was in Heidelberg.[19] During these times, Melanchthon became familiar with this man who represented one of the last vestiges of Heidelberg's former humanist excitement.

Wimpfeling was, in fact, visiting Heidelberg when news of the death of the Strasbourg preacher Johannes Geiler von Kaisersberg arrived. Wimpfeling and Geiler had long been friends, and upon news of Geiler's death, Wimpfeling immediately set about composing a brief biographical sketch in his honor. Melanchthon, who had become familiar with Geiler while at Pforzheim, was likewise moved. During his Heidelberg years, he avidly read Geiler's sermons for personal edification. Later, he often quoted Geiler in his biblical lectures at Wittenberg. As Wimpfeling prepared his brief biography, Melanchthon composed an elegy. Wimpfeling saw it and was impressed—he published it at the end of his biographical sketch.[20] Wimpfeling subsequently recommended Melanchthon to be the tutor of Count von Löwenstein's sons,[21] and published another poem[22] of his in a book dedicated to the defense of the new scholastic theology (the so-called *via moderna*, originating with Ockham, and contravening some of the ideas of Thomas Aquinas and the so-called *via antiqua*).

---

19. Scheible, 17.
20. *Epicedion.* CR 10:469.
21. Count von Löwenstein also knew Georg, Melanchthon's father, through shared military service under Maximilian. Scheible, *Melanchthon*, 20.
22. CR 20:765.

THE HONEYCOMB SCROLL

Jacob Wimpfeling with his students.

Formal Studies

In 1510, Luther was disappointed by what he discovered on his trip to Rome. Likewise, in the same year, Philipp Melanchthon was disappointed by what he discovered at Heidelberg. Perhaps due to his precocious talents and excellent instruction from Unger, Simler, and Hiltebrandt, Melanchthon was over-prepared for his coursework at Heidelberg. Frequent attacks of fever also dampened his enthusiasm for the place. He voiced his displeasure distinctly when he commented, "Almost nothing was taught me except trivia compounded with more of the same."[23] "Nothing was publicly taught there except a wordy dialectic and a pretense of physical science. . . . It was like finding one's way through labyrinths choked with rubbish;

---

23. CR 4:715. Cf. Manschreck, 33.

how little was known of literature and history: of the very subjects men themselves professed to teach!"[24] Further, he found the students to be coarse and of corrupt morals.[25]

Johannes Geiler von Kaiserberg. By Lucas Cranach the Elder.

The fact of the matter was that Melanchthon already had the *trivium* (grammar, dialectics [that is, Aristotelian logic], and rhetoric) well in hand. He also had little trouble with the *quadrivium* of math, geometry, astronomy, and music. These disciplines represented the prerequisites for further studies in theology, law, or medicine.[26] Accordingly, the only professors who made an impression on him were Peter Günther for rhetoric, and Conrad Helvetius for

---

24. MBW 2780. CR 4:715–16. Trans. and qtd. (without attribution) in Wilson, 26. Cf. Stump (also without attribution), 18.
25. CR 4:715.
26. These were the three faculties available at Heidelberg at the time.

astronomy and astrology (which were often viewed as related topics at this time[27]). Influenced by his father's credulous attitude toward astrology, Melanchthon held a lifelong fascination with it. Luther thought this was silly, and told him so.

The required Aristotelian readings at Heidelberg were especially necessary for further studies in theology. The scholastic methods of the *via antiqua* required a good grasp of many Aristotelian concepts, seeing that Thomas Aquinas was the central theologian for the Heidelberg faculty, and his primary achievement was the careful and brilliant integration of Aristotelian philosophical premises with Christian theology.

Aristotle was vital for establishing categories, composition, making distinctions, analysis, and for the pursuit of both physics and metaphysics. Further, in order to advance to theological studies, students had to master a complicated set of technical terminology and become expert in applying it in esoteric argumentation.[28] Melanchthon was ultimately scornful of these practices, and even more so of the poor late-classical and early medieval Latin compilations of Aristotle used in the courses. Nevertheless, despite his approbation, in the end Melanchthon incorporated some assumptions of Aristotelian dialectics and rhetoric into his thinking (especially regarding paradox, or the appearance of contradiction), which contributed to the evolution of his theology over time.[29]

Melanchthon made rapid progress with his studies. Once when a professor grew frustrated with a piece of Greek translation, he grumbled, "Where shall I find a Greek?" A number of students shouted out, "Melanchthon!"[30]

---

27. See MSA 6:383 showing Melanchthon's belief in their interdependence.
28. See Probst, 22.
29. See Graybill, *Evangelical Free Will*, 141–49.
30. CR 4:715. Cf. Richard, 15.

As required, Melanchthon attended numerous public disputations, and participated in some of them.[31] This required a mastery of logic (dialectics) and the art of persuasive public speaking (rhetoric). He was intense about his preparation, and did well in these verbal contests that sometimes resembled the intellectual manifestation of medieval knightly tournaments. At the same time, on an interpersonal level, Melanchthon was always the amiable diplomat. He managed to earn the favor of all the various factions at the university (but especially those inclined toward humanism). Students and professors respected the quality of his work and the modesty of his character.

Informal Studies

Melanchthon learned more outside of the classroom at Heidelberg than within it. Through family connections at the electoral court, he was once present for some of the antics of the court jester, Hänsel Narr. Sent to get wood for the kitchen fires, he approached the pile, stooped down, and began strenuously heaving to pull free a few pieces from the very bottom of the stack. When questioned, he said, "The top pieces come away too easily—I want to get the bottom ones first." Melanchthon drew a moral from this story when he told it later: the jester "wanted to do the difficult part first. A lot of people do the same with studies and other things."[32] Though it did not involve jesters, the home of Pallas Spangel provided an even more significant place of learning. The steady stream of distinguished guests and stimulating conversation was of unmatched quality.

---

31. See Probst, 22.
32. Mühlhaupt, 16. CR 25:516.

THE HONEYCOMB SCROLL

Die Hohe Schul zu Heydelberg. Woodcut by Sebastian Münster, ca. 1588.

Spangel himself was a pious intellectual with a foot in two worlds—medieval scholasticism, and Renaissance humanism. He loved the new learning with its revival of classical studies, but he saw it as running parallel to scholasticism. It was never his intention to utilize the methods of humanism (returning to the original sources in their own languages) as a means to revise scholastic orthodoxies.

He delighted in the excellence of the Latin works of antiquity, but then turned to Thomas Aquinas for spiritual guidance (he did not ever give much time to the new way [*via moderna*] in scholasticism pioneered by William of Ockham). Spangel was quite content simply to accept the authority of the church and its official dogmas. Melanchthon, who was most keen on classical learning, had not studied much theology yet. But he trusted and liked Spangel, and so he tentatively accepted the old way (*via antiqua*) of Thomas while intending to read more about it all later himself.[33]

Melanchthon, indeed, while not impressed with most of the teaching at Heidelberg, *was* impressed with the library. He and some of his friends virtually moved in. He could often be found standing reading a chained book, or seated at a little bench with one of the volumes allowed into limited circulation. Melanchthon began with what was familiar—he started reading modern poets like Mantuan. Then, as he came across references to histories and fables, he dug deeper to get the full story. In this way, he worked into the classical literature. Here he began to pick up a sophisticated vocabulary and style, but he returned repeatedly to contemporary authors like Politan. They valued effective polemic over grace and beauty of composition. Melanchthon's early style took on much of this pugilistic tone, as can be seen later in his first theological treatises at Wittenberg.[34]

Melanchthon read everything he could get his hands on. His interests ranged widely, including philosophy, mathematics, astronomy, and especially the ancient languages of Greek, Latin, and a bit of Hebrew (studied from Reuchlin's grammar). As a result of his tutoring session with the von Löwenstein boys, he even began drafting a *Rudiments of Greek Grammar* of his own.

33. Cf. Greschat, 19.
34. CR 4:715–16. Cf. Stump, 18, and Richard, 14–15.

Through learned conversation at his living situation, along with his private studies, Melanchthon came into contact with some of the powerful emerging ideas of humanism. Nevertheless, Heidelberg University as a whole was not yet prepared to accept these newer ways of thinking, despite having experienced some of it in previous decades. Established universities like Heidelberg tended to be conservative institutions, viewing themselves as guardians of the old ways.[35] Newer universities (like Tübingen) tended to embrace the emerging humanism as a way of distinguishing themselves. It would not be long before Melanchthon would find his way there.

Piety

The piety of Melanchthon's childhood stayed strong at Heidelberg. He immersed himself in the printed sermons of Geiler, and took great delight in public worship. Following his father's example and that of Spangel as well, Melanchthon was known to keep the monastic hours of prayer.[36] He maintained a keen interest, likewise, in the accounts of the lives of the saints. Enamored of the new humanist learning, Melanchthon was also a thoroughgoing adherent of late medieval piety. Perhaps this is part of the reason he got along so well with Luther. Both men helped usher in a new age, but with hearts formed by the last.

Melanchthon hungered to learn more about God, and so thought to pursue graduate studies in theology upon completion of his bachelor's degree. His piety in Heidelberg rested loosely within the general framework of Spangel's old-school Thomism, though his independent studies were beginning to lead him in another direction. As he completed his bachelor's studies, Melanchthon began to pursue the required readings of the theology faculty. He wanted to study

---

35. CR 11:439–42.
36. Greschat, 18. Maurer, 23–24.

it for himself. Meanwhile, he took his responsibilities to others seriously. His tutoring of the von Löwenstein boys quietly marked the start of his teaching career, at age fourteen. At the university, he occasionally had opportunity to compose and deliver speeches before his fellow students.[37] His learning was not to be just for his personal edification, but it was to overflow for the good of others.

View of modern Heidelberg and the Neckar River, from the Castle. Photo by Gregory Graybill.

Laurels and Burrs

In the late spring of 1511, Melanchthon stood the examination for his bachelor of arts degree. All examinations were oral and in Latin at this time. He faced a panel of four professors, led by the rector of the university, Leonhard Dietrich. He had to swear that he had

---

37. Scheible, *Melanchthon*, 20.

completed all the required readings, and then give clear, concise, and complete responses to the grilling prepared for him by the professors.

Melanchthon passed with flying colors and received his bachelor of arts degree (under the category of *via antiqua*) on June 18, 1511.[38] He completed the course in only two years. For the next year he redoubled his efforts on reading scholastic philosophy in preparation for entry to the master's program in theology. However, his application was denied, because he was "still so young and of a childish appearance."[39] While biographers normally depict this as an unfair slight to Melanchthon, it should be remembered that the influential men at the university considered a master's degree to be a great honor—one which normally included a mandatory period of teaching at the university afterwards. They feared that Melanchthon, being such a young boy, did not yet possess the strength, authority, and maturity to be an effective professor.[40]

In any case, the rejection deeply stung Melanchthon. He felt himself fully qualified, and resented being rejected for matters beyond his control. His frustration with Heidelberg University had now reached its limit, and he was prepared to move on. Later in life, he ruminated on this moment, saying,[41] "It is often very good for young persons if their wishes are not all gratified. This I experienced at Heidelberg."

---

38. Some sources say June 11, instead.
39. . . . *noch so jung und kindliches Ansehens war.* CR 10:260.
40. See Urban, 22.
41. Quoted (without attribution) in Ledderhose, 22–23. Also quoted (without attribution) in Urban, 22.

8

Tübingen

1512–1518

The studies flourish, the spirits are awake. It is a luxury to live.
—Ulrich von Hutten[1]

Besides his frustration with being held back from pursuing further studies at Heidelberg, Melanchthon also continued to have attacks of fever. With his slight stature and frequent illnesses, his mother began to become concerned.[2] She strongly advised him to move, if only for a change in climate. Confirmation of this course of action came with the death of Pallas Spangel in the summer of 1512.[3] Now with his living situation at an end and further studies stymied, it was time to move on. Simler and Reuchlin, Melanchthon's mentors,

---

1. Schaff, 108.
2. Some have suggested that Melanchthon's father may have become ill not through a poisoned well, but through lead poisoning over time, as a result of his work as an armorer. While that is unlikely, in light of the simultaneous sudden death or serious illness of Georg's entire artillery company, it does seem likely that young Philipp may have been exposed to elevated levels of lead—*in utero*, in infancy, and in early childhood.
3. The date was likely July 17, 1512. However, Camerarius reports it as May 16, instead.

recommended Tübingen. Melanchthon took their advice, and after stopping over with his family in Bretten, he arrived in Tübingen in September, where he matriculated on the seventeenth.[4]

A World in Flux

Melanchthon would stay in Tübingen for six years, and during that time, events were in motion that would change the world. The Fifth Lateran Council met from 1512–17. However, with the death of Pope Julius II and the accession of Leo X in 1517, the implementation of these modest reforms languished.

Meanwhile, in the region surrounding Tübingen, the "Poor Conrad" Revolt broke out in 1514. The peasants demanded better treatment, but Duke Ulrich put down the rebellion harshly. Melanchthon was sympathetic to the peasants, which is not surprising, considering that Duke Ulrich was the one who had besieged Melanchthon's own hometown a little more than a decade earlier.

More distantly, the Battle of Marignano (1515) reshaped the European political scene. There, Francis I defeated the Swiss, and captured Italy's wealthiest city, Milan. Francis I emerged as a great power on the western European scene, to be counterbalanced by the Holy Roman Empire. As the influence of the papal armies receded, the main power struggle now lay between the houses of Valois and Habsburg.

More obscurely, in 1517, at a newly founded university in northeastern German lands, a professor tacked up some theses for debate. The reforms of the Fifth Lateran Council had not amounted to much, and this professor wanted to debate some of the underlying theology supporting the fundraising efforts that were helping pay

---

4. Maurer provides an extensive treatment of Melanchthon's years in Tübingen: 1:30–83.

for the new basilica in Rome. Philipp Melanchthon would join that debate shortly—but for the time being, he would spend six years toiling in Tübingen.

Town and University

Tübingen, 1643. Woodcut by Matthäus Merian.

Tübingen is located in Württemberg, which, in the sixteenth century, was the most significant territory in the southwestern section of the Holy Roman Empire. The town sat on a ridge, with densely wooded hills rising north of town, and the Neckar River flowing below. By moving from Heidelberg (which was also situated on the Neckar) to Tübingen, Melanchthon traveled upriver, closer to the source. It is a fitting metaphor for his studies, in which he also strove to travel upriver, *ad fontes*—to the wellsprings, to the sources, of ancient learning.

Compared to Heidelberg, Tübingen was a new university, founded only thirty-five years earlier, in 1477. Duke Eberhard the

Bearded had intended for it to be the center of learning for the Duchy of Württemberg, equipped with the most excellent professors. While it had an early reputation for energetic learning, by 1512, the faculty was becoming settled around a predominantly scholastic theology. While Heidelberg University at this time was more committed to the *via antiqua* and its emphasis on a moderate philosophical realism (particularly as mediated by Thomas Aquinas), the faculty at Tübingen was more open to the more recent *via moderna*, with its embrace of nominalism, as articulated by John Duns Scotus, and then mediated by William of Ockham and then especially by a recent faculty member, Gabriel Biel.[5] However, realism also had a champion at Tübingen in professor Konrad Summenhart.[6]

The issue of realism versus nominalism remained fiery at Tübingen—even to the extent that students were separated in *burse* (dormitories providing both room and board) according to which position they held. The realist students had their own banner (an eagle), while the nominalist students did as well (a peacock).

So which was the better approach? To put it simply—did ideas exist eternally somewhere in a perfect form, such that all earthly things are merely imperfect copies (realism)? Or are the individual things we observe in this world unique, and we merely give them names (nominalism)? Can we talk about universals (realism), or only individuals (nominalism)?[7]

---

5. On the theology at Tübingen University during Melanchthon's time there, see Helmut Feld, "Die Tübinger Universitätstheologie im Urteil Melanchthons," in eds. Stefan Rhein, et al., *Philipp Melanchthon in Südwestdeutschland: Bildungsstationen eines Reformators* (Karlsruhe: Badische Landesbibliothek, 1997), 87–100.
6. See Feld, "Die Tübinger Universitätstheologie im Urteil Melanchthons," 92–95.
7. For a good run-down of this issue, see "Nominalism" in the OER.

Student Life

Melanchthon, while he had at first tentatively engaged with Pallas Spangel's moderate Thomistic realism at Heidelberg,[8] now distanced himself from that position and chose to live in the nominalist burse. While he wrote some of his mother's pithy aphorisms on the walls of his room[9] and prepared to settle into his studies, he could not ignore the competition between the nominalist and realist students, which burned with all the violent exuberance peculiar to young men of a certain age. According to Camerarius, Melanchthon acted as something of a mediator between the two sides, tamping down the hostility that sometimes erupted in fighting that was more than nominal in its use of fists, clubs, stones and swords.[10]

Among the other students, Melanchthon did not make the same kind of lasting friendships that he had at Pforzheim (e.g., with Simon Grynaeus) or Heidelberg (e.g., with Johannes Schwebel).[11] However, he did see two fellow students from his Pforzheim days—Matthias Erb, the future Württemberg reformer, and Franciscus Irenicus, who arrived in Tübingen in 1516 and would go on to become a well-known German humanist and historian.

Melanchthon's most significant new friendship among his fellow students at Tübingen was with Ambrosius Blarer (sometimes rendered Blaurer). Blarer came from Alpirsbach, and was the son of a patrician family from Constance. He found his vocation as a Benedictine monk, and departed from Tübingen in 1514. From there, he and Melanchthon began a steady correspondence. For instance, in 1514, Melanchthon wrote to encourage Blarer in his humanistic studies, even offering to help. He affirmed his friendship,

---

8. See Kuropka, *Melanchthon*, 19.
9. Wilson, 41.
10. Cam. *Vita/Das Leben*, chapter 7. Cf. Manschreck, 36.
11. Cf. Mühlhaupt, 19.

praised Blarer's erudition, called him "most beloved brother" (*frater amantissime*), and signed his letter as "your Philipp" (*Philippus tuus*).[12] Later, Blarer would go on to become the reformer of Constance.

Ambrosius Blaurer (1492–1564).

Formal Studies

Two of Melanchthon's professors at Tübingen would have been very familiar: Georg Simler and Iohannes Hiltebrandt—his teachers from the Pforzheim school. Hiltebrandt, though, died a year later, in 1513.[13] In the meantime, Melanchthon studied philosophy (logic) and jurisprudence under Simler. He also heard lectures on medicine and studied Galen on his own.

---

12. MBW 2. July 26, 1514. Additional correspondence with Blarer during Melanchthon's Tübingen years can be found in MBW 4, 5, and 9. Cf. Scheible, *Melanchthon*, 22.
13. Cf. Scheible, *Melanchthon*, 20.

Two of his favorite professors were Francis Stadian (sometimes rendered Franz Kircher) and Johannes Stöffler. Later in life, Melanchthon wrote of Stadian that he loved him as a father.[14] He studied dialectics under him for a couple years. In 1518, in his address, *On Correcting the Studies of Youth*, he praised Stadian, calling him "a friend . . . a person of such erudition and manner of life that he was able to take sure delight in all good and learned men."[15] Stadian was also acquainted with Reuchlin—sometimes Melanchthon passed messages between the two men.[16]

Likewise, Melanchthon was enthralled by his classes on mathematics, astronomy, and astrology with Johannes Stöffler—who was known for establishing and maintaining accurate calendars.[17] In 1513, the young Melanchthon wrote some laudatory Latin verse for one of Stöffler's books.[18] Stöffler taught that the stars *do* affect human events—and Melanchthon enthusiastically agreed.

---

14. Quoted (without attribution) in Wilson, 37.
15. *De corrigendis adolescentiae studiis.* MSA 3:36.1–5. Trans. Keen, 51.
16. E.g., MBW 15.
17. See Günther Oestmann, "Johannes Stoeffler, Melanchthons Lehrer in Tübingen," in eds. Stefan Rhein, et al., *Philipp Melanchthon in Südwestdeutschland: Bildungsstationen eines Reformators* (Karlsruhe: Badische Landesbibliothek, 1997), 75–86. See also Maurer, 129–70.
18. *Elucidatio fabricate ususque astrolabii.* See Manschreck, 39, esp. n. 43.

THE HONEYCOMB SCROLL

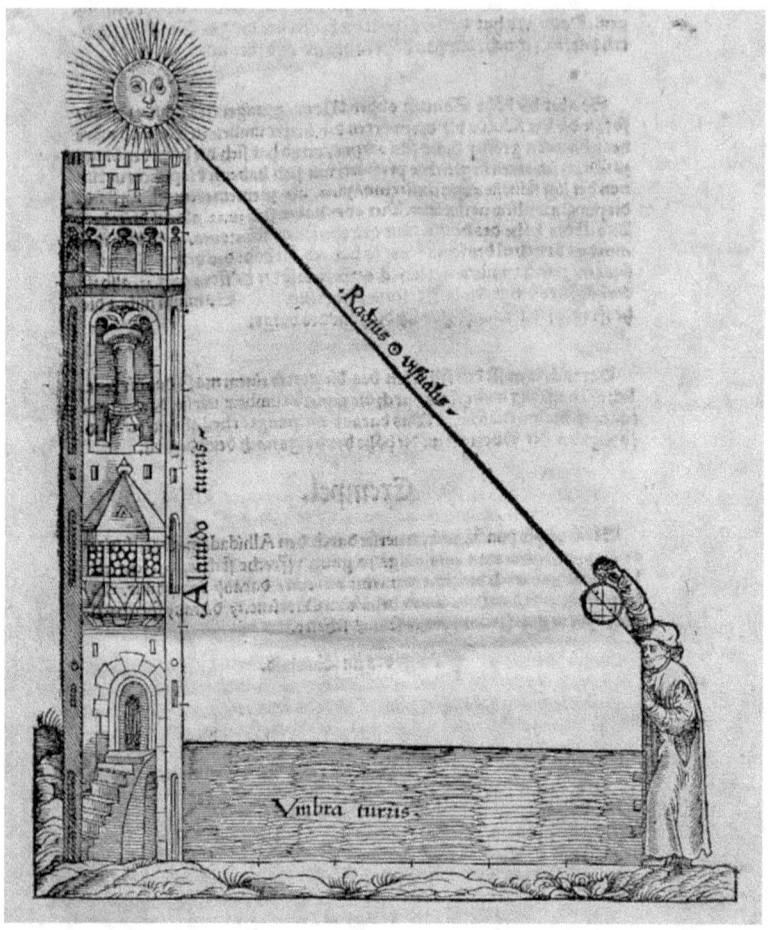

A page from Johannes Stöffler's book, 1536. Vermessung der Höhe eines Gebäudes in der Ebene anhand seines Schattens mit dem Astrolabium.

Philipp also continued his study of Latin with Johannes Brassican of Constance, who taught with a straightforward style similar to Unger. Professor Heinrich Bebel, a well-known early German humanist and poet laureate from the age of twenty (courtesy of Emperor Maximilian), also stood highly in Melanchthon's esteem. Bebel lectured on poetry, and inspired Melanchthon to read Virgil,

Terence, and Cicero on his own. Under his influence, Melanchthon left the lesser-quality modern poets (like Bembo and Baptista Mantuan) in order to pursue the classics more assiduously.[19]

Some professors at Tübingen were excellent, but others were not. Melanchthon was not impressed by Jacob Lemp's attempts to picture transubstantiation on the blackboard.[20] Scholasticism, not the Bible, was the dominant emphasis of the theology faculty at Tübingen.[21] Melanchthon therefore took matters into his own hands with his private self-directed program of study.

Informal Studies

Oecolampadius—who was about fifteen years older than Melanchthon, and whom Melanchthon probably had met at some point in Heidelberg—arrived in Tübingen in March, 1513, and stayed on until 1515, when he moved to Basel. During this time the two developed a close working relationship. He and Blarer, in fact, represented Melanchthon's two most enduring friendships to come out of his Tübingen days.[22]

With no dedicated Greek professor at Tübingen, Oeclampadius agreed to supervise Melanchthon's studies. Together, they worked their way through Hesiod and other Greek works. Later, Melanchthon claimed that no one had helped him more in his youth than Oecolampdius.[23] Meanwhile, Melanchthon also did some independent study of Hebrew—likely using Reuchlin's 1506 textbook, *The Rudiments of Hebrew*.[24]

---

19. CR 10:192, 20:766, 1:938.
20. CR 4:718. See also Feld, "Die Tübinger Universitätstheologie im Urteil Melanchthons," 87–92.
21. Reflecting the more partisan historiography of an earlier age, Cox, in 1817, wrote, "theology, as it was then taught, consisted in little else than scholastic subtleties, knotty questions, unintelligible jargon, and absurdities compounded of superstition and profaneness" (p. 17).
22. See Greschat, 24.
23. CR 4:70, CR 1:87–88. Cf. Manschreck, 39.
24. *De rudimenti hebraicis*

Johannes Oecolampadius (1482–1531).

Rudolf Agricola (1443–1485).

Later, in 1515, once Oecolampadius had moved on to Basel, he sent Melanchthon a three-volume set of Rudolf Agricola's *Dialectics*—an older work, though just published in 1515 in Louvain.[25] Through this work, Agricola became one of Melanchthon's most important influences during his Tübingen years.

A great proponent of classical learning, Agricola had taught Aristotle and Lucian at Heidelberg University.[26] Growing out of these studies, he produced his *Dialectics*. Melanchthon devoured and internalized the work, memorizing large portions of it and applying it to his classical studies. He pored over the order of argumentation in the orations of Cicero and Demosthenes. With Agricola's guidance, Melanchthon made steady gains in his ability to comprehend and make use of these texts. He began mimicking the order of argumentation he found there in his own work, seeking to model his writing and speaking on the best methods of the ancient glories of Greco-Roman civilization. Melanchthon assimilated this material so thoroughly, that when he wrote his own textbooks on rhetoric and dialectics, they strongly echoed Agricola's work. These textbooks were utilized as far afield as Britain, where Queen Elizabeth and Shakespeare both may well have read them.[27] Thus Agricola's influence likely extends further than the present fame of his name.

Agricola's words also began tilling the soil of Melanchthon's mind to prepare the way for the seed of the Reformation gospel. In his *Dialectics,* Agricola leveled attacks on scholasticism—on its philosophy, if not its theology. He denigrated the medieval logic and grammar texts used by scholastic theologians in favor of the best works of ancient Greek and Latin literature. He criticized the scholastics for a faulty grasp of rhetoric and dialectics, combined with

---

25. Also called Löwen in German, and Leuven in Dutch. CR 4:716.
26. CR 11:280, 396; 3:674.
27. Manschreck 35, esp. n. 28.

an unexamined adherence to tradition. Here then, with the help of a return to unsullied Aristotelian dialectics, Melanchthon began to see a way out of the labyrinths of scholastic logic, while at the same time laying a foundation for his famous *loci* method—that is, teaching based on a rational series of topics, or *loci* (commonplaces).[28]

In addition to Agricola, Melanchthon also launched into an exhaustive study of William of Ockham (ca. 1287–1347). There he found confirmation of the principles of nominalism, but he was not convinced of Ockham's *via moderna* scholastic theology.[29] He did, however, begin to become doubtful about a number of church dogmas. He would therefore hold onto nominalistic presuppositions, but with an openness to employing a simpler and cleaner theological system. He became more skeptical of scholastic systems, with an inclination to return to the sources—*ad fontes*—to the Bible itself. Through his own studies, therefore, he was well-positioned to be receptive to Luther's evangelical theology.

To summarize Melanchthon's development in the issues of Christian faith to this point, he had begun with the simple piety of his parents, along with a confidence in the humanistic program of returning to original sources. From there, he was exposed to realism and the distinctive emphases of Thomistic *via antiqua* scholastic theology while at Pforzheim and Heidelberg. Then, beginning with his own studies at Heidelberg, he began to question Thomistic realism, turning instead to nominalism. However, even though he found confirmation of this move through his studies of Ockham at Tübingen, he rejected Ockham's *via moderna* scholastic theology. Meanwhile, his personal devotion to the Lord remained fervent.

---

28. Cf. Stupperich, 29–30.
29. CR 1:321, 1083.

A street in Tübingen's old city, May, 2013. Photo by Gregory Graybill.

Piety

Throughout his university years, Melanchthon remained true to the faith instilled in him as a child. He maintained spiritual disciplines, and combined his humanistic passion for original sources with his devotion to God by sustaining an intensive ongoing study of the Bible.[30] He wrote his own notes in the margins, as well as insights gleaned from the church fathers. While he found the scholastic theology taught at Tübingen to be a wearying exercise in hairsplitting, he found his Bible-reading, by contrast, to be life-giving.

Melanchthon primarily read the Bible in Latin, though he knew his studies of Greek and Hebrew could help him get even closer to the original meaning of the text. He took his Bible with him everywhere—even to church—and when he found the sermon to be unprofitable, he would read his Bible instead. He was reprimanded on more than one occasion for reading his Bible during church.[31] Part of what gave him away was that his Bible was a different size and shape than the prayer book. Others, noticing this variance (and obviously demonstrating just how much *they* were focusing on the sermon), speculated that Melanchthon was reading profane authors during worship. This immersion in Scripture, however, primed Melanchthon to be amenable to Luther's scriptural arguments later. He also found the writings of Jean Gerson and Wessel Gansfort[32] (who anticipated some of Luther's themes) to be profitable—but the

---

30. This report comes mainly from Camerarius (Cam., *Vita,* 11; *Das Leben,* 44). Some, like Wengert, however, suspect Camerarius of painting an overly rosy picture of Melanchthon as a piece of partisan propaganda in the later Philippist-Gnesio-Lutheran controversies. See "'With Friends Like This . . .': The Biography of Philipp Melanchthon by Joachim Camerarius," in Thomas F. Mayer and D. R. Woolf, eds., *The Rhetorics of Life-Writing in Early Modern Europe: Forms of Biography from Cassandra Fedele to Louis XIV* (Ann Arbor: University of Michigan Press, 1995), 115–32.
31. CR 10:259–60. Cam., *Vita,* 16.
32. Manschreck erroneously refers to this figure as "John Wessel," pp. 38–39. See CR 24:309.

Bible in particular began to shape and reshape Melanchthon's thought world. This shows that Melanchthon's embrace of evangelical theology a few years hence was not so much a matter of being overawed by Luther, but rather an instance of Luther providing the last piece in a puzzle that was already almost complete when Melanchthon arrived at Wittenberg.[33]

Reuchlin

Meanwhile, during his Tübingen years, Melanchthon's relationship with his relative, Reuchlin, proved even more significant than his friendships with Blarer and Oecolampadius. Hailing him as "my sweetest Capnio, my Father,"[34] Melanchthon made frequent trips to Stuttgart to visit his famous relative. Often other students would accompany him, and they would discourse with Reuchlin at length in his expansive library or in the pleasant garden.[35] Reuchlin generously made loans of his books, as seen from Melanchthon's letter in January 1518, when he thanked him for allowing him to borrow Simplicius, Ammonius, and Philoponus, while also submitting a request for volumes of Albertus Magnus.[36] Reuchlin likewise made regular trips to Tübingen, where he was known to stay in the burse and hold forth in conversation at meals.

Public affairs often marked Reuchlin and Melanchthon's discussions, and Reuchlin's particular troubles must have been a frequent topic. Since 1509, Johannes Pfefferkorn, a converted Jew, and Jacob Hochstratten, a Dominican Inquisitor, had militated for the banishment of the Jews and the incineration of all their writings

---

33. I have not found any evidence that Melanchthon read Luther before arriving at Wittenberg in the middle of 1518. He may have, though.
34. *Salve, suavissime mi Capnio, mi pater.* MBW 19. July 12, 1518. CR 1:31.
35. See Wilson, 45–46, for an unattributed quotation from Melanchthon to this effect. Cf. Manschreck, 39.
36. MBW 15.

(except the Old Testament). They envisioned bonfires of these books in the city centers throughout the Empire. Jews appealed strenuously to the emperor. Emperor Maximilian, through the Elector of Mainz, ordered Reuchlin to give his opinion. Reuchlin defended the Hebrew literature, saying it should not be destroyed (except for those books specifically attacking Christianity). Maximilian approved of this and ordered it so.

Pfefferkorn then started a pamphlet war, complete with abusive comments. He accused Reuchlin of heresy and had him put him on trial before the Bishop of Speyer with threats of incarceration by the Inquisition. Some even report that *Reuchlin*'s books were burned in Mainz.[37] This dispute began to garner attention throughout western Europe, as humanists (including Willibald Pirckheimer and Johannes Brassican of Tübingen) rushed to defend Reuchlin and the works of Hebrew antiquity, while others (such as Hochstratten's fellow Dominicans in Cologne) made a case for the purging of Jewish literature. The ecclesiastical court eventually exonerated Reuchlin, though the controversy would continue to plague him, even in light of support from Ulrich von Hutten and the knight Francis von Sickingen.

In the midst of this ongoing controversy in 1514, Melanchthon wrote a foreword[38] praising Reuchlin for a book called *The Letters of Eminent Men.*[39] It was a collection of epistles from famous and learned scholars in support of Reuchlin's position on preserving ancient Hebrew literature. Melanchthon wrote, "Germany can behold nothing more glorious than the person of Reuchlin, whom the goddess of wisdom has adorned with the most splendid gifts."[40]

---

37. E.g., Deane, 23.
38. MBW 1. See also Greschat, 22.
39. *Clarorum virorum Epistolae Latinae Graecae et Hebraicae variis Temporibus missae ad Iohannem Reuchlin Phorcensem LL. Doctorem.* Tübingen, Thomas Anshelm, March, 1514. See esp. MBWT 2:7–13.

Melanchthon's role in this controversy did not exactly endear him to the other faculty at Tübingen, who by and large were not keen humanists. Traditional scholastic theologians, they were more than likely to be sympathetic to Pfefforkorn and the Cologne monks over Reuchlin. This confident and precocious "boy" was beginning to grate on them as a bit of an upstart.

Shortly after the publication of *The Letters of Eminent Men*, a satirical *Letters of Obscure Men*[41] appeared, also in support of Reuchlin, in which the doctrines and lifestyles of monks and scholastics were systematically mocked. Published anonymously, Melanchthon has occasionally been accused of being a contributor to this work,[42] which helped stoke popular sentiment to see a reformation—at least of pious living and morals—among professional churchmen.

Magister

Once, while Melanchthon was in Tübingen, the well-known Renaissance humanist, Willibald Pirckheimer wrote to him to express concern over his health, warning him not to damage himself through an excessive zeal for work.[43] Today, Melanchthon might be called a workaholic. Undeniably, though, he got things accomplished—quickly. On January 25, 1514, he took his master's examination while still sixteen years old. He passed, ranking first among eleven candidates. His degree came under the category of *via moderna*—but one must bear in mind that this did not fully encompass Melanchthon's shifting thoughts on theology. One must remember

---

40. MBWT 2:7–13. Trans., Richard, 24.
41. *Epistolarum obscurorum virorum*
42. One can only speculate about Melanchthon's involvement with the *Letters of Obscure Men* (more likely culprits include Ulrich von Hutten and Crotus Rubianus [cf. Cam., *Das Leben*, 49, n. 36]). However, he did send a letter to Reuchlin in January, 1518 in which he said he planned to polemicize on Reuchlin's behalf, and that he was true to him. MBW 15. See also CR 10:472ff. Scheible, *Melanchthon*, 24, however, points out that Melanchthon never completed this task.
43. MBW 14.

that this was a degree in Greek, and could better be described as a credential in philosophy rather than theology. It wasn't until he reached Wittenberg that Melanchthon acquired the degree of *baccalaureus biblicus*. So, philosophically speaking, Melanchthon agreed with nominalism rather than realism, and so *via moderna* fit him better than *via antiqua*. But he still rejected the theological systems of Ockham, Biel, and other *moderni*.

With his degree of *magister atrium*, Melanchthon also received a license to be a *Privatdocent*. In other words, he was allowed to lecture on the ancient classics in his own burse. Hence, his formal teaching career began when he was not quite seventeen.[44] This was both a privilege, and also likely a requirement. It was a common practice at universities at this time to oblige former students to spend two to five years teaching in the college. Then (as now), using graduate students to teach saved the university money.[45]

Melanchthon taught well, lecturing on Virgil, Terence, Livy, and Cicero. He came to be known as a sophisticated, excellent teacher. He also provided instruction in rhetoric, dialectics, and Greek,[46] and was known as enthusiastic and thorough. His classes were popular. One face in particular in these classes was quite familiar—Franciscus Irenicus, Melanchthon's peer at Pforzheim. He matriculated at Tübingen on May 16, 1516, and became Philipp's student! Two other familiar faces also appeared outside of Melanchthon's formal lecturing duties. The von Löwenstein boys, whom he had tutored in Heidelberg, matriculated at Tübingen in the summer of 1514, and he resumed helping them with their studies.[47]

---

44. CR 1:13; 10:297.
45. See OER, "Universities."
46. Mühlhaupt, 18. Kuropka, 20.
47. Greschat, 22.

Moving beyond studying with just the von Löwenstein boys, Melanchthon gathered a small humanist study group (or sodality) around himself.[48] The goal of this little group was to cultivate a purer mastery of Latin, and to pursue knowledge of the Greek language. Ambrose Blarer participated, as did Johann Setzer (Secerius), who ended up marrying the daughter of the printer Thomas Anshelm. Another student, Bernhard Maurus, became a lasting friend, and Melanchthon later dedicated several writings to him.

Scholarly Publishing

Besides teaching and continuing his own studies, Melanchthon now entered more fully into the world of scholarly publishing. Thomas Anshelm, the printer from Pforzheim, moved his press to Tübingen in 1511. Upon the move, Melanchthon's old Pforzheim instructor, Hiltebrandt, worked for Anshelm as a copy editor. However, after Hiltebrandt's death in 1513, Anshelm needed a new employee. Melanchthon seemed to a natural fit for the job, and he readily agreed to it.[49] Not only would the work allow him access to interesting new humanistic publications, but it would also boost his modest income. This turned out to be a lasting relationship—Melanchthon helped Anshelm until his death in 1523, and then continued to work with Anshelm's son-in-law, the same Johann Setzer who was a member of Melanchthon's Tübingen sodality, until *his* death in 1532. Anshelm and Setzer published numerous treatises from both Luther and Melanchthon.

---

48. See Richard, 22, and Wilson, 42.
49. See Stefan Rhein, "Buchdruck und Humanismus—Melanchthon als Korrektor in der Druckerei des Thomas Anshelm," in eds. Stefan Rhein, et al., *Philipp Melanchthon in Südwestdeutschland: Bildungsstationen eines Reformators* (Karlsruhe: Badische Landesbibliothek, 1997), 63–74.

The printer's mark of Thomas Anshelm, 1515. Courtesy of the Digital Image Archive, Pitts Theology Library, Candler School of Theology, Emory University.

Melanchthon's work for Anshelm during these Tübingen years involved more than copy editing, however. One major project involved the extensive editing of Johannes Nauclerus's *Chronicon* ("Universal History.") The former chancellor of the University of Tübingen (and friend of Reuchlin) had not been able to complete this blend of fiction and history before he died. Upon Reuchlin's recommendation, Melanchthon completed it, and Reuchlin wrote a preface.[50] The work appeared in 1516 and became widely read. Anshelm published a similar work, Franciscus Irenicus's *Exegesis Germaniae*, in 1518, following Melanchthon's proofreading work.

---

50. CR 10:260.

In 1516 Melanchthon also produced a version of Terence's comedies in meter (formerly they were only available in prose) with a preface.[51] He praised Terence for fine colloquial Latin and good morals. Melanchthon likely appreciated the moral tone both because of his pious convictions and also because of the strong emphasis on the moral aspect to be found in Wimpfeling's pedagogy—a pedagogy Melanchthon had been trained under at Pforzheim (through Simler, who considered Wimpfeling a mentor) and also from the communications and writings of Wimpfeling himself, whom Melanchthon met in Heidelberg. This production of Terence in meter was a significant accomplishment, and it would not go unnoticed.

Meanwhile, in 1517, Melanchthon translated some of Plutarch, Pythagoras, and Lycidas.[52] He also responded positively to Stöffler's suggestion to issue the works of Aratus, but he would soon move on to even more ambitious projects.

Less ambitiously, Melanchthon also wrote forewords for a number of humanist publications (including his own).[53] For example, in addition to his essay defending Reuchlin in *The Letters of Eminent Men*, Melanchthon wrote a foreword in 1514 for Bartholomaeus Coloniensis's *Dialogus mythologicus*.[54] He recommended it to younger students as an example of the perfection of the rhetorical arts. But although Bartholomaeus Coloniensis had provided an example of the perfection of the rhetorical arts, the field of Greek studies literature frankly lay in a shambles. Melanchthon himself decided to set out to provide some order here.

---

51. See Richard Wetzel, "Melanchthons Verdienst um Terenz unter besonderer Berücksichtigung 'seiner' Ausgaben des Dicthers," in *Philipp Melanchthon in Südwestdeutschland: Bildungsstationen eines Reformators,* eds. Stefan Rhein, et al. (Karlsruhe: Badische Landesbibliothek, 1997), 101–28. Melanchthon's preface can be found in MBW 7.
52. See MBW 13.
53. MBW 3, 6, 6a, 7, 13, 16, 17 (as an afterword), 18.
54. Tübingen, Thomas Anshelm, August, 1514.

To Purify Greek Studies

Melanchthon now brought to fruition the ideas that had flowed from his work in Greek tutoring with the von Löwenstein boys, beginning back in Heidelberg. He continued work on his *Rudiments of Greek Grammar* throughout his time in Tübingen, finally offering it for publication through Anshelm's press in 1518 (who had since moved his operation to Hagenau).[55] It proved very successful and went through numerous editions. In his foreword to this work, Melanchthon lamented the lack of language education in Germany, thus leading to an impoverished philosophy. He dedicated the work to his students and expressed his hope that it would be useful even for complete beginners. He then conveyed his wish for a greater renewal of Greek philosophy.[56]

In the afterword to his *Rudiments of Greek Grammar*, Melanchthon announced his new project of restoring the original text of Aristotle.[57] The Latin translations of the day were inadequate, and Melanchthon hoped to provide a purer text, using the best manuscripts, taking effort for accuracy.

---

55. *Institutiones graecae grammaticae* (Hagenau: Thomas Anshelm, 1518). Cf. CR 1:24; 18:124; 20:3.
56. MBW 16.
57. MBW 17.

Detail from the Melanchthon statue outside the Stiftskirche in Bretten. Photo by Gregory Graybill.

Further, this was important in that scholastic realists were citing Aristotle in their support, and so perhaps a better edition would provide a stronger rationale for a nominalist approach.[58] By returning to the original sources, Melanchthon hoped to circumvent scholastic distortions. For this mammoth project, Melanchthon was encouraged by his professor, Stadian,[59] who had promised to help, along with Willibald Pirckheimer, Reuchlin, Georg Simler, Wolfgang Capito, and Oecolampadius. Unfortunately, the project became stalled (perhaps due to the Reuchlin affair), and when Melanchthon moved to Wittenberg in 1518, he soon became engrossed in other concerns.

---

58. Cf. Manschreck, 37.
59. See *De corrigendis adolescentiae studiis* (1518), in MSA 3:35–36. Trans. Keen, 51–52.

A Rising Star

In 1516, professor Heinrich Bebel died. The university called on Brassican to fill his chair, which left *his* former responsibilities open. The university, in turn, called on Melanchthon to take up Brassican's former teaching load in Latin, rhetoric, and history. As part of this new formal responsibility, he began drafting his own textbook on rhetoric,[60] along with an updated edition of Agricola's work on the matter. Both would appear a few years later in 1519.

Willibald Pirckheimer (1470–1530).
Engraving by Albrecht Dürer, 1524.

---

60. *De rhetorica libri tres.*

Erasmus of Rotterdam (1466–1536). Painting by Hans Holbein, 1523.

During these years, Melanchthon was rising rapidly in reputation and responsibility, and, through his publications, he was starting to receive notice outside of Württemberg. In about 1516, Melanchthon dedicated a Greek ode to Willibald Pirckheimer.[61] Pirckheimer responded with a letter praising Melanchthon and his learning, calling him a most intimate friend on account of his talents and studious habits.[62] At the same time, when Melanchthon published his version of Terence in meter, he included a preface in which he praised Erasmus as one of the greatest masters of the word.[63] Erasmus, after seeing Melanchthon's Terence edition, lavished praise on the young scholar from Bretten: "Eternal God, what promising

---

61. CR 1:22. MBW 10.
62. CR 1:23–24. MBW 14.
63. *Neque vero de poetae artificio aliud, quam quod Erasmus Roterodamus, optimus maximus literarum praeses...* MBWT 7:90–92.

hopes does not Philipp Melanchthon raise, who though only a youth, indeed, scarcely more than a boy, deserves equal esteem for his knowledge of both Latin and Greek! What wisdom in argument, what purity of expression and style, what comprehensive knowledge, what varied reading, what delicacy and mental elegance he displays!"[64]

Not long after, in July 1517, Erasmus said even more in a letter to Oecolampadius: "Of Melanchthon I entertain the most distinguished and splendid expectations. God grant this young man may long survive us. He will entirely eclipse Erasmus."[65] In a letter to Julius Pflug, he added, "[Melanchthon] not only excels in learning and eloquence, but by a certain fatality is a general favorite. Honest and candid men are fond of him, and even his adversaries cannot hate him!"[66] At about this time, Erasmus likewise wrote to Reuchlin suggesting that Melanchthon could teach at Cambridge: "If you send your young friend Philipp to the Bishop of Rochester with a letter of recommendation from you, believe me, he will be most kindly treated, and advanced to an ample fortune. There is no place where he will enjoy more leisure for the best studies."[67] Word of Erasmus's plaudits filtered back to Melanchthon, who gratefully published a Greek epigram in his honor in March, 1518.[68]

---

64. *Annotat. ad Nov. Test.*, Basel, 1516, fol. 555. Trans., Manschreck, 26. Oecolampadius, who was helping Erasmus draft these annotations at the time, may have had a hand in drawing Erasmus's attention to Melanchthon. See OER, "Oecolampadius."
65. EE 3:18.32–34, Nr. 605.
66. Quoted in Ledderhose (1855), p. 27, n. 1.
67. Calais, 27 August, 1516 (epistle 446). In Nichols, ed., 2:375. EE 2:331.55–57, Nr. 457. The editor of the EE concurs that Erasmus was talking about the University of Cambridge here (2:319).
68. See EE 2:319–20, Nr. 454.

Jealous Colleagues

In 1517, at the age of 20, Melanchthon gave an oration on the liberal arts,[69] dedicated to his professor, Stöffler. In his oration, Melanchthon spoke of the seven-stringed lyre and the origin of the liberal arts. He included a ringing call for deep study of the classics and the Bible, combined with moral integrity. Many praised the excellence of this speech. Others increasingly grew envious of this young achiever. Following on the heels of his involvement in the Reuchlin affair, some of Melanchthon's colleagues began to grow jealous of him. Some coarsely satirized him for his role in the Reuchlin dispute. A few even hinted that he might be a dangerous man. Melanchthon did not take kindly to these rumblings of abuse, and his letters near the end of 1517 show him feeling wounded, unhappy, and threatened. While he sought to pursue humanistic learning to new vistas, he experienced snubbing and hostility from colleagues more interested in retrenching in the scholastic thought of the *moderni*. When Luther posted his *Ninety-Five Theses* and began to make a stir, the Tübingen theologian Jacob Lemp took it upon himself to fight this new heresy. Meanwhile, some of Melanchthon's allies, such as Simler and Stadian, kept a low profile.

The year 1518 saw humanistic learning being tarred with a pejorative connotation through its perceived connection with the disturbances Luther was causing. In the face of this professional and social pressure, Simler even backed off of his earlier enthusiasm for humanism somewhat, embracing instead a more thoroughgoing support for scholasticism. For some people, Melanchthon's calls for humanistic learning began to sound suspiciously like Luther. Although he was popular with his students, the faculty at Tübingen

---

69. *De artibus liberalibus*. MSA 3:17–28. For his intellectual development, it is interesting to note that he called dialectics the mother of all the arts. See Scheible, *Melanchthon*, 26.

began to foster a dim assessment of the young scholar from Bretten. Their disapproval of humanistic studies began to irritate Melanchthon. He chafed at the thought of continuing to teach in an institution where it was "a major offence to study good literature."[70] He wrote a letter to the former student and member of his sodality, Bernhard Maurus, saying, "The method of teaching which ought to improve both the understanding and the manners is neglected here. What is called philosophy is a weak and empty speculation, which produces strife and contention! The true wisdom of heaven which should regulate human affections is banished!"[71] It was clear that Melanchthon was ready for a change—and in an age when letters were often public documents, his colleagues were soon aware that he was ready to go.

Time for a Change

In 1517 and 1518, Melanchthon was busy with his teaching, but dissatisfied. Being associated with the burse was growing old, too. One can only take adolescent antics for so long. It was becoming obnoxious and confining. He definitely was letting it be known that he would be glad to teach somewhere else, and Reuchlin proved to be his main networking contact.[72] When an opening became available at Ingolstadt, Melanchthon was invited to fill it. However, the intellectual atmosphere there was too similar to that of Tübingen, and so Melanchthon turned it down. But then, Reuchlin received a letter from the Elector Friedrich of Saxony looking for a recommendation for a Greek professor. Melanchthon was the obvious choice. Not only did he have the skills to do the job, but his

---

70. CR 1:31–32, MBW 19.
71. MBW 16. See Manschreck, 41.
72. MBW 19.

recent publication of a *Rudiments of Greek Grammar* further burnished his Greek credentials. Reuchlin made the recommendation.

When positive word came back from Saxony regarding Melanchthon, Reuchlin wrote his young relative right away. He told him the news of the invitation to teach at Wittenberg and urged him to accept it, quoting the Lord's words to Abram: "Go from your land and from your relatives and the house of your father, and come to the land I will show you. I will make you into a great nation, and I will bless you and magnify your name, and you will be blessed."[73]

Reuchlin continued with a few practical suggestions for a quick move, and ended with a nod to Melanchthon's frustrating situation at Tübingen by reminding him of the words of Jesus that a prophet is not accepted in his own country.[74] With that, he bid Melanchthon a fond farewell: *Vale feliciter.*

---

73. MBWT 20:4–9. Reuchlin was paraphrasing Genesis 12:1–2.
74. *Non est acceptus propheta in patria sua.* MBW.T 20:27. Cf. Matthew 13:57.

9

Wittenberg

1518–1519

This school is a foundation and ground of pure religion, therefore she ought justly to be preserved and maintained with lectures and with stipends against the raging and swelling of Satan.
—Martin Luther[1]

Duke Ulrich was not pleased to see Melanchthon go. In an attempt to retain his services, he dispatched Conrad von Sickingen to Bretten to lobby Philipp's mother. He promised her that out of respect for her pious late husband, he would be glad to make provision for Melanchthon to enter the priesthood and receive a generous benefice—so long as he stayed in Württemberg. Melanchthon, however, did not feel called to enter ordained ministry.[2]

Despite Ulrich's distress, the reaction from Melanchthon's colleagues at the university was distinctly more tepid. Few deplored

---

1. Martin Luther, *The Table Talk of Martin Luther*, trans. William Hazlitt (Philadelphia: The Lutheran Publication Society, 1902), Nr. DCCXC. www.ccel.org/ccel/luther/tabletalk.html.
2. CR 10:260–61.

his departure. Melanchthon would later maintain some slight contact with theology professor Balthasar Käuffelin[3] and former student Bernard Maurus,[4] but this was the exception rather than the rule.[5] Simler remarked that "though there were many learned men there, they were not learned enough to understand how great was the learning of him who had gone from the midst of them."[6] Camerarius later commented that the professors at Tübingen simply failed to grasp what an adornment to the university they were losing.[7]

Street sign in modern-day Tübingen, near the university.

The Road to Wittenberg

Melanchthon did not linger in Tübingen. He was on the road within a couple days of receiving Reuchlin's letter of July 24.[8] He stopped in to see his learned relative briefly in Stuttgart, and then visited Elisabeth Reuchlin in Pforzheim before making his way home to Bretten. He could only stay a few days, and it must have been a

---

3. E.g., MBW 38a, 1795, 3160.
4. MBW 40.
5. He also later wrote Caspar Churrer in Tübingen to assure him of his friendship. MBW 304. 1523/4.
6. CR 1:31. Trans. Richard, 34.
7. Chapter 7. Cam., *Vita*, 25; *Das Leben*, 53.
8. Greschat (p. 26) erroneously lists this as July 4, 1518.

bittersweet time—it was a relief to move on from Tübingen, and it was exciting to be going to the intellectual hot-spot of Wittenberg. But mother and son were close, and Wittenberg lay a vast distance from Bretten (by sixteenth-century standards)—about 340 miles. Today, it takes about eight hours to make the journey by train (even using the high-speed Inter-City Express). Indeed, it would take Melanchthon about three weeks to get there on horseback, with a few stopovers. He would only see his mother again a bare handful of times before she died.

At the start of August, 1518, Melanchthon bid farewell to his family and hometown.[9] He retraced his steps to Stuttgart, where he saw Reuchlin for the last time. Then he traveled onward to Augsburg, where an imperial diet (*Reichstag*) was underway. These gatherings held a pseudo-parliamentary function for the Holy Roman Empire. They helped, at least nominally, to preserve some sense of cohesion to the empire (not least through ratifying imperial taxes). Although a host of political and ecclesiastical delegates attended, these affairs were increasingly becoming dominated by Germans, with others showing their indifference by their absence.

At this particular gathering, which lasted for several months, Cardinal Cajetan served as the papal legate. His major task was to drum up financial support from Emperor Maximilian and the German princes for a new crusade. The reports from the east showed the Ottomans to be highly aggressive, presenting a severe danger to Christians not only in that region, but in central and western Europe as well.

In the midst of these proceedings, Melanchthon arrived and introduced himself to the electoral party from Saxony. Elector Friedrich was the most significant elector present, due to his power

---

9. Some locals, speaking the Badisch dialect, still affectionately refer to the town as "Bretta."

and influence. His secretary, confidante, and chaplain, Georg Spalatin (originally called Burckhardt, but hailing from the mid-Franconian town of Spalt), held primary responsibility for the university. He took this new professor from Bretten under his wing. Departing most likely on Tuesday, August 10, 1518, Melanchthon and Spalatin now made their way to Wittenberg.

During the long ride from Augsburg to Wittenberg, Melanchthon had ample opportunity to get to know Spalatin. The two held many like-minded ideas about education and theology, and they soon became lasting friends and close coworkers, forming a tight circle with Luther.[10] In 1560, Melanchthon's Wittenberg colleagues looked back on this relationship and characterized it as a fruitful one of love, peace, and unity.[11] Certainly, Spalatin would become one of Melanchthon's most important professional contacts, both in person and by letter. While only eighteen epistles are extant from Spalatin to Melanchthon, more than two hundred can still be found from Melanchthon to Spalatin, dated between Melanchthon's arrival at Wittenberg in 1518 and Spalatin's death in early 1545. (However, this disparity in extant letters may have had more to do with Spalatin's organization in filing incoming mail, rather than a dearth of letters in reply. Melanchthon was notorious for his messy work space, after all.)

The little party bound for Wittenberg would not have been alone on the roads as they slowly rode north. During this era, before confessional divides began to create barriers to travel, one could move about relatively freely in central Europe—though one still needed a

---

10. In German, a significant difference exists between *Freund* and *Bekannter* (friend and acquaintance). Some in the literature (such as Scheible and Wengert) make a big deal about this—especially when it comes to the relationship between Luther and Melanchthon. However, this is an unnecessarily fine distinction, especially for an English-speaking audience where the word "friend" covers much wider ground than the German *Freund*. Accordingly, throughout this book, I use the word "friend" in an American sense to describe a cordial relationship ranging anywhere from cheerful collegiality to deep intimacy.
11. CR 10:261.

license to travel. Tens of thousands of travelers from many walks of life were on the roads at any particular time.[12]

About three days out from Augsburg, Melanchthon and Spalatin arrived in Nuremberg,[13] the place where Melanchthon's father had once served a term of apprenticeship to a master armorer. Though their schedule only permitted a stop of one night, they took the opportunity to visit Willibald Pirckheimer, with whom Melanchthon had already established an epistolary friendship. This was the first time they had met in person. On the same evening, they also met with Christoph Scheurl, a former law professor at Wittenberg (1505-12), with whom Melanchthon would later correspond.[14] The famous painter Albrecht Dürer also lived in Nuremberg, but there is no evidence that Melanchthon met him in this brief overnight visit. The city of Nuremberg, however, would become important in Melanchthon's life—he would help found the first German *gymnasium* (high school) here in 1526, with his friend Camerarius as rector of the upper school. Much correspondence would subsequently go back and forth between Wittenberg and Nuremberg.

Following another week of northward travel, Melanchthon and Spalatin reached Leipzig—the location of the university that served as Wittenberg's main regional competition. The faculty of the university honored Philipp with an elaborate formal meal. Camerarius later reported, "Philipp used to tell what occurred at a banquet given in his honor by the University. The courses were many, and as each was served, some person would get up with a prepared speech and address him. Having observed this for a while and having responded once and again, Philipp said: 'I pray you,

---

12. See OER, "Travel." See also Norbert Ohler, "Reisen zur Zeit Melanchthons," in ed. Peter Bahn, *Als ich ein Kind war...: Bretten 1497–Alltag im Spätmettelalter* (Ubstadt-Weiher: Verlag Regionalkultur, 1997), 111–32.
13. Usually rendered in German as *Nürnberg*.
14. E.g., MBW 25.

illustrious sirs, allow me to respond once and for all to your speeches, for I am not prepared to speak so often with the proper variety.'"[15]

During the course of the evening, the Leipzig faculty urged Melanchthon to stay and teach at their university rather than carrying on to that other less-remunerative backwater institution on the Elbe River. In fact, they offered to double his pay.[16] Although Melanchthon turned down their offers, he did become concerned about the adequacy of his pay at Wittenberg, and later confided in both Spalatin and Luther about the issue.

Besides being fêted by the faculty at Leipzig, Melanchthon also had the slightly awkward yet nevertheless interesting opportunity to meet the twenty-five year-old Petrus Mosellanus. Born with the name Schade, Petrus changed his name in humanistic fashion to Mosellanus in honor of the Mosselle River, which flowed through Koblenz some fifty miles from his home village. He succeeded the English classicist Richard Croke (Crocus) as professor of Greek at Leipzig. When the position of professor of Greek opened at Wittenberg, Mosellanus was the other leading contender in addition to Melanchthon. In fact, Luther and the rest of the faculty had *preferred* that Mosellanus get the job, and Melanchthon's success was due primarily to Reuchlin's ringing endorsement. However, when Melanchthon and Mosellanus met, the awkwardness of the situation soon gave way to their shared enthusiasm for Greek and classical studies. They quickly came to value and honor each other, such that in a letter not long after this time, Melanchthon called Mosellanus *amicissimo mihi* ("a most dear friend to me.")[17] However, even Mosellanus warned Melanchthon

---

15. Trans. Richard, 35. Cam., *Vita*, 26; *Das Leben*, 54.
16. CR 1:42, cxlviii.
17. MBW 21. A memorial fountain for Peter Mosellanus can be found at Hauptstraße 23, in Bruttig-Fankel, in Rheinland-Pfalz, Germany. See Cam., *Das Leben*, 53. On this stopover, Melanchthon also made the acquaintance of Andreas Francus Camicianus, who later achieved excellence and honor.

about the low salary in Wittenberg, and they discussed how Philipp might get by on it.[18]

St. Peter's Basilica, under construction.

Indulgences and Ninety-Five Theses

Meanwhile, as Melanchthon chatted about Greek with Mosellanus in August, 1518, other events were well underway—events that would soon loom large in Melanchthon's life.

In 1506, Pope Julius II commissioned the building of St. Peter's,[19] in order to replace for Christendom the loss of the Hagia Sophia in Constantinople in 1453. It was not fitting that Europe's most glorious cathedral should be adorned as a mosque. Pragmatically,

---

18. MBW 21.
19. For a book-length treatment of this subject, see Scotti, R. A., *Basilica: The Splendor and the Scandal: Building St. Peter's* (New York: Viking, 2006).

Julius employed indulgences as a funding stream to finance the elaborate construction.

This sale of indulgences (not only to finance Albert's attempt at the archbishopric of Mainz, but also the funding of St. Peter's) drew ire north of the Alps, where many Germans felt that their hard-earned money was being drained away to serve Italian vanity projects. Luther articulated this sentiment in his *Ninety-Five Theses* and their explanation in 1517, when he said, "The revenues of all Christendom are being sucked into this insatiable basilica. The Germans laugh at calling this the common treasure of Christendom. Before long all the churches, palaces, walls, and bridges of Rome will be built out of our money. First of all we should rear living temples, next local churches, and only last of all St. Peter's. Better that it should never be built than that our parochial churches should be despoiled. . . . Why doesn't the pope build the basilica of St. Peter out of his own money? He is richer than Croesus. . . . If the pope knew the exactions of these vendors, he would rather that St. Peter's should lie in ashes than that it should be built out of the blood and hide of his sheep."[20]

According to the *Oxford Encyclopedia of the Reformation,* "an indulgence is the complete or partial remission by the church of temporal punishment (as opposed to the eternal punishment of hell) for sins that have already been forgiven, provided that certain conditions (for example, going on a pilgrimage, going on or supporting a crusade, almsgiving, making a contribution toward the building of a church or of a hospital) have been fulfilled. The debt of punishment is paid off from the treasury of merit that has been acquired by Christ, the Blessed Virgin, and the saints."[21] By the time the Dominican Tetzel came hawking indulgences in the

---

20. Trans. Bainton, 80. No original citation provided.
21. OER, "Indulgences."

vicinity of Wittenberg in 1517, however, they were being marketed straightforwardly as time off of purgatory in exchange for cash—hence, Luther's *Ninety-Five Theses* nailed to the door of the Castle Church on October 31, 1517.

Castle Church Door, with Luther's Ninety-Five Theses. The picture above the door depicts Luther and Melanchthon kneeling before Christ. (Photo by Gregory Graybill May, 2013—the church was undergoing repairs at the time of the photo.)

Martin Luther (1483–1546), at age 37.
Engraving by Lucas Cranach, 1520.

Heidelberg Disputation

In April, 1518, the Augustinian Order was set to meet in Heidelberg. Luther proposed that they hold a disputation on the issue of indulgences, and his mentor (who was also the head of the order), Johannes von Staupitz, approved. This disappointed those who simply wanted Luther silenced. Some thought he we would be burned at the stake soon. Sensible of the controversy, Staupitz and Luther traveled the 330 miles to Heidelberg in disguise. Elector Friedrich, also aware of the danger, was determined to defend his star professor—he would not tolerate him being carted off to Rome. Accordingly, the Elector Palatinate treated Luther very well upon his arrival—hosting a dinner for him and giving him a tour of the chapel and armaments.

When Luther spoke on April 26 in Heidelberg, he not only defended his views on indulgences, but he also developed his ideas to pit a "theology of the cross" against the corrupt "theology of glory" widely promulgated in the church. Some in the audience found his arguments very compelling. Among them were three future reformers whom Melanchthon knew from his student days in Heidelberg—Johannes Brenz, Martin Bucer, and Erhard Schnepf. Bucer commented, "Luther has a marvelous graciousness in response and unconquerable patience in listening. In argument he shows the acumen of the apostle Paul. That which Erasmus insinuates he speaks openly and freely."[22] Additionally, Melanchthon's classmate from both Pforzheim and Heidelberg, Franciscus Irenicus (now on the Heidelberg University council) was present. All in all, Luther felt the entire endeavor was a success. He noted drily: "I went on foot. I came back in a wagon."[23]

---

22. Quoted in Bainton, 87—however the primary source citation he gives is incorrect. The source is a letter from Martin Bucer to Beatus Rhenaeus, soon after he heard Luther speak at the Heidelberg Disputation, around May 1, 1518.
23. WABR 1:172–74, Nr. 75.

WITTENBERG

Wittenberg. Illustration by Jeffrey Mathison.

Wittenberg

After spending several days in Leipzig, Melanchthon and Spalatin again set out for Wittenberg on Tuesday, August 24, 1518. They arrived the next day, on Wednesday, August 25, at about ten o'clock in the morning. This town would be Melanchthon's home for the next forty-two years, and, in 1556, he would call it a "special jewel."[24]

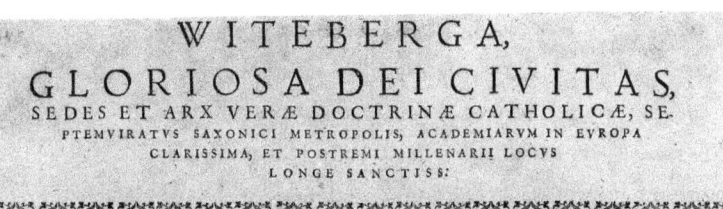

Stadtansicht von Wittenberg, um 1558. Stiftung Luthergedenkstätten in Sachen-Anhalt.

At this time, Wittenberg was a backwater just beginning to make a name for itself. Most residents lived in poorly-constructed, unattractive low clay dwellings. Compared to the grandeurs of Heidelberg and Tübingen, this place was but a village. Humble shops and public baths with dishpans hung out to indicate that they were open could be found here. Two main cobbled streets ran roughly parallel for about a mile, just north of the Elbe River. Each contained a small stream, brought into the city by aqueducts. The two roads

---

24. From a history of Wittenberg, written by Melanchthon in 1556, and sealed up in a steeple ball at the top of the city church in Wittenberg. It was discovered in 1910.

began at the Castle Church in the west, widened to permit the marketplace and City Church (where Luther preached) in the middle, and again gently converged on the university buildings and the Augustinian monastery in the east, where Luther lived with his fellow monks.

Named for the white soil of the area, the town was founded by Flemish settlers in the twelfth century. A low wall and moat surrounded the west, north, and east sides of the town, with the Elbe River providing a natural barrier to the south. Markets could frequently be found along this waterfront, selling grain, vegetables, fruit, and game from the nearby woods. Fairs, plays, and executions also happened here. A grinding mill was located at the west end of town.[25]

The Elector Friedrich the Wise owned a massive collection of relics, stored mainly at the Castle Church. This collection expressed a deep concern for spiritual matters, which was also reflected by the thousands of masses he arranged to be said at the two churches each year. Friedrich's relic collection additionally provided a large level of income from pilgrims coming to reduce their sentences in purgatory.[26] In fact, due in large part to this income, Friedrich was able to improve the Castle Church from 1490 to 1509, and found the University of Wittenberg in 1502. He also showed a taste for fine art, by hiring the famous painter Lucas Cranach the Elder, whose house (which was the largest in town in 1518) and pharmacy can still be found just off the marketplace, across from the city hall. Cranach was forty-six years old when Melanchthon arrived.

---

25. WATR 2:669.
26. Skeptical modern readers are often quick to cite the financial motive as primary. However, by all accounts, Friedrich was also a pious man. Rather than attributing the motivations for his collection of relics either to his piety *or* a financial motive, it surely comes closer to the truth to remind the reader that even the best of people often have deeply mixed motives.

A scene in Wittenberg, looking west toward the Castle Church. Notice the small stream in the foreground. Photo by Gregory Graybill.

Leucorea—Wittenberg University

Friedrich certainly had a reason to found a university in Wittenberg. The Wettin family at one point had controlled the region around Leipzig (with its university) as well as the region around Wittenberg. But in 1485, the domain was divided between two branches of the family—such that when Friedrich inherited his title and rule, he found himself without a university. He set himself to improving Wittenberg in a number of ways. His chief passions were education, art, and religion. His most notable improvements included the renovation of the Castle Church, and the chartering of a new university. This new university could be staffed to some extent by the learned Augustinian and Franciscan monks who lived in town. Friedrich hoped that it would rival Leipzig University, located only forty-five miles away. In true humanist fashion, by translating the name "Wittenberg" into Greek, the result was "Leucorea"—the official name of Friedrich's new university.

Once the university was founded in 1502, Friedrich's next ambition was to build it into one of the most excellent universities anywhere. This led to his search in 1518 for professors of Greek and Hebrew, and Friedrich's inquiry to Reuchlin—the leading Hebrew expert of his day. For Hebrew, Reuchlin recommended Paul Riccius, a converted Jew, a former student of Reuchlin, and a physician to Cardinal von Gurk. He also recommended another former student, Conrad Pellican, who had published his own Hebrew grammar in 1507. A third name was that of Oecolampadius.[27] Of course, Reuchlin's *only* recommendation for Greek was the author of a recent Greek grammar—his relative Philipp Melanchthon.

---

27. Reuchlin, *Briefwechsel*, ed. Matthias Dall'Asta and Gerald Dörner, Nr. 256.

Friedrich the Wise (1463–1525), by Albrecht Dürer, 1524.

Soon after Melanchthon's arrival in town, he met the rest of the Wittenberg faculty—most of whom were in their thirties: Andreas Bodenstein von Karlstadt (age 32, theology), Nicholas von Amsdorf (age 35, theology), Martin Luther (age 32, theology), Jerome Schurf (a lawyer from Tübingen, whom Melanchthon had met before), Johannes Rhagius and Otto Beckman (Latin classics), Caspar Borner (mathematics and astronomy), Jakob Premsel, and Johannes Gunkel (Thomistic physics and logic). Melanchthon, by contrast, was only twenty-one years old. When his colleagues first met him, they were anything but impressed.

First Impressions

After dropping off and commending the new professor, Spalatin headed almost immediately back to the diet at Augsburg. In the university record, it read, "Philipp Melanchthon of Bretten, a Tübingen Master of Arts, was registered as the first professor of the Greek language."[28] He would have to give his inaugural lecture within three days. Meanwhile, he tried to settle into his modest dwelling. Some thought it was more than modest—"dilapidated cabin" was probably a better description.[29] Perhaps the warnings of the Leipzig faculty held some merit. Christoph Scheurl later wrote from Nuremberg to commiserate, commenting that when he lived in Wittenberg, the beer was bad, too.[30]

When Melanchthon emerged from his little cabin, the rest of the Wittenberg faculty coolly began to size him up. Luther had not been the only one who had preferred Petrus Mosellanus. They saw a skinny, frail young man who was not quite five feet tall. He had uneven shoulders, a high forehead, a modest demeanor, and sharp blue eyes. Some privately called him *Männchen* ("little man"), or "the little Greek." Luther was prepared to write him off, stating, "I fear that his delicate constitution may not bear the mode of life in this country."[31] Some students winked and made circular gestures with their fingers about him.[32] "Poor, scrawny little man," remarked Luther.[33]

---

28. CR 1:cxlviii.
29. OER, "Wittenberg."
30. MBW 56.
31. WABR 1:192.19–20. Nr. 88. This quotation actually came after Luther heard Melanchthon's inaugural address, and was now enthusiastic about him. Nevertheless, it still represented a negative initial impression of Melanchthon—one that endured, despite a general reversal in outlook following the successful initial lecture.
32. CR 1:52, 10:531.
33. Luther's impression of Melanchthon as a "poor, scrawny little man" was enduring, but not unaffectionate. The context of his remark was in a dinner table conversation, when someone asked him what he thought the apostle Paul looked like. He said he thought the apostle was probably a "poor, scrawny little man"—like Philipp: *ein armes dürres Männlin wie Magister Philippus*. WATR 1245.

A view of the Castle Church tower from the west, the likely scene of Melanchthon's inaugural lecture. An evening in May, 2013. Photo by Gregory Graybill.

On Saturday, August 28,[34] the university gathered at the Castle Church to hear Melanchthon's inaugural lecture (*Antrittsrede*), titled, "On Reforming the Studies."[35] With the best Latin he could muster, and with the powerful, emphatic rhetoric of a serious student of the art, Melanchthon made a clear and passionate call for the purification of every discipline. He advocated for classical learning, denigrated scholastic scholarship, and argued for the mastery of Hebrew, Greek, Latin, and original Christianity. This learned and impassioned oration put to flight all the negative impressions that initially swirled around the Bretten native.

Skepticism about Melanchthon now gave way to enthusiasm. Luther sent a report to Spalatin, who was still on the road back to Augsburg. "Regarding our Philipp Melanchthon, about whom you write and advise, have no doubts that everything has been done and will be done. On the fourth day after his arrival he delivered clearly the most educated, most pure oration, and there was so much favor and admiration from everybody that you don't have to think up reasons to commend him to us anymore. We swiftly disabused ourselves of opinions and notions based on his stature and personality. We rejoice and are amazed at the actual reality in him. We give our thanks and regards to the illustrious Prince and to you as well. Certainly the one for whom we have such enthusiasm ought to be better taken care of. Please give the Prince our highest commendation. I clearly desire no other teacher of Greek but this one.... The man is worthy of all honor."[36]

Upon hearing the reports of Melanchthon's enthusiastic reception in Wittenberg, Spalatin was both pleased and worried. In Luther's same letter, he warned about the low pay promised to Melanchthon,

---

34. Some sources suggest it was Sunday, August 29, instead.
35. *De corrigendis adolescentiae studiis.* CR 11:15–25. MSA 3:29–42.
36. WABR 1:192.11–28. Nr. 88. Cf. Manschreck, 24, and Richard, 40–41—both of whom employ slightly varying English translations of this passage.

noting that both Ingolstadt and Leipzig had offered him much more. Spalatin voiced his concern to Melanchthon, who, despite his anxieties on the topic, responded with a letter on September 14 reassuring Spalatin that he fully intended to honor his commitment to the elector to teach at Wittenberg. He had indeed been worried about the pay, but his mind was now at rest.[37] It seems that for Melanchthon, the intellectual and spiritual climate of Wittenberg outweighed the increase in pay available elsewhere. Wittenberg was exactly where he wanted to be.

Professor of Greek

Melanchthon threw himself into his work at Wittenberg with the all-consuming energy that would characterize his entire forty-two-year career at the Leucorea. It is a telling detail that Luther—who was himself known to work to excess—often chided Melanchthon to slow down and take appropriate rest. Melanchthon, however, often rose at 2:00 a.m. to get a jump on the day. He began with devotions, letters,[38] and private study before heading to his first lectures, which usually started punctually at 6:00 a.m. Teaching requirements were normally complete by early afternoon, leaving the rest of the day for study and writing, capped off by a strict 9:00 p.m. bedtime (which allowed a luxurious five hours of sleep until the 2:00 a.m. wakeup).

As outlined in his inaugural lecture, Melanchthon began his Greek courses with Homer's *Iliad*[39] and the New Testament book of Titus. His teaching emphasized language, logic, and classical literature. After these courses, he moved on to Plutarch and Pindar, possibly James, and then definitely to the Pauline letters of Romans and

---

37. MBW 21.
38. Melanchthon never dealt with letters in the evening, because otherwise it would disturb his sleep.
39. For the *Iliad*, Melanchthon worked with Johannes Rhagius Aesticampianus. As of April 3, 1519, a transcript was in process. MBW 50. Cf. Scheible, *Melanchthon*, 32–33.

Galatians (of which student notes remain). He was also planning courses in Greek grammar, and reading Plato.[40]

In the meantime, Melanchthon wrote to Spalatin in October, noting that his inaugural lecture had been published, and asking his valued colleague's opinion on it. Melanchthon seems to have also heard rumors that some were still ridiculing him to some extent, and he urged Spalatin not to listen to them, but instead to seek the opinions of more qualified observers in the University of Wittenberg.[41] His aim was to do his work well, for the glory of Saxony and the University.[42]

But while Melanchthon showed concern for negative reviews, the positive feedback on his teaching was overwhelming. Camerarius says that Melanchthon quickly won the affection and admiration of all.[43] He taught excellently, gaining love and respect, despite being a demanding teacher. He gathered increasing numbers of students, and did his best to build networks and cultivate relationships—both locally and on the broader European stage.[44] His aims and the goals of the university were in synch, as seen by the humanistic transition in the curriculum that continued after his arrival—classes in scholasticism were reduced, language studies multiplied, courses in the classics were added, and interest in the Bible was on the increase.[45] Melanchthon's friend, Camerarius, later claimed that while Crocus and Mosellanus had established good reputations at Leipzig, Melanchthon quickly outshone them at Wittenberg.[46]

---

40. Melanchthon said as much in a letter to Spalatin in December, 1518. MBW 35.
41. MBW 31.
42. MBW 29, 31.
43. Cam., *Das Leben*, 54.
44. For example, he wrote to Erasmus (MBW 38), and introduced himself by letter to Wolfgang Capito (MBW 57).
45. CR 1:75, 203.
46. Chapter 8. Cam, *Das Leben*, 55.

At this time, Melanchthon also tutored Luther in Greek (who tutored Melanchthon in theology in return). Luther was impressed. He claimed, "No one living is gifted with such talents. He is to be esteemed. God himself will despise anyone who despises this man."[47] Further, "Whoever does not recognize Philipp as his instructor is a stolid, stupid donkey, carried away by his own vanity and self-conceit. Whatever we know in the arts and in true philosophy, Philipp has taught us. He has only the humble title of Master, but he excels all the Doctors."[48] Luther held a very definite opinion.

With a flair that can only be communicated with Latin superlatives, Luther further wrote to Spalatin on September 2, *Philippum Graecissimum, eruditissimum, humanissimum habe commendatissiumum* ("Philipp is the very best Greek scholar, the most erudite, and the very best humanist—I give him my highest commendation.")[49] He went on to conclude by noting the growing popularity of Greek for theology students, stemming from Melanchthon's teaching.

Indeed, class sizes were not merely growing for Melanchthon (as well as for Luther), but more and more students were flocking to Wittenberg itself. In the winter semester, 1518, at Wittenberg, student enrollment stood at 120. It doubled by the next semester, and climbed to 333 by the summer of 1520.[50] Students and visitors from distant regions began to arrive—from German lands outside Saxony, and even beyond. In fact, by 1520, Wittenberg was the largest university in the German-speaking lands. As the *Oxford Encyclopedia of the Reformation* puts it, "Luther and Melanchthon attracted so many students that the Leucorea became the most highly

---

47. CR 10:302. Trans Manschreck, 44.
48. CR 10:302. Trans. Richard, 44–45.
49. WABR 1:196:40–41, Nr. 90.
50. CR 10:301.

attended German university."⁵¹ In fact, some reports can be found that on occasion, Melanchthon had two thousand hearers for some of his lectures—including many people of high rank. He taught such a variety of subjects to such a high degree of skill, that he did the work of several professors all by himself.⁵² In fact, when he died, it would take four professors to take over his teaching load.

Interim Professor of Hebrew

Although Melanchthon was hired to teach Greek at Wittenberg, the chair of Hebrew was vacant when he arrived. Accordingly, he stepped into the breach and picked up these courses as well, until a suitable professor could be found. This did not take long, as a famous Hebraist named Johannes Böschenstein arrived at the end of October to take up the Hebrew duties. He was twenty-five years older than Melanchthon, and Philipp was happy to work with him.⁵³ Melanchthon wrote a recommending afterword (really just a jacket blurb) for Böschenstein's Hebrew grammar, which appeared in December. He called it "an excellent and useful little book."⁵⁴ He also recommended Böschenstein in a letter to Christoph Scheurl.⁵⁵

Unfortunately, though, on the very day in January when Melanchthon wrote to Scheurl, Böschenstein went on vacation and never came back. As a result, Melanchthon once again stepped in to take over courses in Hebrew. He dealt with the Psalms,⁵⁶ sections of Genesis, and Hebrew grammar. He continued these classes until April, 1520, when a new professor, Mattäus Adrianus, finally arrived.⁵⁷

---

51. OER, "Wittenberg."
52. CR 10:301. Cf. Manschreck, 43.
53. See MBW 22. Cf. Scheible, *Melanchthon*, 33.
54. MBWT 34:4. *Hebraica grammaticae institutiones*. Wittenberg: Johannes Grunenberg, 1518.
55. Jan. 20, 1519. MBW 39.
56. MBW 50.

Publications

For Melanchthon, teaching involved not just lecturing, but also publishing. He often worked with the Wittenberg printer Johannes Grunenberg, who had set up his press in the Augustinian monastery at the east end of town in 1508. Melanchthon helped keep the press very busy.

Grunenberg published Melanchthon's inaugural lecture in 1518[58]—for which Philipp contributed a foreword.[59] Before he had been in Wittenberg for a month, Melanchthon dedicated a translation of one of Lucian's works to Elector Friedrich.[60] Also right after his arrival, he set himself an ambitious publication program that included a Greek lexicon, writings from Plutarch and Pindar,[61] *Hymnus in angelos*, Athenagoras, and Plato's *Symposium*. He also had a plan to work with the incoming professor, Böschenstein, on a trilingual edition of the Psalms (in Greek, Hebrew, and Latin).[62] To help with this project, he wrote to Spalatin in Augsburg and Scheurl in Nuremberg asking for their help in acquiring copies of Hebrew and Greek Bibles.[63] Additionally, in October he was still talking about his grand Aristotle project that he had first mentioned in Tübingen. By cleansing Aristotle, he hoped to make a contribution to theology.[64] However this project would prove too ambitious even

---

57. During the search process, Melanchthon wrote to Spalatin in May, 1519, suggesting that Johannes Cellarius would be a suitable pick, according to him and Luther. MBW 58.
58. *De corrigendis adolescentiae studiis.* MSA 3:29–42.
59. MBW 30.
60. MBW 23 (for the dedication). The text of the short book can be found in CR 17:979–98. See also MBW 29.
61. MBW 48, and 52. Melanchthon admired the emphasis on ethical formation in Plutarch.
62. MBW 24. CR 1:44, 50, 52.
63. MBW 24, 25, and 32.
64. MBWT 29:24–26. See also MBW 35. See also Günter Frank, "*Accingimur enim non vano conatu ad instauranda Aristotelica*: Melanchthons Tübinger Plan einer neuen Aristoteles-Ausgabe," in *Der frühe Melanchthon und der Humanismus*, ed. Franz Fuchs (Wiesbaden: Harrassowitz, 2011), 51–72.

for Melanchthon—who was simultaneously gaining an increased interest in theology. His Greek edition of Titus appeared in October.[65]

Also in 1518, some thought that Melanchthon was the author of the bitingly satirical *Letters of Obscure Men*, which supported Reuchlin and cleverly attacked those who sought the destruction of Hebrew literature. However, while he may have helped edit the work, Melanchthon was not the author. He did agree, however, that Pfefferkorn and his Dominican allies were "base, flattering parasites and greedy dolts."[66]

Moving into 1519, Melanchthon was working on a textbook on rhetoric,[67] to which he added a foreword,[68] and sent a copy to his former Tübingen student, Bernard Maurus. He took the time also to warn Maurus of the corrupt philosophy at Tübingen. Melanchthon's disciplined study of rhetoric and dialectics would provide him the background and tools for his later disciplined and well-delineated theological textbook, the *Loci communes*. Meanwhile, Melanchthon's teachings on Paul and James also went to press in 1519[69] (and in his free time, he dabbled in medical studies).[70]

Luther in Augsburg

In the autumn of 1518, at the same time that Melanchthon was launching himself into teaching and scholarship at Wittenberg, the diet at Augsburg continued to run its course. Spalatin patiently

---

65. Wittenberg: John Grunenberg, 1518. See MBW 29.
66. CR 11:1006.
67. *De rhetorica libri tres*.
68. MBW 40.
69. See, e.g., MBW 50.
70. Melanchthon wrote a foreword to Peter Burckhard, *Parva Hippocratis tabula* (Wittenberg: Johannes Grunenberg, 1519). MBW 37. Burckhard was a friend of Scheurl's and was a senior professor on the medical faculty at Wittenberg. Melanchthon also liked and recommended the medical scholar Ulrich Pinder (MBW 22, 24, 31, 39, 42–44).

assisted the elector in navigating these political and religious waters. Pope Leo X kept insisting on a new crusade, but the German princes, with their gaze firmly fixed on central Europe rather than eastern Europe, were recalcitrant. Likewise, the issue of Martin Luther's writings continued to cause a considerable stir. Seeing the diet as a possible forum for resolving the conflict, Elector Friedrich agreed to ask Luther to come to Augsburg to discuss the matter with representatives of the Roman Church. After all, this was German, rather than Italian, soil. On September 26, Luther obediently departed for Augsburg, where Staupitz, the head of the Augustinian Order, sought to guide and counsel him.

Friedrich, though, remained cautious. He had a genuine piety and desire to do right as a Christian prince, and he was also aware that this monk was helping the new university in Saxony rise to international prominence. He made sure that Emperor Maximilian provided a guarantee of safe-conduct for Luther. Nevertheless, Luther's thoughts drifted to martyrdom at the stake, and he steeled himself to stay true to his convictions. He wrote to his Wittenberg colleagues, "I will remain steadfast in the truth, remembering, 'Thy will be done, Lord.' . . . God is true, even if people are false."[71]

If the worst did come to pass, then Luther viewed Melanchthon as a divinely-appointed successor in his gospel work.[72] He wrote to him, "Play the man, as you do. Teach the youth the things that are right. For you and for them, I will be immolated, if it please the Lord. I prefer to perish—which would be a great sorrow to me, even to lose your sweetest society forever—rather than recant."[73]

A recantation, though, was precisely what Cardinal Cajetan intended to extract from the obstreperous monk. This was not a

---

71. MBWT 27:4–5. He alludes to Romans 3:4.
72. Stupperich, 36.
73. MBWT 28:11–14. Augsburg, Oct. 11, 1518.

matter of doctrinal debate—it was a matter of submission to duly constituted authorities (meaning the Church), who had the power and responsibility to articulate Christian doctrine.

Cajetan was a student of Aristotle, and a Dominican expert on Thomas Aquinas. He published a thorough commentary on Thomas's *Summa theologiae* in four parts between 1508 and 1522. From 1508 until 1518, he served as the master general of the Dominican Order. He was no lightweight.

While Luther could afford the luxury of a sole focus on doctrinal questions, Cajetan also represented a pope with geopolitical concerns revolving around the gathering Turkish Muslim storm in the east. The Christian outpost of Rhodes faced an existential threat. The Balkans, Hungary, and even Austria could field only modest forces in the face of a mighty janissary-fortified Turkish force intent on conquest, subjugation, and the expansion of Islam at the expense of Christianity. It was essential to have Christian harmony in central Europe for the sake of providing a unified front against the invaders. The rebellious monk from the outposts of Germany needed to recant and submit, or else get bound and hauled back to Rome. While Cajetan did examine Luther's writings, his instructions were to reconcile him only if he recanted.

The interview between Luther and Cajetan took place at the newly built house of the banker Jakob Fugger. Cajetan simply asked Luther to recant. He refused, unless shown his errors. Cajetan engaged him briefly, but then returned to his simple call to recant. Luther would not.

Over supper, Cajetan spoke of Luther to Staupitz, saying, "I am not going to talk with him anymore. His eyes are as deep as a lake, and there are amazing speculations in his head."[74] Staupitz realized that

---

74. Walch edition of Luther's works, XV, 208. Bainton, 96.

neither side was going to budge. So he released Luther of his vow of obedience to the Augustinian Order, and told him to flee Augsburg. Luther did so—in the dead of night, October 20-21.

The next day, Luther issued an appeal to the pope. He continued on his journey, and arrived back in Wittenberg on October 30. On November 9, the papal bull *Cum postquam* was promulgated, more clearly defining indulgences. On November 18, Luther publicly appealed to a general council of the church. Technically, this call for a general council was considered to be a heretical attack on the position of the pope. A week later, Luther wrote to Spalatin, "I am expecting the curses of Rome any day. I have everything in readiness. When they come, I am girded like Abraham to go I know not where, but sure of this, that God is everywhere."[75]

Cajetan quickly demanded that Elector Friedrich put Luther in chains and send him to Rome. Luther prepared to go into exile. However, much to Luther's joy, the elector was unwilling to give him up, and told the Roman *curia* just that in a letter on December 18.[76] The *curia* sent Charles Miltitz to lobby the elector, replete with the coveted Golden Rose as a sop. Miltitz spoke with Luther, on January 4-6, 1519, and gained an assurance from him that he would stop polemicizing if his opponents did as well. In the end, Luther's opponents kept right on attacking, so he did, too.

Meanwhile, Melanchthon defended Luther and agreed with his call for a general council. He wrote to Spalatin, "Do not fear the raging of the Romanists. That is what such men usually do. Unless they act like tyrants they do not think they rule. But, good God! There is a difference between such ruling and serving as stewards."[77]

---

75. Bainton, 100. WABR 1:253–54, Nr. 112.
76. WABR 1:250.
77. March 5, 1519. MBW 45.

Humanism and Erasmus

The humanistic movement that had brought Melanchthon to Wittenberg continued after his arrival. The focus on languages and history strengthened, while the old emphases on Aristotle and the scholastics weakened. It was an exciting time of transformation, and Melanchthon viewed it as fully in line with the teachings of the famous Erasmus of Rotterdam.

In the foreword to his book on rhetoric, in January 1519, Melanchthon praised Erasmus, along with Reuchlin and Luther.[78] In the same month, he wrote to Erasmus to recommend Luther to him, and deferentially denied that he had criticized Erasmus's paraphrase of Romans.[79] Erasmus's reply was a bit prickly, but he praised Melanchthon for his *Hymnus*, calling for the cohesion of the educated. On the topic of Luther, Erasmus was guarded. Likewise, he was critical of the polemic in Melanchthon's own inaugural address at Wittenberg. Erasmus concluded with an admonition to Melanchthon to take care of himself, and not to work to excess on his studies—thereby demonstrating that word of Melanchthon's torrid work habits had already traveled far and wide.[80]

Despite Erasmus's somewhat cautious words, Melanchthon continued to look for unity between him and Luther. In March, he wrote Spalatin, saying that he saw great theological agreement between Erasmus and Luther.[81] A couple months later he again told Spalatin that he discerned Erasmus's support for the Lutheran cause.[82] At this stage, Melanchthon was enthusiastic about both Erasmus and Luther, and hoped that they could make common cause.

---

78. MBW 40.
79. MBW 38.
80. April 22, 1519. MBW 53.
81. MBW 46. He had recently read Erasmus's *Ratio seu verae compendium theologiae* (LB 5:75–138; *Selected Writings* 3:117–495).
82. MBW 58.

Along with Erasmus, Melanchthon believed that the humanistic endeavor of returning to high-quality original sources helped to enhance the ethical imperative in readers. He wrote an admiring foreword to Plutarch, lauding his high ethical teachings.[83] This meshed nicely with the strong ethical emphasis in the pedagogy Melanchthon had imbibed first from Simler in Pforzheim, and then from the writings of Wimpfeling.

For Melanchthon, the humanistic endeavor of going to the sources led not only to a salutary ethical system, but to Christ himself. "And when we apply our minds to the sources, let us begin to understand Christ, who made his clear mandate to us, and we shall pour forth the blessed nectar of divine wisdom."[84] For Melanchthon, humanism was vital not for its own sake, but for the deepening and strengthening of Christianity. This is one of the key factors that differentiated much of northern European humanism from its Italian cousin.[85] "For I feel that there is absolutely nothing more important than what is approved by the decrees of the Evangelical church."[86]

Theology and Luther

Melanchthon never shed his childhood Christian faith. Instead of subordinating it to his studies and teaching, rather, his studies and teaching supported it. The exhaustive study of the Bible he had begun at Tübingen continued at Wittenberg. This was both a matter of personal conviction and of professional responsibility.

As a professor of Greek (and interim professor of Hebrew), Melanchthon could hardly escape the biblical texts. In 1519, Melanchthon wrote a foreword to Luther's *Operationes in Psalmos*.[87]

---

83. July 6, 1519. MBW 48. Plutarch, *De liberorum institutione* (Köln: Eucharius Cervicornus, 1519).
84. *De corrigendis adolescentiae studiis*. MSA 3:40.19–22. Keen, 55.
85. See James R. Payton, *Getting the Reformation Wrong* (Downers Grove, IL: InterVarsity, 2010): 68–69.
86. *De corrigendis adolescentiae studiis*. MSA 3:41.10–11. Keen, 55–56.

In it, he told his readers that after a four-hundred-year reign by scholasticism, true theology—despite resistance—was finally being brought once again into the light (thanks to Erasmus, Reuchlin, Capito, Oecolampadius, Karlstadt, and especially Luther).[88]

Melanchthon began having theological conversations with Luther as soon as he arrived in Wittenberg. While he continued his own wide reading, he also soon started work on his *baccalaureas biblicus*, which he would complete in about a year (in September, 1519). His own theological development, which we have already seen at Heidelberg and Tübingen, now merged nicely with Luther's emphases. The two men found themselves in broad agreement, and Melanchthon learned much from his new theological mentor. They spent a good deal of time together—for example, they traveled together to Leipzig for four days (January 6-10, 1519), where they celebrated a New Year's mass and visited with Mosellanus. Pirckheimer also came up from Nuremberg to join the small group.

By the spring, Melanchthon was sufficiently advanced in theology to write a complimentary foreword for Luther's commentary on Galatians (although he also protected himself by using a pseudonym).[89] It was probably due to Luther's influence that Melanchthon began to develop a negative judgment of Aristotle's *Physics*. In his foreword to Luther's commentary, he argued that Aristotle blocks the teachings of Christ, displacing true theology (especially among the scholastic admirers). Melanchthon's grand plans for a new Aristotle edition gradually fell by the wayside. He did, however, still speak positively of Aristotle's dialectics.[90] Increasingly,

---

87. Wittenberg: Johannes Grunenberg, 1519.
88. March 27, 1519. MBW 47.
89. "Otho Germanus." MBW 54. Luther, *In epistolam Pauli ad Galatas commentaries* (Leipzig: Melchior Lotter the Elder, 1519). See also his afterword, under the name "Paulus Commodus Brettanus" in MBW 65.
90. MBW 46.

Melanchthon favored the Bible as sole authority, and he only valued Aristotle insofar as he provided exegetical techniques for better understanding the biblical text.

But now, these studies were about to be interrupted by fallout from Luther's Heidelberg Disputation from the previous spring.

Eck Throws Down the Gauntlet

In October, 1518, when Luther was on his way to Augsburg, he expressed suspicion of the Ingolstadt professor Johannes Eck.[91] This suspicion was justified. Eck read Luther's Heidelberg Disputation with great disapproval, then challenged both Luther and Karlstadt to a new disputation at Leipzig—a site located between Ingoldstadt and Wittenberg.[92] While Christoph Scheurl tried to build bridges between Eck and the Wittenbergers,[93] he was not successful. Melanchthon claimed that Eck was proud of the disputes he stirred up, and he urged Spalatin to be steadfast in supporting Luther.[94] The disputation was set for June 27, 1519, at the University of Leipzig.

---

91. MBW 27.
92. Feb. 19, 1519. WABR 1:342–43, Nr. 151.
93. MBW 56.
94. May 21, 1519. MBW 58.

10

All In. The Wittenberg Movement

1519–1520

"That's stupid."
—Melanchthon (in print) to Johannes Eck[1]

Prior to 1518, Martin Luther was on friendly terms with Johannes Eck. However, when Luther published his *Ninety-Five Theses*, Eck became critical. His *Obelisci* defending indulgences appeared and swiftly drew a response from both Luther and Karlstadt. Luther replied with his own *Asterisks,* and Karlstadt attacked Eck on free will in his *Apologeticae conclusiones* of May, 1518.[2] Not one to back down, Eck then set forth theses on penance, grace, free will, and indulgences. He topped it off by challenging Karlstadt to a public disputation. Luther still thought he might mediate between Karlstadt and Eck at this point, but in December, Eck published additional

---

1. Paraphrased. *Defensio Phil. Melanchthonis contra Joh. Eckium.* 1519. MSA 1:16.19: *nemo tam stupidus est . . .*
2. In his *Chrysopassus* (1514), Eck argued that God predestines rewards and punishments on the basis of foreknowledge (which implies free will).

theses against Karlstadt, in which he took the opportunity to broadside Luther as well. Now piqued, Luther responded with additional theses of his own. Eck began to center the debate with Luther on the issue of papal primacy, which Luther declared was a relatively recent innovation from only a few centuries prior. He began an in-depth historical study in an attempt to prove it.

Leipzig Disputation. Woodcut, 1557. Leipziger Religionsgespräch, kolorierter Holzschnitt. Stiftung Luthergedenkstätten in Sachen-Anhalt.

Leipzig Disputation

The disputation was set for June, 1519, in Leipzig. Duke Georg of Saxony sponsored the debate, and he only gave permission for Luther to participate at the last moment. The venue was the Pleissenberg Castle, which had a hall great enough to accommodate the large audience.[3] Eck arrived early in Leipzig, and was greeted with honors

---

3. See Camerarius, chapter 10, for his take on the Leipzig Disputation.

by the university faculty. The official Wittenberg contingent arrived on June 24 in two open wagons. It included Karlstadt, Luther, Melanchthon, Johannes Lang (vicar of the Augustinians), Nicholas von Amsdorf, Johannes Agricola, and three doctors of law. The *unofficial* Wittenberg contingent also included several hundred students on foot, many of whom carried weapons—just in case. Seeing that, Eck requested (and was granted) a substantial armed bodyguard—just in case. In the end, thousands of people came to hear this heated disputation.

As the proceedings got underway, the ground rules were laid down at great length.[4] Due to the high interest in the topic throughout western Europe, it was proposed to have stenographers record the entire debate. Eck protested that this might interfere with the heat of the moment. Melanchthon demurred, arguing that the truth might fare better at a lower temperature.[5]

Karlstadt, Eck, and Luther were all about thirty-three years old. Eck, though often caricatured since Reformation times, was a formidable opponent. Much like Melanchthon, he was a high achiever since childhood. Eck entered the University of Heidelberg at age eleven. He was interested in a wide variety of topics, ranging from logic and dialectics to economics and canon law. He became a doctor of theology at the University of Freiburg in 1510, and then received a second doctorate at the University of Ingolstadt, where he began teaching and quickly became the dominant presence in the theology faculty. He was also an ordained priest, as well as an excellent debater. There was a reason *he* had been the one to throw down the gauntlet and challenge the Wittenberg professors to a public debate—he was confident in his skills and sure that he would win. Eck possessed a quick mind, remarkable recall, and an

---

4. WA 2:251.
5. MBW 59. CR 1:91.

ability to deliver passionate and effective rhetoric at a moment's notice. Melanchthon, though, came with a healthy skepticism about Eck. Having looked into the Ingoldstadt professor's previous controversies, Philipp thought he came off as proud.[6]

Others may have had reservations about the highly-credentialed Karlstadt. He was well-spoken, open to learning new things, and bold to the point of disaster in pursuing ideas to their full logical extent. A serious student of Augustine; and influenced by Luther, Reuchlin, and Bernard of Clairvaux; Karlstadt was a doctor of theology (1510), as well as the archdeacon of All Saints' Collegiate Church (the Castle Church) in Wittenberg. He also held doctorates in both civil and canon law, which he had received from the *curia* in Rome in 1516. Barrel-chested, stocky, and with a deep Germanic delivery to his speech, he brought force to his argumentation. Karlstadt was an intellectual pugilist of intemperate tenacity. This, combined with his short fuse, provided numerous opportunities for drama over the course of his career. Luther, by contrast, while famous for intemperate interludes in his printed works, was known at this time for his cheerful and friendly personal demeanor, even when pressed in serious public circumstances.

The first part of the debate began on June 27 and extended until July 3, with Eck and Karlstadt arguing about the roles of grace and free will in justification. Eck sought to defend free will, while Karlstadt denied it, maintaining that an unregenerate person cannot will the good, and that the soul is passive in the reception of God's grace.

---

6. MBW 58.

Andreas Bodenstein von Karlstadt (1486–1541). Universitätsbibliothek, Universität Basel.

Johannes Eck (1486–1543).

On June 29, the feast day of Peter and Paul, Luther preached on Matthew 16, arguing that the office of the keys is given to every Christian, and not just the pope. Then, from July 4–14 he and Eck argued on the issue of papal primacy. Thin and gaunt, Luther nevertheless struck an upbeat, even humorous, demeanor. Essentially, Eck maintained that the pope was divinely appointed as head of the church (*iure divino*). Luther responded that only *Christ* is the head of the church, and the pope is only in authority by a *human* decision (*iure humano*).

During the debate, Melanchthon sat as an observer, but he remained active nonetheless. Even since his boyhood experiences at the fountain in Bretten debating passing scholars, Melanchthon had relished the back and forth of scholarly argument. His mind stayed fully engaged, and he provided Karlstadt and Luther with steady streams of ideas, information, and arguments to support them in the debate. This irritated Eck. He thought that this adolescent grammarian was arrogantly butting in far more often than was appropriate.[7]

While the intellectual and doctrinal issue of papal primacy made the debate interesting on its own, other unspoken factors added to the tension. Should Germans really be subject to a distant Italian potentate? Did God truly ordain this situation, or was it merely a human invention resulting in the exploitation of the German nation? Further, what *was* the truth of the matter? In an age when average life expectancy hovered in the mid-thirties, death and the life to come loomed large. *Did* indulgences help speed one through purgatory, as the pope claimed?

Eck upped the ante when he broached a new line of argumentation. He began to link Luther's ideas with those of the fifteenth-century Bohemian Jan Huss. In 1415, the Council of Constance had condemned Huss, and he had been captured (by deception), and burned at the stake. If Eck could equate Luther's arguments with Huss's, then that would disqualify Luther, and perhaps even lead to his own live incineration, should he fail to recant. Huss, too, had denied the authority of the pope. Eck forced Luther to admit that Huss might have been right on some things, and that the Council of Constance might have made an error. Duke Georg of Saxony was impressed with this line of thinking, and ever after stood as an implacable opponent to Luther.

Luther and Eck went on to debate purgatory, indulgences, and confession, but these all served as secondary topics in relation to the primary issue of papal authority. As the disputation wound down, Karlstadt and Eck briefly revisited their theses on grace and free will on July 14 and 15. Afterward, the Wittenberg delegation made

---

7. CR 1:cxlix.

the one-day trip home, and Melanchthon found himself back in his cramped cabin by July 16.

Luther wanted the transcripts of the disputation published right away. Eck wanted judgments from theological faculties first. Erfurt and Paris were asked to do so, but never quite got around to it. However, though unasked, the theologians at Louvain and Cologne provided condemnations of Luther. At the same time, some who had been in the audience at Leipzig had taken copious notes, which they released to the public. Melanchthon, too, sent a copy of the transcript of the disputation to Spalatin, recommending that he arrange for it to be published.[8]

During these months following the disputation, Christoph Scheurl reported that general opinion at least in Nuremberg had crystallized around a positive valuation of Luther over Eck.[9] Many students from the University of Leipzig voted with their feet—a large number transferred to the University of Wittenberg.[10] This included Caspar Cruciger, a Hebrew specialist, who would become a close friend of Melanchthon and help Luther with translating the Old Testament.

Luther, mulling over the disputation and how Eck had boxed him into confessing agreement with Huss, came to embrace the idea. In February, 1520, he wrote, "We are all Hussites without knowing it."[11] Putting it more forcefully, he continued in the same letter, "Paul and Augustine, taken at their word, are Hussites."

As to Melanchthon's advisory role at the Leipzig Disputation, Luther couldn't have been happier. Eck had accused Melanchthon of being arrogant, distracting, and an unqualified mere master (not doctor)—a teacher only of the peripheral topics of Greek and rhetoric.[12] This did nothing to dampen Luther's enthusiasm for his

---

8. MBW 61.
9. MBW 80.
10. An outbreak of plague in Leipzig in 1521 likely hastened the exodus.
11. WABR 2:42, Nr. 254.

young colleague: "I return to Philipp, whom no Eck can make me hate. In my profession I count nothing better than his favorable testimony. This one man's opinion and authority mean more to me than many thousands of miserable Ecks. I would not hesitate to yield my opinion to this ingenious grammarian, if he should disagree with me, even though I am a master of arts, philosophy and theology and adorned with nearly all of Eck's titles. I have often done this, and I do it daily, on account of the divine gift, bountifully blessed, which God has placed in this frail vessel, so contemptible to Eck. I do not laud Philipp, however, for he is a creature of God, and nothing. I revere in him the work of my God!"[13]

For his part, Melanchthon reciprocated Eck's acrimony. In a letter to Spalatin, he accused Eck not just of error, but of moral turpitude.[14] He said much the same to Johannes Lang.[15] Finally, he attempted to publish an even-handed account of the debate, in the form of a long letter addressed to Oecolampadius.[16] It didn't go over too well—at least, not in Ingolstadt.

A Literary Fight with Eck

Melanchthon sent his letter summarizing the Leipzig Disputation to Oecolampadius on July 21, 1519. Because it was a public document and the public had great interest in the matter, the letter was swiftly published in Wittenberg, Augsburg, and Froben. In it, Melanchthon framed the debate as a contest between the early theology of Christ and the Aristotelian ideas of scholasticism. While he was complimentary of Eck, he also noted that he attempted to incite the crowd against Luther.

12. See esp. WABR 1:456 (Cf. 402).
13. CR 1:85. Cf. WABR 1:435–58, Nr. 191. Trans. Manschreck, 48.
14. MBW 60.
15. MBW 62.
16. *Epistola de Lipsica Disputation*. MBW 59.

The letter wounded and angered Eck. Oecolampadius confided that nothing had hurt Eck more than this letter.[17] Melanchthon's former student in Tübingen, Martin Cellarius, was now at Ingolstadt. He thought "Melanchthon's" letter must be a fake. He was appalled at the attacks on Eck and asked Melanchthon to clear up the matter.[18] Eck himself, however, wasted no time in reaching for his feather and inkwell. Melanchthon's letter was dated July 21. Eck's response came on July 25.

In the very title of his tract, Eck called Melanchthon false, and none-too-obliquely declared him to be a mere "Wittenberg grammarian" unqualified to enter the lists of his betters.[19] Eck declared the young scholar to be in over his head, and that he had misunderstood the debate. He should have kept quiet rather than open himself to ridicule by broadcasting his ignorance.

Melanchthon, as we have seen, inherited a bit of a temper, most likely from his mother. Though he worked to keep it under control—and usually succeeded—he was not entirely prepared to turn the other cheek in response to Eck's backhand. Besides, the public understanding of the gospel was at stake. While he mulled over his response, Melanchthon wrote to the Augustinian Johannes Lang, saying he would not write to Eck as he deserved, but simply in order to defend the Wittenberg character and cause.[20] Nevertheless, by the time he was finished, the tone was sharp.[21] He declared, in fact, that no one who had heard Karlstadt's arguments could be so stupid as to accept Eck's solutions.[22] Further, he accused Eck of abusing

---

17. MBW 73a—before Feb. 27, 1520.
18. MBW 66. Cellarius is also known as Borrhaus.
19. *Excusatio Eckii ad ea, quae falso sibi philippus Melanchthon grammaticus Vvitembergensis super Theologica disputatione Lipsica adscripsit.* 1519. CR 1:97–103. Suppl. Mel. 6:1.71.
20. MBW 62.
21. *Defensio Phil. Melanchthonis contra Joh. Eckium.* 1519. MSA 1:11–22.
22. "Quod lectorum ad suam conclusionem relegat, nemo tam stupidus est, qui putet Carolostadium Eckianam conclusionem defendendam suscepisse." MSA 1:16.

words by employing such non-scriptural terms as "free choice"—a fiction originating with Ockham.[23] Regarding Luther's portion of the disputation, Melanchthon summarized the arguments and gave his full support to his Wittenberg colleague. The papacy was a relatively recent human invention, some things Huss said were correct, and popes and councils certainly could err.[24] Significantly, Melanchthon insisted on scriptural authority. Eck cited church fathers, but Melanchthon asserted that they had no binding authority—they were only secondary because they could err, even when well-meaning. In the end, the Bible had to trump human reason. Upon completion, Melanchthon sent this *Defensio* against Eck to Spalatin, the Elector Friedrich, and Lang.[25] He was now no longer a mere observer in the broader debates of the nascent Reformation.

Eck, for his part, thought he had won not only the Leipzig Disputation, but also his pamphlet war with Melanchthon. As winter approached, he pursued his cause by other means—he made his way to Rome to advocate to the pope for the suppression of Luther and his supporters. There, he pressured the *curia* to investigate Luther for heresy. Word of this made its way back to Wittenberg,[26] where the daily rounds of university life continued, even as political and religious storm clouds continued to gather over western Europe.

A New Holy Roman Emperor

In addition to the theological drama emanating from Wittenberg, Leipzig, and Ingolstadt, 1519 also proved to be a significant year

---

23. "Porro, quid necesse erat novis glossematis et plane fictitiis asserere vim liberi arbitrii, qua bonum efficiat, cum receptissimum sit et apud scholasticos vel summae notae, nempe Occamicos, quosdam voluntatis actus tantum recipi." MSA 1:17. Cf. Graybill, *Evangelical Free Will*, 84.
24. Cf. Manschreck, 50.
25. MBW 61 and 63. See also MBW 67a.
26. MBW 84.

for political events. On January 12, 1519, the Holy Roman Emperor Maximilian died. Melanchthon gave an oration in his honor in Wittenberg.[27] This was an immensely significant event, because it now meant the seven electors had the opportunity to choose the next sovereign. At this point, the papacy was still a major political (and military) force to be reckoned with. Likewise Francis I of France and Charles V of Spain represented the other two main powers on the western European stage. Just whom the Electors selected to be the next Emperor could be decisive for tipping the balance of power one way or the other. The pope (and of course Francis) favored the election of the French sovereign. Elector Friedrich kept his own counsel—seeking to follow his conscience, but also being interested in continuing to bolster the fame and prestige of his new university in Wittenberg. If Luther was a heretic, then he wanted him condemned. But if he was not, then he should be vindicated. Either way, Friedrich insisted that Luther receive a fair hearing, and not be condemned unheard. In this season of an uncertain transition of power at the head of the Holy Roman Empire, Friedrich's desires carried much weight.

As the question of succession grew over the course of the spring of 1519, half a world away a Spanish explorer named Cortez landed in Mexico. That summer, Francisco Pizarro received royal charter for the west coast of South America. Two weeks later, Ferdinand Magellan set sail from Seville on his voyage to circumnavigate the globe. While the crowned heads of Europe contended for power and influence on the Continent, Charles's domains were growing overseas. At the same time, the expansionist threats of the Ottomans could not be ignored. They set their sights upon the Balkans, Bulgaria, Hungary, Austria, and even the German lands all the way to the Rhine. At the same time, they sent invading armies into north

---

27. *Oratio funebris dicta divo Maximiliano Caesari* (Wittenberg: Johannes Grunenberg, 1519). CR 11:26–34. His foreword to this oration can be found in MBW 41.

Africa, and unleashed Muslim pirates headed by Barbarossa to terrify, kidnap, and enslave throughout the Mediterranean. Entire coastal villages were destroyed, and their citizens taken away to row slave ships or to be sold at market in Algiers. At Rhodes, the remnants of Crusader forces stood their ground, with the Knights of St. John proving to be especially effective irritants as pirates themselves operating against grain supplies bound from Egypt to Istanbul.

On June 28, the Electors finally met in Frankfurt am Main to decide on the next emperor of the Holy Roman Empire. In the end, the choice was unanimous—it was Charles V. He was crowned at Aachen in October, 1520.

Charles V crowned in Aachen. Woodcut, 1520.

Baccalareus Biblicus

During this year, Melanchthon, in addition to his teaching, was engaged in the formal study of theology. He published twenty-four theses on justification[28] for his *baccalaureus biblicus* degree, and defended them on September 9, 1519. Luther called them "audacious but true."[29] However, after the Leipzig Disputation and the ongoing pamphlet war with Eck, Melanchthon was in no mood to straddle the fence. He emphatically affirmed the authority of scripture alone, and stated that councils could err.

Broadening the controversy out from the Leipzig Disputation, Melanchthon also chose to pronounce on the Lord's Supper. At Tübingen, Philipp had been scornful of Professor Jakob Lemp's attempts to depict transubstantiation on a blackboard. Now he went beyond didactic scorn to flatly arguing that it is no heresy to doubt transubstantiation, with its Aristotelian underpinnings. Some who read this thought it was an entirely unchristian position to take, and Melanchthon reported to Johannes Heß in early 1520 that he had taken some sharp criticism for it.[30] Naturally, Eck was one of these critics. He took it upon himself to write to Elector Friedrich to warn him of this heresy in his midst.[31]

Melanchthon defended his theses in a disputation on September 9, 1519. Luther was present, of course, and he was most impressed. He reported to Staupitz, "[Philipp] responded in such a way that it seemed to all of us to be a miracle."[32] Moreover, "Christ willing, he will surpass many Martins and will be a mighty foe of the devil and of the scholastic theology. He knows their tricks, and also the Rock of

---

28. MSA 1:23–25. See also MBW 76.
29. WABR 1:514, Nr. 202. See Scheible, *Melanchthon*, 137.
30. MBW 76.
31. Nov. 8, 1519. WABR 1:492, Nr. 192.
32. *Ita respondit, ut omnibus nobis esset id quod est scilicet miraculum.* WABR 1:514, Nr. 202.

Christ (*Christi petram*). Therefore he mightily prevails [1 Macc. 5:40]. Amen."[33]

Ten days after the disputation, Melanchthon received his degree. This both enabled and obligated him to teach on the Bible—a responsibility he discharged through lectures on Romans in 1520 and 1521.

Falling out with Reuchlin

At the same time that Melanchthon was becoming increasingly integrated into the Wittenberg movement, his relationships further south were progressively *dis*-integrating—not just with Eck at Ingolstadt, but also—sadly—even with Reuchlin himself.

To put it mildly, all was not well in Württemberg following Melanchthon's departure from Tübingen. Duke Ulrich, ruling from Stuttgart, had always possessed a tempestuous character. He was the one responsible for the siege of Bretten during Melanchthon's childhood. He also offended public sensibilities through marital infidelity, personal violence, oppressive measures, and deficit spending. Even though he had rendered military service to the Holy Roman Empire, he was twice placed under the imperial ban. Further, while rulers may have been willing to overlook Ulrich's private sins, they decided to tolerate it no further when he added the provocation of attacking, occupying, and annexing the free imperial city of Reutlingen (situated between Tübingen and Stuttgart). Perhaps it made sense when Ulrich looked at a map, but he miscalculated the political realities surrounding this situation. Reutlingen happened to be a member of the Swabian League—which was founded on a mutual self-defense pact of several regional German principalities.

---

33. WABR 1:514, Nr. 202.

The member states honored their pact, and banded together to go to war against Duke Ulrich.

By September, 1519, the conflict had come to Stuttgart. Reuchlin wrote to Melanchthon, speaking of the atrocities being committed by the armies of the Swabian League, but noting that Ulrich still eluded them. He sought the mediation of Elector Friedrich to end the conflict and sorrowfully related that his attempts to secure the safety of his Greek and Hebrew manuscripts had failed. Reuchlin's great library (which he had once promised that Melanchthon would inherit) was under serious threat. He himself was also in danger. Reuchlin concluded with greetings to Luther, and said that he had also sent twenty florins to Melanchthon's mother in Bretten.[34]

The Swabian League pressed the attack, and Reuchlin ended up fleeing to the nearby city of Ingolstadt. Duke Ulrich eventually found himself cornered, and then driven into exile. The Swabian League sold off his territory to Charles V in order to pay their expenses for the military operation.

A few months later, in December, Melanchthon passed along greetings to Reuchlin via Johannes Schwebel in Pforzheim.[35] Less than two weeks later, though, Melanchthon received a letter from Reuchlin that must surely have caused him surprise and grief. Reuchlin had become involved at the University of Ingoldstadt—the very place where Johannes Eck dominated. Further, Reuchlin was living in Eck's house! The two apparently had numerous conversations, and Reuchlin related to Melanchthon that he was sure he could secure Eck's forgiveness for him following the aftermath of the Leipzig Disputation. In fact, Reuchlin wanted Melanchthon to leave Wittenberg (both physically and intellectually), in order to join the faculty at Ingoldstadt.[36]

---

34. MBW 67.
35. MBW 68.

Melanchthon put off answering Reuchlin's letter for three months. He must have known it would break their relationship. To go to Ingolstadt would mean supporting the pope instead of Luther. This Melanchthon could not do—even for love of family. He finally replied on March 18, 1520.[37] He congratulated Reuchlin on his professorship at Ingolstadt, and spoke positively about Dukes Wilhelm and Ludwig in Bavaria and their desire to promote the sciences—much like Elector Friedrich. However, Melanchthon went on to say that although living in Wittenberg did not seem to be good for his health, he could not come to Ingolstadt. He had given his word to the elector that he would teach in Wittenberg, and he would keep it. He didn't think he should make another change, especially after having made friends in Wittenberg. "I love my homeland, but I must also heed whither Christ calls me, not whither my own pleasure may draw me."[38] He explained, "Many things call me to you—the desire to be near you, love of home, the prospect of association with many learned men, a wonderful library to use, and my health. However, I cannot break my pledged word to the Elector, and I do not want to do anything to cause him to doubt my veracity. I love my native land certainly, but I must consider what Christ has called me to do more than my own inclinations. Trusting in the Holy Spirit, I shall do my work here until the same Spirit calls me away. I ask not to live happily but righteously and Christlike."[39]

With this decision, Melanchthon would certainly *not* live happily—at least insofar as his relationship with Reuchlin was concerned. He expressed concern about the situation a month later in a letter to another contact in Worms.[40] The next mention of the

36. Dec. 21, 1519. MBW 68a.
37. MBW 77.
38. MBW 77. Trans., Stupperich, 35.
39. MBW 77. Trans., Manschreck, 53.
40. MBW 82.

situation comes a year later, in March, 1521, when Melanchthon related to Spalatin that he had received word from Ingolstadt (possibly through Martin Cellarius), that Reuchlin no longer wanted any contact with Philipp at all. Reuchlin asked that Melanchthon never write him again.[41] Melanchthon later wrote to Pirckheimer that the whole situation baffled him.[42]

This alienation from Reuchlin clearly showed that Melanchthon's primary allegiance was to the gospel as he understood it, rather than to the scholarly humanistic movement as a whole that Reuchlin so ably represented. The disciplines of humanism were not ends in themselves, but tools to dig for truth in service of the gospel. Not surprisingly, Melanchthon never inherited Reuchlin's library.

Falling in with Luther

As Melanchthon was falling out with Reuchlin, he was falling in with Luther. The two were not only collegial colleagues, but also friends.[43] In 1520, Melanchthon wrote, "A Christian heart that knows no guile is the foundation of friendship."[44] This certainly seemed to be the case between these two Wittenberg colleagues, and it remained so throughout their lives, despite the remarkable strains of the early

---

41. MBW 130.
42. Sept., 1521. MBW 171.
43. See Graybill, *Evangelical Free Will*, 58–63, for more on their relationship and references to further literature on the subject. Scheible and Wengert argue it goes too far to label them "friends," but outside of a German context where *Freund* and *Bekannter* are important distinctions, modern American usage of "friends" would certainly apply to Luther and Melanchthon. See also Camerarius, chapter 9, and Heinz Scheible, "Melanchthon als theologischer Gesprächspartner Luthers," in ed. Heinz Scheible, *Aufsätze zu Melanchthon* (Tübingen: Mohr Siebeck, 2010), 1–27. Richard, (p. 41), though, goes too far in the other direction by idealizing and perhaps mythologizing Luther and Melanchthon's relationship: "The great men were at once drawn to each other. Luther's clear understanding, deep feeling, pious spirit, heroic courage, overwhelmed Melanchthon with wonder, so that he reverenced him as a father. Melanchthon's great learning, fine culture, philosophical clearness, his beautiful character and tender heart, acted as a charm upon Luther. Each found the complement of his own nature in the other."
44. MBW 85. April 27, 1520.

Reformation movement. To this day, they are buried next to each other in the Castle Church in Wittenberg.

Crucially, Luther and Melanchthon were on the same page theologically. Melanchthon's thought on theology had developed independently before he arrived in Wittenberg, and once there, he found that Luther's thinking meshed neatly with his own growing ideas.

Hence, Melanchthon viewed Luther's theology as essentially that of Augustine, of whom he certainly approved. He called Augustine "a man of both singular genius and great experience in sacred matters."[45] Melanchthon claimed that only Augustine and some of the Greek theologians represented true biblical theology. Origen and Jerome certainly did not.[46] In 1521, Melanchthon explicitly connected Luther with Augustine, writing, "Is not Luther's view on free will and grace the whole view of Augustine, if you rightly judge the matter? And besides, Luther follows him throughout in his commentary on Galatians."[47]

Simultaneously, Melanchthon castigated scholasticism and metaphysical philosophy, declaring, "The dregs of philosophers, the scholastic theologians of our age, think that the minds of men are excited [by the Law] to the pursuit of virtue. What dreams! . . . Philosophy is in error; our minds are not equal to divine laws."[48] Additionally, "There is a common statement to the effect that a drink of water is not to be found in water which has been rendered turbid

---

45. "Divus Augustinus, vir et ingenio singulari et magno sacrarum rerum usu...' Declamatiuncula in Divi Pauli doctrinam. Epistola ad Johannem Hessum Theologum." 1520. MSA 1:40.2–3.
46. Feb. 12, 1521. MBW 124. Melanchthon continued by saying that of course, the scriptures are above all. For more on Melanchthon's use of patristic thought, see E. P. Meijering, *Melanchthon and Patristic Thought: The Doctrines of Christ and Grace, the Trinity, and the Creation* (Leiden: E. J. Brill, 1983).
47. *Widder das wuetende urteyl der Pariser Theologisten. Schutzred Phil. Melanchthon fuer Doctor Mart. Luther*, WA 8.299.36–39. Trans. Hill, 74.
48. *Declamatiuncula* (1520). MSA 1.36:14–17; 37:1–2. Trans. Hill, 40.

with filth. Just so no faithful man has ever satisfied his mind with scholastic theology which has become polluted by so many human arguments, nonsense, tricks, and trifling traditions."[49] Elsewhere, he derided Bonaventure, Thomas, Scotus, and Ockham by name.[50] He also demonstrated a passion for *sola scriptura*, saying, "What madness is it, therefore, what blindness, since the Scriptures alone point out a succinct way of salvation, if you seek the beauty and structure of virtue from the clever thoughts of philosophers when they are obsolete!"[51]

In addition to theological comity, Luther and Melanchthon also had great professional respect for one another, undergirded by the conviction of spiritual kinship in Christ. In 1521, Melanchthon wrote, "When we speak for Luther, we speak for your sacred vessel, for the doctrine of Christ."[52] Melanchthon believed that Luther was on a divine mission.[53] He was sent by God.[54] Some wanted to dissociate from Luther because he was too controversial. Melanchthon rejected the idea, admitting further that even though some were offended by Luther's coarse joking, Melanchthon said he could always find a kernel of truth in it.[55] Moreover, "Martin seems

---

49. *Declamatiuncula.* MSA 1:38.38–39.3. Trans. Hill, 42. See also MBW 87 (1520), and MBW 89—Melanchthon's foreword to Aristophanes's *Nubae* (Wittenberg: Melchior Lotter, 1521).
50. In 1521, when he wrote to the theologians of the Sorbonne, Melanchthon accused, "But what do you do? Anything other than let the minds of Christians become great in the formalities of Scotus and in the connotations of Ockham rather than in Christ?" *Widder das wuetende urteyl der Pariser Theologisten,* WA 8:300.19–22. Trans. Hill, 74. See also "On Correcting the Studies of Youth" (1518), where Melanchthon indulged in a little further name calling, not only of Scotus and Ockham, but also of Thomas and Bonaventure: "Gradually the better disciplines were neglected, we left Greek learning behind, and everywhere bad things began to be taught as if they were good. From this proceeded Thomases, Scotuses, seraphic doctors [Bonaventure], cherubic doctors [joke], and the rest of their followers, more numerous than the offspring of Cadmus." Keen, 49. MSA 3:32.23–27.
51. *Declamatiuncula.* MSA 1:34.21–25. Trans. Hill, 38. Cf. Graybill, 81–84.
52. *Didymus Faventinus.* MSA 1:59.36–37. Cf. Stupperich, 43, where his translation does not quite follow the Latin.
53. Aug. 18, 1520. MBW 105.
54. Nov. 4, 1520. MBW 109.
55. April, 1520. MBW 81.

to be driven by a spirit. He accomplishes more by prayer than we do by considered deliberation. Nothing worse could happen than for us to be deprived of him."[56] Again, "I would rather die than be separated from this man; nothing worse could happen than to have to do without Martin."[57]

As we have seen above, Luther also had nothing but praise for Melanchthon. He often recommended Philipp's books second only to the Bible,[58] and he was known to gush that Melanchthon had surpassed him in theology.[59] As a pair of workaholics with a shared theological worldview, Martin and Philipp got along famously.

---

56. MBW 109. Trans. Manschreck, 62.
57. April 27, 1520. MBW 84. Trans. Manschreck, 54.
58. WATR 5:5511, 5647, 5787, 5827, 6439, 6458.
59. E.g., CR 10:260. CR 1:cxlvi.

11

Wedding Bells and Papal Bulls

1520–1521

You say that so much work will kill you? Well, that's quite all right. God has plenty of work for clever men to do in heaven.
—Johann von Staupitz[1]

In the early sixteenth century, the German lands were not unified. For Melanchthon, living in Saxony was like living in a foreign country—complete with unfamiliar customs, food, and drink. Young Philipp was thin when he arrived at Wittenberg, and he continued to lose weight. By all accounts, keeping house was never at the top of Melanchthon's to-do list. In fact, when he came to Wittenberg, it was the first time in his life that Melanchthon had been responsible for maintaining his own household. He did not excel at this. In all reality, he lived in a shambolic bachelor pad.

---

1. Spoken to Martin Luther, upon commanding him to become a theology professor. Quotation adapted from Bainton, 59. Otto Scheel, ed., *Dokumente zu Luthers Entwicklung* (1929), Nos. 174, 230, 444, 485.

Philipp normally dressed in an undershirt, pleated skirt, doublet, leggings, cap, overcoat, and cow-mouth shoes. Visitors to his workspace reported that the professor usually left letters, books, and manuscripts lying around. His desk was a mess, and whenever he wanted a specific item, he had to hunt for it.[2] Luther, who lived two doors down, was of the opinion that this young man needed some serious help right away. He thought he was overexerting himself, and that Melanchthon would burn out, or get sick, or maybe even die. In 1520, Erasmus, too, praised Melanchthon's studies, but again warned him against pushing himself too hard.[3] If word was reaching distant cities like Louvain about Melanchthon's constant habits of work, then it must have been remarkable indeed.

Melanchthon himself did not share these opinions. He immersed himself in work, and was happy to do it. As to any overexertion, Melanchthon gave at least partial blame to insomnia compounded by anxiety. Throughout his life he had trouble sleeping. And if one can't sleep, then why not get up and be productive? Philipp was known to start the day at 2:00 a.m. He would devote himself to prayer and devotions, through which he effectively battled his worries. He explained, "If I never worried, I would never invoke God. But because piety through prayer puts an end to worries, I cannot be altogether indifferent to all this. Thus, I am driven through worries toward prayer, and through prayer I drive out the worries."[4] For Melanchthon, his piety and studies went together—for his primary concern was both to live and promote true Christianity.[5] After praising and seeking God, Melanchthon would deal with correspondence. His personal correspondence was vast (his extant

---

2. These descriptions can be found on the official displays at the Melanchthon House in Wittenberg.
3. MBW 97.
4. Quotation posted at the Melanchthon House, Wittenberg.
5. E.g., MBW 125. Feb. 19, 1521.

letters number nearly ten thousand—and many more are surely lost to the exigencies of time). He also often handled official correspondence for the University of Wittenberg. With his growing fame also came burgeoning requests for letters of recommendation from his students and others. Eventually, it all became unmanageable. But, each day, he did what he could, and finally turned from letters to preparing to teach. Lectures usually started at 6:00 a.m.

From the beginning, Luther was convinced that not only was Melanchthon overworked, but he was also underpaid. He voiced worries that his colleague would depart to take up better-paying job offers. He wrote to Spalatin, "Although I hope Melanchthon will not go to Bavaria, yet I have always wished that he might have a larger salary, so that they might lose the hope they have conceived of getting him, since they see that he is paid less here than he would be there. If there is any chance, be vigilant."[6]

Melanchthon was not unaware of Luther's efforts. However, he was determined to be content with his modest pay. On July 10, 1520, he wrote to Spalatin to reject his proposal of applying to the elector for a salary increase, noting that his pay was generous in comparison to what other people locally were making.[7] Melanchthon repeated this on July 22, telling Spalatin that the students needed an example of someone loving the studies apart from pay. Humanism was not a mercenary endeavor. It had value in its own right.[8] Further, if the fine arts were to perish, then everything would fall prey to barbarism.[9]

Luther, sounding exasperated, wrote to Spalatin at the beginning of August, saying, "If you are not successful, I will write nothing to the elector about Melanchthon's salary. What I wrote formerly I did so that the man might have no reason for leaving us; but if

---

6. June 25, 1520, to Spalatin. WABR 2:130, Nr. 305. Trans. Manschreck, 59.
7. MBW 99.
8. This is still an argument today for a liberal arts education.
9. MBW 101.

nothing can come of it, the Lord's will be done."¹⁰ Luther remained convinced, however, that Melanchthon needed both a raise in his salary, and an improvement in his domestic situation. To put it plainly, Philipp was in dire need of a wife. As Martin began pestering Melanchthon about this,¹¹ Philipp wrote to Spalatin one more time to claim a caveat on his demurral regarding an increased salary—he said that his present salary was adequate—*so long as his martial situation did not change.*¹²

Engagement

The family Krapp was well-respected in Wittenberg. Hieronimus (Hans) Krapp had been a dressmaker and the mayor of Wittenberg until his death in 1515. His widow, Katharina, was a vigorous woman. They had several children—one of whom was a son named after the father (Hieronimus),¹³ and another was a daughter named after the mother (Katharina). This daughter, born in October, 1497, was only a few months younger than Philipp Melanchthon. She came from a good house, and at the swiftly-advancing age of twenty-three, was still unmarried. Luther thought she would make a fine match for his young colleague.¹⁴ Philipp was not so sure.

Luther merrily kept after Philipp, this rising star of Wittenberg, who wanted nothing more than to lose himself in his work. Martin wanted to make sure that Philipp had help taking care of his household—and of his health, for he was *not* taking good care of himself.¹⁵ In June, Luther confided to Spalatin, "I know not what

---

10. WABR 2:163–64 Nr. 324. Trans. Manschreck, 59–60.
11. Feb. 5, 1520. Letter to Spalatin. WABR 2:30–31, Nr. 249.
12. July 14, 1520. MBW 100.
13. He, too, went on to be a dressmaker and the mayor of Wittenberg.
14. See Stefan Rhein, "Katharina Melanchthon, geborene Krapp—Ein Frauenschicksal der Reformationszeit," in *Melanchthon: neu entdeckt*, eds. Stefan Rhein and Johannes Weiß (Stuttgart: Quell Verlag, 1997), 164–89. Unfortunately, no pictures or letters of Katharina remain.

Melanchthon will do about marrying, especially the girl you suggest. I want him to take a wife, but wish neither to dictate nor to advise whom he shall marry, nor do I see that he is particularly anxious to marry."[16] More than a month later, Luther reported again, saying, "I tried to get him to marry for the profit of the Gospel, for I thought he would live longer in this state; but if nothing comes of this, let it pass. I fear he will not long survive his present manner of life. I try to do what I can for the Word; perhaps I am unworthy to accomplish anything."[17] Luther apparently let his frustrations be known at this point, for rumors of Melanchthon's engagement began circulating in Wittenberg.[18]

Within two weeks, these rumors turned to fact. On August 18, 1520, Melanchthon wrote to Lang in Erfurt. He expressed frustration with this step of getting engaged to Katharina Krapp, but said he was going through with it on account of the counsel of his friends (and of one in particular!) and because of the weakness of the flesh and the dangers of iniquity in fleshly liberty. He was neither hopeful nor cold toward the idea, and was pleased with Katharina, of whom he approved and considered to be a gift from God. He did, though, want to make sure he was following Galatians 5:13 in its admonition, "Do not use your liberty as an opportunity for the flesh." Further, he viewed the vows of marriage with great seriousness.[19] The one who kept his word to serve in Wittenberg would also keep his word to his wife.

Luther, too, wrote Lang on August 18, 1520, speaking of Melanchthon's decision to marry. He acknowledged the chatter of

---

15. Feb. 5, 1520. Letter to Spalatin. WABR 2:30–31, Nr. 249. See also Rhein, "Katharina Melanchthon," 166.
16. June 25, 1520, WABR 2:130, Nr. 305. Trans. Manschreck, 59.
17. August 5, 1520. WABR 2:163–34, Nr. 324. Trans. Manschreck, 60.
18. Rhein, "Katharina Melanchthon," 166.
19. MBW 105. Cf. Camerarius, chap. 12.

gossips blaming him for his friend's engagement, but protested that he only wanted the best for him.[20]

Philipp and Katharina did, in fact, become engaged—officially on August 26 or 28.[21] However, we have little evidence of any sort of romantic connection. Nevertheless, in an age when the average lifespan extended only to the mid-thirties, sometimes the practical aspects of marriage took precedence over romantic notions. Marriage in this age was an institution focused more on children and housekeeping than personal fulfillment.[22] Economics and politics often loomed larger than "chemistry." Shared experience and common values—more than personal attraction—undergirded the relationship. Further, marriage at this time was less the expression of a preexisting love than of a safe sanctuary in which that love could grow.

The "safe sanctuary," however was soon threatened as the Wittenberg rumor mill churned back into action. Some in town tried to foment scandal by questioning Katharina's virtue. They pointed to a close relationship she had recently ended with another man (of good reputation), and speculated wildly. Philipp was wounded by these ugly rumors, but Luther insisted they were untrue, and counseled Melanchthon to go forward, rather than break it off based on the lies of men. Later, Luther discussed the incident at his dinner table, and marked the whole thing up to a satanic attack.[23] Stephan Rhein notes that no evidence can be found to corroborate the rumors, and that the most reliable accounts show nothing but an honorable, upright marriage.[24] Nevertheless, Philipp and Katharina moved forward the wedding date, setting it for November 27, 1520.[25] As

20. WABR 2:167, Nr. 327. See Rhein, "Katharina Melanchthon," 166.
21. Rhein, "Katharina Melanchthon," 169.
22. See OER, "Family."
23. WATR 2:383, Nr. 3538. Cf. Rhein, "Katharina Melanchthon," 167–68.
24. Rhein, "Katharina Melanchthon," 167–68.

Luther explained, the wedding was hastened to restrain the danger of evil tongues.[26] Melanchthon, though, had to be cajoled to some extent to take this step. He saw nothing wrong with delay instead of haste, but the Krapp relatives argued for moving things along,[27] especially in light of a possible papal ban, that would have prevented a priest from performing the ceremony (some priests had already left town, in anticipation of just such an action).

Melanchthon's initial urge to delay the wedding was not an isolated incident. Perhaps reflecting the impetuous nature of a driven young man, or the single-minded focus of public figure caught up in momentous times, Melanchthon's reflections on his engagement period can only be described as ungracious. A few days after the engagement, Melanchthon told Spalatin that his friends pressured him into it, and that he was determined that the engagement and marriage would not interfere with his studies.[28]

In September, Melanchthon wrote to Günter von Bünau in Merseburg. In a postscript, he mentioned his engagement on account of the fact that Katharina Krapp was also an acquaintance of von Bünau. Melanchthon, however, did not content himself with sharing the news, but went on to say that he was pushed into this arrangement by his friends, and that they were trying to cheat him out of pleasure and study.[29] Likewise, in mid-October, Melanchthon wrote another acquaintance, sharing his nuptial plans, but insisting he was only going through with it based on outside advice (it certainly wasn't *his* idea), in order to provide a role model for youth.[30]

---

25. MBW 111. Cf. Rhein, "Katharina Melanchthon," 169.
26. Nov. 13, 1520. WABR 2:214.15–16, Nr. 352.
27. MBW 112.
28. Aug. 31, 1520, letter to Spalatin. MBW 106.
29. MBW 107.
30. MBW 108.

Luther's table and living room. Photo by Gregory Graybill.

Finally, a month later, with the wedding day itself now looming, Melanchthon referred to the upcoming event as "a day of affliction." Perhaps by writing in Greek, Melanchthon felt a little freer to express himself strongly. In any case, despite the anticipated misery of marriage, Melanchthon nevertheless continued in this letter by inviting Dominicus Schleupner of Leipzig to attend the festivities. Melanchthon went on to ruminate that although he was not looking forward to marriage, he still had to acknowledge the reality of sexual desire and concluded that he found consolation about the whole thing through Scripture's positive teachings on marriage. He would just have to trust in what the Bible said.

Marriage

The day of the wedding finally arrived. We know Melanchthon was reluctant, but what about Katharina? We have no record of her thoughts on the matter. All we know is that she showed up.

November 27, 1520, was a weekday.[31] Accordingly, Melanchthon posted a note in Latin verse on the university bulletin board cancelling his lectures on Paul for the day.[32] The guests at the wedding included Luther, Luther's parents and sisters, and a few faculty colleagues from Wittenberg and Leipzig. None of Philipp's family were able to make the long trek from Bretten on such short notice. Philipp's mother was miffed about the situation. On the bride's side, guests included Katharina's mother, one or two sisters, and four brothers.

Both Melanchthon and his bride were twenty-three years old. A student, writing at the time, described Katharina as of modest looks, petite, a bit austere, but esteemed, honorable, and upright.[33] She came with a small dowry. The simple ceremony included a promised wedding poem, composed and delivered by the poet-botanist Euricius Cordus.[34]

---

31. Some sources list Sunday, Nov. 25 as the wedding date, instead. MBW *Itinerar* gives the date of the wedding as Nov. 26–27 (inclusive).
32. CR 10:143, 552, 560.
33. Karl Hartfelder, *Melanchthoniana Paedagogica* (Leipzig, 1892), 111.
34. MBW 105.

THE HONEYCOMB SCROLL

The Elector Friedrich was in town, but he did not attend the wedding. In his place, he sent a representative bearing notice of a substantial raise in Melanchthon's salary (from 60 guilders per year to 100).³⁵ Friedrich also sent a rich supply of wine, wild game, and fish for the reception. Melanchthon later sent the elector a couple of thank you notes for the gifts and the raise, expressing his satisfaction in the elector's approval of the marriage, and also stating his hopes that his new status would be a benefit to the University in Wittenberg.³⁶

In the end, Melanchthon married a mayor's daughter (which helped root him to the area), much as his own father had married a mayor's daughter (which had helped root *him* to the area). Just as Elector Philipp the Upright had been glad to bind the father to his region, so Elector Friedrich must have been glad to bind the son to *his* region. The increase in salary only sealed the deal. Melanchthon wrote to Spalatin the next summer, saying that he was managing just fine on his new salary, despite price inflation in Wittenberg.³⁷

Family crests for Melanchthon and Krapp [Crapp], united through marriage. The Latin slogan underneath was Melanchthon's motto, taken from Romans 8:31, "If God is for us, who can be against us?" Photo by Gregory Graybill, taken in Melanchthon's study, at the Melanchthonhaus, Wittenberg.

35. MBW 115.
36. MBW 114–15. Melanchthon moved with alacrity—his thank you note was dated within about a week of the wedding itself. He was also busy the very day after the wedding (Nov. 28), sending news to Georg Spalatin. MBW 112.
37. MBW 155.

Family Life

Camerarius described Katharina as "a most pious woman, ardently devoted to her husband, generous and kind to all."[38] Characterized by the highest purity of lifestyle and character, she showed constant concern for the religious performance of duties and respectability. In this, she proved a great match for Philipp, who, in addition to his vibrant Christian faith, was known for his generosity with recommendations, money, and food. For example, he frequently gave away the coins he received as honoraria to whoever needed them.

While Philipp and Katharina were united in faith and generosity, they apparently also shared a general lack of interest in the details of daily life and domestic furnishings. Contemporaries reported that Katharina had few talents for cooking.[39] Hence, the domestic help Luther had sought for Melanchthon in a wife was not fully realized in Katharina.

She did, however, bring more than just herself to the marriage—her mother was part of the package deal. Frau Krapp had been a widow for three years—and she lived for another twenty-eight with her daughter and son-in-law. Melanchthon's mother-in-law reached the age of eighty—which was extraordinary by sixteenth-century standards. She died on May 3, 1548.

But the early marital situation continued to be more of a burden than a joy to the single-minded young scholar. Melanchthon, for his part, kept complaining to friends that he had been locked into marriage through outside pressure.[40] Apart from the obvious culprit of Luther, Melanchthon also fingered Johannes Agricola (1494–1566) of Wittenberg. Agricola had served as Luther's secretary at the

---

38. Cam., *Vita*, 38. See Camerarius, chapter 13 throughout, for a description of Melanchthon's family life.
39. Display signage, Melanchthon House, Wittenberg, 2013.
40. E.g., Jan. 1, 1521. Letter to Ambrosius Blarer. MBW 118.

Leipzig Disputation, he had received his *baccalaureas biblicus* on the same day as did Melanchthon, and he would soon become rector of the faculty of the arts and a professor of pedagogy. After his wedding, Melanchthon wrote Agricola, telling him that he was "not without guilt" in the whole affair, and that he was entirely blameworthy for depriving Melanchthon of his freedom.[41] By this point, Agricola was freshly married himself, and with a final count of fourteen children (one of whom he named Philipp), Agricola did not seem to be as dour about his nuptial situation as his colleague.[42] Bucking up a bit, by February of 1521, Melanchthon was stoutly telling Johannes Heß that although he suffered from his marriage, his studies were hardly affected at all.[43]

Meanwhile, despite the jeremiads conveyed to Agricola, Melanchthon apparently got along well with him, because he tried to move Agricola and his family into the little cabin with him that he called home. Noting the already cramped quarters, however, Melanchthon's wife and mother-in-law firmly opposed the maneuver, and Melanchthon had to write an apologetic letter explaining the impossibility of incorporating the two households. He, Melanchthon, was completely willing to do it—but his immediate relatives would not permit it. Melanchthon was just sick about it—so much so, that he couldn't handle breaking the news to Agricola in person, and instead had to send a letter.[44]

Nevertheless, Melanchthon proved himself ever hospitable. He attended student socials, and regularly hosted gatherings of colleagues and students in his home. He also took in a number of unmarried student boarders over the years. The increasing popularity of the University of Wittenberg created a shortage in student housing, and

41. MBW 113.
42. See MBW *Personen*, "Agricola, Johannes."
43. MBW 126.
44. MBW 113.

this was one way Melanchthon thought he could help. He was also happy to host friends and foreign visitors to his home, and he reveled in lively table conversation. Melanchthon turned his home into a kind of school in its own right, where he sought to offer help to new students, and where he staged the readings of ancient plays.

These lively but cramped quarters were located at the east end of town, close to the Augustinian monastery that served as Luther's home. It sat on the same site as the present-day Melanchthon House, which was built beginning in 1536 when the elector decided that Melanchthon needed a larger residence. The small home of the Melanchthon family of 1520, however, was anything but spacious. It was a definite come-down for Katharina. But, they made do.

The Melanchthon household normally had two main meals each day—an early lunch around 11, and then dinner around 5:00 p.m. They probably had at least one live-in maid, who helped with the cooking. The food came mainly from the town market, with occasional gifts of game from princes and colleagues. They also cultivated a small herb garden in the backyard. Many in this era ate a diet dominated by meat. Melanchthon, however, preferred porridge, fresh fish, hard-boiled eggs, and a variety of vegetables. He ate only a little meat. He also enjoyed a good wine—preferably from his home region, or if that was unavailable, from Hungary. He said the wine helped with his insomnia.

Mealtimes were family affairs, where the entire household sat down together—Philipp, Katharina, children (in time), servants, and boarders. Earnest, detailed prayers would be said both before and after each meal, along with the Apostles' Creed.

The most important boarder in the Melanchthon household moved in in 1519, a year before the marriage. Johannes Koch[45] came from Ilsfeld, near Heilbronn, which was only twenty-eight miles from

---

45. Mentioned, for example, in MBW 68.

Melanchthon's hometown of Bretten. This fellow countryman ended up serving as Melanchthon's assistant (though he did not write for Melanchthon or take dictation). Moreover, Koch became the manager of all the Melanchthon household affairs. A sign in the Melanchthon House in Wittenberg explains, "[Koch] took care of everything in the household whereby he bought, stored, guarded the goods, and occupied himself with all domestic commodities and considerations."

Koch managed the affairs of the Melanchthon house for thirty-four years. He began each morning with Scripture and prayer, and then went on to train the children in their early education. In his own time, he also read theology. He became a central figure in the Melanchthon household. Philipp later wrote, "He accompanied us in all our times of exile, labors and afflictions."[46] Thanks in large measure to this friend, Melanchthon was freed of most domestic responsibilities and was able to devote himself almost entirely to scholarship and teaching. His veritable avalanche of extant books and letters surely confirms the favorable status of his domestic arrangements. When Koch died in 1553, Melanchthon invited university officials to the funeral, and gave a Latin oration at the grave.

Although Melanchthon was private about his family, it seems clear that trust and love grew between Philipp and Katharina. In the end, they were married thirty-seven years (until Katharina's death in 1557) and had four children,[47] whom they raised with a strong emphasis on faith in Christ, prayer, and devotion to God.

Melanchthon especially emphasized the importance of prayer. He valued careful composition, for the glory of God. He favored the

---

46. CR 8:65. Trans. Manschreck, 306.
47. Numerous descendants of the Schwartzerdt/Melanchthon family can be found to this day. I met one while staffing the Melanchthonhaus-Bretten booth at the Hamburg *Kirchentag* in 2013.

balanced integration of all the major types of prayer—praise, thanksgiving, confession, petition, and adoration. Prayer proved ever needful, because outside the walls of the family home, dramatic events were underway that have since helped shape the development of Christianity worldwide.

Exsurge Domine

In 1517, Luther posted his theses. In 1518, they were discussed. In 1519, they were disputed. In 1520, it was finally time for Pope Leo X to intervene.

The *Catholic Encyclopedia* offers a mixed personal portrait of this pontiff: "He was not a handsome man. He [had a] fat, shiny, effeminate countenance with weak eyes. . . . The unwieldy body was supported by thin legs. His movements were sluggish and during ecclesiastical functions his corpulence made him constantly wipe the perspiration from his face and hands, to the distress of bystanders. But when he laughed or spoke the unpleasant impression vanished. He had an agreeable voice, knew how to express himself with elegance and vivacity, and his manner was easy and gracious." Leo X, a scion of the Medici family of Florence, was cultured and politically astute. He was both a patron of Michelangelo and also the (unsuccessful) preacher of a crusade in 1518 to resist the violent Muslim invasions of Christian lands. Between France, the Holy Roman Empire, and the Ottomans, Leo X had more than enough to keep himself occupied—especially when he sought to live life in style. Bainton once described Leo "as elegant and indolent as a Persian cat."[48] His chief concern was to preserve papal power and protect papal prestige,[49] and so the theological strife with Luther must have been an annoying distraction.

48. Bainton, 74.
49. OER, "Leo X"

THE HONEYCOMB SCROLL

In the German lands, though, Luther was not a distraction—he was the main event. His religious ideas were important, but they also touched a nationalistic nerve at a key moment in European history. Many Germans were confident in their own language and culture, and were sensitive to the idea of being ill-used by Italian potentates of worldly motives draining German resources for their own aggrandizement. The fiery knights Ulrich von Hutten and Franz von Sickingen had a notable military force at their disposal along the Rhine. Previously they had supported Reuchlin in the Pfefferkorn affair, and now they strongly endorsed Luther. They showed a willingness to add the power of the sword to Luther's trust in God and power of the pen. On January 20, 1520, Hutten wrote Melanchthon on behalf of Franz von Sickingen. They offered their swords to Luther. The letter was sent to Melanchthon as a middleman for the sake of public discretion.[50] They asked Melanchthon to keep this quiet, but they were also serious.[51]

Meanwhile, having heard the reports from Cajetan's meeting with Luther in Augsburg in 1518, and now from Eck's debate with Luther in Leipzig in the summer of 1519, Leo X was stirring himself to take action to deal with this insubordinate German monk. It was hard *not* to, with Eck personally present in Rome doing his best to stir the pot with the *curia* and with anyone who would listen.

Eck even helpfully donated his services for drafting a papal bull condemning Luther. He worked with a committee, which soon presented the finished product to Leo X for his consideration. Leo ordered it published on June 15, 1520. In this bull, Leo denounced forty-one of Luther's theses as heretical, and gave Martin (and his supporters) sixty days to recant. If he did not recant, then he would be excommunicated.

---

50. MBW 72.
51. See also MBW 74 and 98.

Exsurge Domine. Title page of the papal bull condemning Luther, 1520.

Eck and Girolamo Aleander were given the task of publishing the bull in Germany. Eck received the additional authority to add names for excommunication at his discretion. In the end, he added Karlstadt, Pirckheimer, and Spengler. Although some of Luther's books were burned at Mainz, many people clearly opposed the action. In fact, they tried to stone Eck and threatened him with death if he tried to burn any more of Luther's books.

Northern European sentiment was strongly sympathetic to Luther. Even Erasmus told Melanchthon that he felt friendly toward Luther.[52] He related that through a letter to Thomas Wolsey in York, he prevented Luther's books from being burned in England. His only reservation was that Luther opposed the divine law to papal primacy. On this basis, Erasmus saw a revolution coming, and he wanted no part of it.

Aleander and Eck accordingly found it difficult to get the bull published north of the Alps. Many cities delayed or declined publication. In Leipzig, students insulted Eck in verse. Duke Georg and the city government prevented Eck from publishing the bull in the city, and he fled by night. Aleander, for his part, reported that nine-tenths of the German populace shouted, "Luther!" and the other tenth shouted, "Death to the pope!"[53]

The papal bull reached Wittenberg on October 10. Luther doubted its authenticity. Its arrival created tension between Eck and the papal emissary Miltitz, who was still industriously trying to win some sort of rapprochement with Luther, whereas Eck sought only to condemn. After hearing of the papal bull, Melanchthon and Luther immediately traveled a day's journey to confer with Miltitz in Lichtenberg. Elector Friedrich, skilled politician that he was, sought

---

52. MBW 97.
53. Paul Kalkoff, ed., *Die Depeschen des Nuntius vom Wormser Reichstage 1521* (Halle, Verein für Reformationsgeschichte, 1886), 48.

to play Eck and Miltitz off of each other, with their differing agendas. Miltitz seemed to be taken off guard by Eck's appearance bearing such a papal bull.

After considering his options, Luther declared that whether the bull was authentic or not, he would never obey the Antichrist.[54] He did not recant for Cajetan, and he was not going to recant for Leo. Of course, this made life difficult for Elector Friedrich, who was in transit to Aachen for the October 23 coronation of Charles V as Holy Roman Emperor. On November 8, Friedrich's councilors wrote to Melanchthon, recommending that Luther appeal the papal bull, and asking what Luther's intentions were going forward.[55] Charles V, only twenty years old at the time, was merely an observer in this religious controversy. That, however, would soon change.

The Pen and the Sword

Staupitz resigned as vicar general of the Augustinian Order in 1520. He was replaced by Wenzeslaus Linck (who stayed in this role until 1523). Staupitz thereby removed himself from the coming storm. Luther, however, did no such thing. Throughout 1520, he remained very active with teaching and writing, producing a number of key publications. Throughout, Melanchthon vigorously supported him, and no doubt had conversations with Luther as he was composing these important tracts. For example, when Hieronymus Emser, the chaplain to Duke Georg of Saxony (and whose coat of arms included an image of a goat) wrote under the penname of "Radinus" to attack Luther,[56] Melanchthon replied by taking up the penname of "Didymus Faventinus." He managed to work many sarcastic references to goats into this oration,[57] but in his central point,

---

54. WA 6:570–93, 597–612.
55. MBW 110.
56. *Oration of Thomas Rhadinus Against the Heretic Martin Luther* (Leipzig: October, 1520).

Melanchthon maintained that Luther did not intend to disrupt the peace of Christian unity. Rather, it was the tyranny of the Roman Antichrist that was doing that. Luther was not rejecting the solid old faith, but rather the much newer innovations placed upon it from medieval times. Luther in fact stood for the gospel, and not the doctrines of men. Scripture fully supported his case. Melanchthon's essay proved to be highly effective and widely read.

Luther's three most significant tracts of 1520 included the *Address to the Christian Nobility of Germany* (August), *The Babylonian Captivity of the Church* (October), and *The Freedom of the Christian* (November).

The first printing of *The Address to the Christian Nobility* included seven thousand copies, and it sold out quickly. In it, Luther claimed that the papacy had become corrupt, and that it was therefore the responsibility of Christian princes to reform the church. After all, through the priesthood of all believers, they, too, had the right to do so. Melanchthon, for his part, enthusiastically endorsed this argument. In a letter to Johannes Lang, he wrote, "The purpose of writing the letter to the German nobility I approved from the beginning. Luther was encouraged in it by those on whom we both rely. Besides, it is of a nature to glorify God. I was not willing to have it delayed. I did not want to curb the spirit of Martin in a matter to which he seems to have been divinely appointed. The book is now published and circulated and cannot be recalled."[58]

Melanchthon also supported the idea of the priesthood of all believers in its practical applications through letters of personal advice. For example, in July, 1521, he wrote to a certain brother Melchior, suggesting that the monastery accept a lay brother working as a baker, so long as he could keep to the chastity

---

57. MSA 1:56–140.
58. MBW 105.

requirement. However, Melanchthon went on to say that one should not suppose that being a monk is a particularly Christian life. He recommended that his correspondent read Luther's writings.[59]

Luther took the practical application of the doctrine of the priesthood of all believers a good deal further than Melanchthon. He applied it in the most dramatic way possible to his current situation. Having now set forth an argument for having secular princes reform the church if necessary, he proposed that they do exactly that. Echoing the words of Paul (Acts 25:11), Luther declared, "I appeal to Caesar." He set his case before the putative heir to the Roman Caesars, the newly elected (though not yet crowned) Emperor Charles V.[60] If the pope refused to stand for Christ, then surely the emperor would do so. A few months later, in November, 1520, Charles wrote to "uncle" Friedrich the elector, requesting that Luther be brought to Worms so that his case might be heard. Luther's appeal to Caesar had been granted.[61]

Meanwhile, as the controversy was heating up along with the summer temperatures in 1520, Melanchthon reported that Luther's devotions and theological studies were increasingly centering on the idea of consolation in exile.[62] He clearly understood that his positions might have very real personal consequences.

Luther's next significant writing came in October: *The Babylonian Captivity of the Church*. In it, he attacked the sacramental system, reducing the sacraments from seven to two. When Erasmus saw this, he declared, "The breech is irreparable."[63] Melanchthon, too, was seriously studying the idea of the sacraments. He had expressed doubt about transubstantiation in his baccalaureate theses of 1519, and now,

---

59. MBW 154.
60. August, 1520. WABR 2:172–78, Nr. 332.
61. *Deutsche Reichstagsakten*, II, Nr. 61.
62. MBW 104.
63. EE 1203.

in 1520, in an open letter to Johannes Heß in Nuremberg, he said that transubstantiation should not be believed, and that it could not be biblically substantiated.[64]

After reading *The Babylonian Captivity*, a certain Pomeranian preacher named Johannes Bugenhagen began to exchange letters with Luther. He ended up coming to Wittenberg in 1521, arriving shortly before Luther departed for Worms. He matriculated on April 29, 1521, and began to give private lectures on the Psalms—which were of such quality that even Melanchthon himself attended.[65] Beginning in 1525, Bugenhagen would become pastor of the town of Wittenberg, and would go on to play an integral role not only in Wittenberg, but also in the wider Reformation.

Luther's *Freedom of a Christian* followed in November, 1520. Here he taught that justification came by faith—and not by keeping certain rules (though of course Christians would follow rules). Writings such as these showed that Luther was in no way prepared to recant. Instead, he continued to develop his theological ideas and their practical applications.

Fighting Fire with Fire

In the summer of 1520, Luther resigned himself to irreconcilable differences with the pope. He wrote, "For me the die is cast. I despise alike Roman fury and Roman favor. I will not be reconciled or communicate with them. Let them damn and burn my books. I for my part, unless I cannot find a fire, will publicly damn and burn the whole canon law."[66] Catholic officials had indeed been burning Luther's books. The publication of the papal bull in Rome coincided with a bonfire of Luther's writings.

---

64. MBW 76.
65. "Bugenhagen," in *Contemporaries of Erasmus*, 218.
66. WABR 2:137.25–29. Nr. 310. Trans., Bainton, 151.

Statue of Johannes Bugenhagen, located outside the City Church in Wittenberg. Photo by Gregory Graybill.

Because the bull arrived in Wittenberg on October 10, that meant Luther's sixty-day grace period to recant ran out on Monday, December 10. He did not recant. Instead, the Wittenbergers marked the expiration of the ultimatum in a memorable way. Early that morning, Melanchthon posted a note on the university bulletin board: "All friends of evangelical truth are invited to assemble, about 9:00, at the church of the Holy Cross, beyond the city wall. There, according to ancient, apostolic usage, the godless books of the papal constitutions and the scholastic theology will be burned inasmuch as the presumption of the enemies of the Gospel has advanced to such a degree that they have cast the godly, evangelical books of Luther into the fire. Let all earnest students, therefore, appear at the spectacle; for it is now the time when Antichrist will be exposed."[67]

Just east of town, not far from Melanchthon's house and the Augustinian monastery where Luther lived, a fire was indeed kindled. Professors, students, and townspeople gathered and watched the burning of the canon law and the theological writings of Eck and Emser. Luther himself consigned the papal bull to the flames. After the singing of a couple hymns, the gathering broke up, but the students, flush with excitement, celebrated uproariously. They continued the festivities by burning the pope in effigy, and by conducting a funeral for a six-foot copy of the bull. These unbridled student energies would later present a problem for the Wittenberg reformers.

In the meantime, Aleander spoke out, saying, "Has the whole world gone wrong, and Martin only has the eyes to see?"[68] Within a week, Charles V got wind of the burning of the papal bull at Wittenberg. Fearing that the scheduled diet in Worms could fall under a papal interdict in retaliation, on December 17 he rescinded Luther's invitation to Worms. Elector Friedrich's reply was to refuse Charles's original invitation from November 28 in any case—citing as rationale the fact that Luther's books were burned in Mainz the same day as the invitation. That seemed to indicate that Luther's case had been prejudged, and Friedrich would not subject his professor to such treatment.[69]

Finally, in the midst of these dramatic events in December, Melanchthon received news of one more. His mother, Barbara, who had recently been widowed again, had just married Melchior Hechel in Bretten—the owner of the Krone guesthouse across the street from the family home. If Philipp saw fit to give his mother short notice for his wedding, then she would give short notice of hers!

---

67. Cf. WABR 2:234; WA 7:183–6. Trans. Manschreck, 60.
68. Kalkoff, ed., 34.
69. *Deutsche Reichstagsakten*, II, Nr. 61.

Pen and Lectern

Between 1519 and 1521, Melanchthon stayed extremely busy, professionally. In 1519, he made the acquaintance of Johannes Heß (1490–1547), who had recently earned a doctorate in theology from Ferrara. A former student and professor, he visited Wittenberg to see Luther and Spalatin for a few weeks. During this time, he made a close connection with Melanchthon. The two would henceforth correspond regularly, and in great detail.[70] Melanchthon viewed him as a confidante, worthy of such information as Hutten and von Sickingen's offers of armed aid. Heß was also a knowledgeable sounding board for academic matters. Heß was like-minded with Philipp in that they both supported Lutheran theology, but also saw the value of diplomatic caution and tolerance.

In his teaching and writing, Melanchthon remained active in biblical studies, theology (including public controversy), and philosophy. Upon completion of his *baccalaureas biblicus* in the fall of 1519, Melanchthon gained teaching rights in the theology faculty, though without giving up his rights and duties in the philosophical faculty. His new credential obligated him to teach based on the Latin Vulgate text of the Bible, and so he lectured on Matthew's Gospel as well as Romans.[71] For him, no scripture was as clear as Romans—and the scholastics had completely missed it. In 1521, he went on to lecture on 1 and 2 Corinthians, for which he produced original Latin translations.[72] Melanchthon also interpreted Old Testament

---

70. E.g., between 1520 and 1521, MBW 76, 83–84, 86, 95, 102, 126, 135, and 169.
71. Cf. MBW 126. Around May, 1521, Melanchthon published a Greek edition of Romans: *Pauli apostolic ad Romanos epistola* (Wittenberg: Melchior Lotter, 1521). His foreword can be found in MBW 142 (with a letter to Bugenhagen). Cf. MBW 156.
72. See Scheible, *Melanchthon*, 61. His Latin translation of 1 Corinthians appeared in late spring, 1521: *Pauli apostoli ad Corinthios prior epistola* (Wittenberg: Melchior Lotter, 1521). The foreword he wrote for it can be found in MBW 138. The Latin translation of 2 Corinthians appeared in the fall of 1521: *Pauli apostoli ad Corinthios secunda epistola* (Wittenberg: Melchior Lotter, 1521). Foreword in MBW 172.

texts. This teaching load was significantly more than was required, but he was enthusiastic and excited about the work.[73]

While Wittenberg was without a Hebrew professor, Melanchthon had stood in the breech, adding these teaching duties to his other activities. His load lessened in April, 1520, when Matthäus Adrianus arrived to teach Hebrew.[74] Adrianus was a baptized Spanish Jew, who had taught Hebrew earlier in Louvain.[75] However, a few months after Adrianus's arrival, Melanchthon reported difficulties with him to Spalatin. He pointed out a "poor harvest" as a result of Adrianus's teaching.[76] Adrianus had a falling out with Luther in October, 1520, and by February of the next year, he gave up his place. At that point, Melanchthon spoke of everything being fine in Wittenberg, "apart from the case of Adrianus."[77] Naturally, Melanchthon was the one to step back in to take over Hebrew teaching once again. He dug out his personal copy of Reuchlin's *Rudiments of Hebrew Grammar* and went back to work.

Around this time in 1521, both Johannes Bugenhagen and Justas Jonas joined the theology faculty at Wittenberg. They would be steadfast allies in the ongoing theological controversies. Melanchthon was equipping himself for these battles with all his copious energy and zeal. In January, 1521, he said he was working on theology as much as possible.[78] A few months previously, he had held a disputation over eighteen theses on justification. He argued for justification by faith, the idea that love flows *from* faith (and is not a natural action), the doctrine that works are not meritorious, and the undergirding importance of scriptural authority.[79]

---

73. MBW 68.
74. See Scheible, *Melanchthon*, 33.
75. MBW 87.
76. MBW 109, 112.
77. MBW 127.
78. MBW 118.
79. *Themata circularia*. MSA 1:54–55.

As his studies progressed, he recommended Augustine, but warned against Origen.[80] He produced a Latin translation of selections from Gregory of Nazianzus (focusing on the content rather than the style),[81] and wrote against monastic vows.[82] He set out to explore church history, as well.[83]

At the same time, Melanchthon busied himself with teaching and writing in the philosophical faculty. He published influential texts on rhetoric and dialectics.[84] These disciplines were critical for approaching biblical interpretation, and they needed to be freed from the sophistic corruptions of the scholastics. He also issued a new edition of his Greek grammar,[85] as well as editions of Demosthenes,[86] Virgil, Aristophanes,[87] Thucydides,[88] Lucian,[89] Arat, and Hesiod.[90]

Though not a pastor or priest, Melanchthon showed a pastor's heart for the student Bartholmäus Schaller, whose father died unexpectedly, leaving him the responsibility of settling family affairs.[91] He wrote Schaller a second time to offer Christian consolation on February 1, 1520. Melanchthon said he would take care of Schaller's two brothers, Caspar and Hieronymus. He

---

80. MBW 84.
81. *Sermo in secunda Encenia quae verna quoque dicuntur* (Erfurt: Matthäus Maler, 1519). Foreword in MBW 64.
82. *Apologia Bartholomaei Bernhardi Feldkirchensis*. CR 1:422–40. See Stupperich, 53.
83. MBW 128.
84. E.g., *Institutiones rhetoricae* (Wittenberg: Melchior Lotter, 1521). Foreword in MBW 161. This printing happened against Melanchthon's will, through the agency of friends. *Compendiaria dialectics ratio* (Wittenberg: Melchior Lotter, 1520). Foreword in MBW 78.
85. *Integrae graecae institutiones* (Hagenau: Thomas Anshelm, 1520). Foreword at MBW 116. Cf. MBW 130. Notice that this is a sequel to the earlier Greek grammar he published in Tübingen—it is published through Anshelm, and not Lotter. This was the new edition urged by Anshelm.
86. *Epistolae duae elegantissimae* (Hagenau: Thomas Anshelm, 1519/20). Foreword in MBW 71.
87. MBW 89.
88. On Thucydides, see MBW 35 and 79. Cf. Greschat, 30.
89. MBW 79. *Luciani oratio adversus calumniam mire elegans* (Wittenberg: Melchior Lotter, 1521). Foreword in MBW 133.
90. See Scheible, *Melanchthon*, 33.
91. MBW 69.

encouraged his student to return to his studies when he was able.[92] He sent additional letters, encouraging Schaller—as he had learned in his studies—to love the cross of Christ. Sadly, though, Melanchthon had to report that one of Schaller's brothers was out of control in Wittenberg—though he offered a reassuring report on the state of the other brother.[93]

Melanchthon clearly cared for his students, and by all accounts, he taught very well. Karlstadt praised his teaching and writing in the fall of 1521.[94] Melanchthon was demanding and well-respected by his students. In 1520, Spalatin reported that one of Melanchthon's lectures had six hundred people in attendance.[95] Nevertheless, Melanchthon's intensity and submerged temper occasionally got the better of him, and he was known to yell at lazy students.[96] These were, however, stressful times for an overworked, newly-married young professor who had thrown in his lot with a colleague who had thumbed his nose at the pope. Luther was courting the very real danger of being burned at the stake. In these momentous days, Melanchthon was not the only person tempted to yell.

---

92. MBW 73.
93. See MBW 88 and 117.
94. MBW 170.
95. CR 10:301.
96. Display text at the Melanchthon House in Wittenberg.

12

Taking a Stand

1521

Organize for yourself collections of *loci theologici*. You can find in the Bible two hundred and even three hundred such concepts. Each one of these must be supported by biblical passages. *Loci* are little nests in which you place the fruit of your reading.
—Erasmus[1]

Upon hearing of Luther's burning of the papal bull, Charles V rescinded his invitation to the Diet of Worms. However, he thought better of it, and in February, 1521, he reinstated the invitation.

Many competing agendas were at play in the lead-up to Worms. The Elector Friedrich wanted his professor to get a fair hearing. Melanchthon was also convinced that Friedrich intended to engage in secret negotiations with the emperor at Worms, and he fully expected them to go well.[2] The pope, for his part, was not thrilled

---

1. Quoted in LCC 19:12. Erasmus, *De copia,* in Hajo Holborn, ed., *Ausgewählte Werke* (Munich, 1933), 158. Also in (English trans.) *On Copia of Words and Ideas*, ed. and trans. Donald B King and H. David Rix (Milwaukee, WI: Marquette University Press, 1963), 291.
2. MBW 120.

with the emperor's decision to hear Luther's appeal at Worms. He had, after all, already decided the case himself through his papal bull. Wasn't that sufficient? Charles's decision to invite Luther to Worms therefore was an attack on papal authority. This, combined with the fact that the papacy had *not* supported the election of Charles as emperor must have caused some level of unease in Rome.

The knights Hutten and Franz von Sickingen enthusiastically favored increasing papal unease in any way possible. They vocally supported Luther and viewed the conflict through a nationalistic lens. Charles must surely have been tempted to at least countenance a similar perspective. After all, the pope represented a rival political power on the European scene. Nevertheless, when it came to matters of faith, Charles viewed himself as a good Catholic who would obey the pope. However, by keeping Luther in German territory rather than sending him to Rome, Charles elevated his own significance in relation to the Roman pontiff. Luther was duly summoned to Worms—with an arrival date set in mid-April.

In late February, Melanchthon wrote to Johannes Heß, saying that Luther was thriving, despite Leo's wrath. The papal bull would achieve nothing, because the Roman bishops didn't dare pass through the territory. They would be in danger if they did—public opinion was too riled against them.[3] Luther was fearless and still publishing tracts with alacrity. Yet, Melanchthon also reported regional opposition to the Wittenberg movement. Emser raged in Leipzig, and at least a few individuals had the gumption to burn Luther's books there.[4]

Melanchthon was convinced that at the heart of this dispute, the cause of the gospel was under threat.[5] For him, this was not a matter

---

3. MBW 126.
4. MBW 127–8.
5. MBW 130.

of mere professional disputation about secondary matters—it lay at the heart of his faith and teaching as a disciple of Jesus Christ. Luther felt the same way. He was nervous that the Catholic party would have undue influence on Charles and the diet. However, he remained defiant: "They labor for the revocation of many articles, but my revocation will be this: 'Earlier I said that the pope is the vicar of Christ. Now, I recant and say, 'The pope is the adversary of Christ and the apostle of the Devil.'"[6]

At the end of March, Melanchthon received an additional piece of communication that complicated matters. A letter arrived from King Christian II of Denmark, Norway, and Sweden. The brother-in-law of Charles V, he threw his support behind Luther.[7] However, Melanchthon was not impressed. While this might look good on paper, the fact of the matter was that Christian II was damaged goods. In the previous November, he had engaged in a bloodbath in Stockholm, in which he methodically slaughtered the leading Swedish nobility. The Swedes considered him a tyrant, and Christian was in dire need of friends on the wider European scene. He would not be a helpful ally for the Wittenberg cause. In fact, he would shortly be deposed and exiled to the Netherlands.

Melanchthon wished to accompany Luther to Worms (it would, incidentally, give him an opportunity to browse through some nice libraries along the Rhine),[8] but it was decided that he should stay and continue teaching his courses. Melanchthon was also busy bringing his important theological textbook, the *Loci communes* to press (see below). Luther, for his part, contemplated martyrdom and viewed Melanchthon as his successor.

---

6. March 24, 1521. WABR 2:293.13–16, Nr. 391.
7. MBW 131.
8. MBW 134.

Christian II, King of Denmark, Norway, and Sweden (1481–1559).

"If I should not return, and my enemies should kill me at Worms, as may very easily come to pass, I adjure you, dear brother, not to neglect teaching, nor to fail to stand by the truth. In the meantime also do my work, because I cannot be here. You can do it better than I can. Therefore it will not be a great loss, provided you remain. The Lord still finds a learned champion in you."[9] When Luther departed for Worms, Melanchthon would not see him again for almost a year.[10]

Elector Friedrich and Spalatin had departed for Worms several months earlier, in January, 1521.[11] In early April, Luther set out for Worms, exegeting for his traveling companions the Book of Joshua along the way.[12] Appropriately, it begins with the admonition to be

---

9. Quoted in Manschreck, 65 (without attributing a primary source).
10. See Camerarius, chap. 14.
11. MBW 119.

strong and courageous.[13] Justas Jonas (1493–1555), appointed just a few weeks early as professor and provost in Wittenberg, met the party in Weimar and traveled with Luther onward to Worms.

Jonas would himself become a notable figure in the Reformation. A tall and cultured humanist, he was approved by Erasmus[14] and had been offended by Eck's attacks on him at the Leipzig Disputation. Later, Jonas would translate some of Luther and Melanchthon's most important theological works from Latin into German. Shortly after he was appointed to Wittenberg, he was supposed to teach canon law, but he refused. His position was thereafter transitioned to biblical theology.[15] Obviously, Jonas was Luther's kind of guy—and no doubt he was an encouragement in the trial that was to come.

While Luther, Jonas, and the Wittenberg party were still on the road to Worms, the theology faculty of the Sorbonne in Paris issued a scathing attack on Luther. They had been asked to judge the Leipzig Disputation and say who won, but they did not engage the arguments on papal primacy—the central point. Instead, they simply condemned Luther as a heretic.[16] Melanchthon read this document when a copy made its way to Wittenberg. He became angry, and wrote a pungent response.

Luther and his party arrived in Worms on April 16, 1521. Two thousand people turned out to meet them. The stakes were indeed high.

Before the Emperor at the Diet of Worms, Luther was shown his books and asked if they were his. He acknowledged them, and said he had written more. He was asked if he defended them all, or rejected them in part. Some advisors had been pressing him behind the scenes,

---

12. MBW 136.
13. Joshua 1:6–7.
14. Allen Ep. 985; CWE Ep. 967A.
15. MBW 143–5.
16. CR 1:366–88.

thinking that if he just recanted on this work or that work, then all could be smoothed over. Before the diet, he was challenged, "Do you alone understand the Bible?"

Luther, feeling the gravity of the moment, asked for a day to think the matter over before replying. Though some were surprised by this response, the emperor granted it to him. The next day, Luther came back with a bold reply: "Unless I am convinced by Scripture and plain reason—I do not accept the authority of popes and councils, for they have contradicted each other—my conscience is captive to the Word of God. I cannot and I will not recant anything, for to go against conscience is neither right nor safe. God help me. Amen."[17] He spoke in German, and then, when asked, repeated it in Latin.

Now all eyes turned to Emperor Charles V. Luther had clearly stated where he stood. The pope had made his own case. Now where would this brand-new twenty-year-old emperor stand? Feeling the gravity of the moment, he took a day to think about it.

---

17. Wrede, ed., *Deutsche Reichstagsakten*, 2:555. Trans. Bainton, 185.

TAKING A STAND

Luther at the Diet of Worms. Wood cut, 1557. The German text reads, "Here I stand. I can do no other. God help me. Amen."

The next day, April 19, 1521, Charles V stood and read out a declaration he had prepared himself in French. If Luther would stand boldly, then so would he:

> I am descended from a long line of Christian emperors of this noble German nation, and of the Catholic kings of Spain, the archdukes of Austria, and the dukes of Burgundy. They were all faithful to the death to the Church of Rome, and they defended the Catholic faith and the honor of God. I have resolved to follow in their steps. A single friar who goes counter to all Christianity for a thousand years must be wrong. Therefore I am resolved to stake my lands, my friends, my body, my blood, my life, and my soul. Not only I, but you of this noble German nation, would be forever disgraced if by our negligence not only heresy but the very suspicion of heresy were to survive. After having heard yesterday the obstinate defense of Luther, I regret that I have so long delayed in proceeding against him and his false teaching. I will have no more to do with him. He may return under his safe conduct, but without preaching or making any tumult. I will proceed against him as

235

a notorious heretic, and ask you to declare yourselves as you promised me.[18]

Charles could have moved against Luther immediately, but instead he chose to honor the safe conduct he had given him. In this, then, Luther was spared the fate of Huss. Some attribute Charles's decision to chivalry,[19] but it also conformed with the political reality that immediate hostilities directed at Luther would have alienated and angered several of the electors present. Luther departed Worms about a week later.

A few days after Luther's departure, on April 30, Charles took steps to place Luther under the imperial ban. He had Aleander, the papal delegate, draft an edict, dated May 6. However, it was not officially issued until May 26, the day after the diet was adjourned (and incidentally, well after those who were inclined to support Luther had left). Even though this was a political council pronouncing on heresy (and thereby undercutting papal preeminence), the fact that the emperor *agreed* with the pope made it in Leo X's interest to support this Edict of Worms, despite his normal hostility to any hint of conciliar authority. Plus, the fact that the edict was drafted by the papal delegate gave the pope even more cover for supporting it.

On May 29, Leo X gave the Edict of Worms his full backing. The pope and the emperor were now agreed that Luther was a devil, that he belonged under the imperial ban, and that he should henceforth be delivered without delay to the proper authorities—dead or alive. His supporters were to be subject to the same treatment, and their property was to be confiscated.

Grand pronouncements were one thing, but turning these dictates into reality was something else altogether. The Edict of Worms

---

18. Wrede, ed., *Deutsche Reichstagsakten*, 2:595–6. Trans. (from French) by Bainton, 186.
19. E.g., see OER, "Charles V."

received a cautious welcome at best in the Swabian League,[20] and among Luther's political supporters, bold steps were undertaken to circumvent it.

Wartburg

On the evening of May 3, when the Wittenberg party found themselves in an isolated stretch of woods on their journey home, a group of brigands suddenly descended on them, taking Luther captive and riding off with him. At least, that's how it appeared. In actual fact, Elector Friedrich arranged the whole affair, in order to take Luther into hiding, for his own protection. He had Luther transported to the Wartburg Castle, where the monk grew a beard and adopted the persona of the knight, "Junker Jörg."

When the news of the attack of the "brigands" reached Wittenberg, Melanchthon and many others thought that Luther had been murdered. He learned otherwise, however, when he received a letter from Luther dated May 12.[21] Luther wrote about involuntary exile, and his distress for the church. He lamented, "God, what a horrendous apparition of the wrath of God is this abominable kingdom of the Roman Antichrist!"[22] He now viewed Melanchthon as his deputy in Wittenberg. Luther exhorted his colleague, writing, "As a servant of the Word, *stand* in the meantime, and defend the walls and towers of Jerusalem until they attack you, too. You know your calling and your gifts. I pray for you especially—if it's in any way possible, I pray without doubt. Therefore return the favor, and let us bear one another's burdens.[23] As yet, we stand alone in the battle. After me, they will be looking for you."[24]

20. MBW 164.
21. MBW 139.1. WABR 2:332–33, Nr. 407.
22. MBWT 139.1:11–12. WABR 2:332–3.11–13, Nr. 407.
23. Gal. 6:2.
24. MBWT 139.1:17–22.

Melanchthon joyfully wrote Wenzeslaus Linck, exulting, "Luther lives! May he remain true."[25] For almost a year, only a select few would know what had really happened to Luther. Melanchthon, Spalatin, and Amsdorf were Luther's primary correspondents at this time.

Luther went on in a second missive to Melanchthon, also dated May 12, to relate that he had heard of the Edict of Worms from Spalatin, and also how Emperor Charles was determined to prevent people sympathetic to Luther from fleeing to Christian II in Denmark.[26] Having an awareness of the political realities, Luther supposed that the Edict of Worms would only really go into effect in the territories of Duke Georg of Saxony and Elector Joachim of Brandenburg. Luther closed by relating his poor health (insomnia and intestinal woes), and with greetings to Katharina, Melanchthon's wife. Luther, at least, was happy about the marriage, even if Philipp still occasionally grumbled.

Melanchthon apparently responded soon after, noting that Luther's preaching at the City Church was sorely missed.[27] Luther replied that as long as Melanchthon and Amsdorf were there, the City Church would not be without shepherds.[28] Nevertheless, with Luther gone, the best preaching in Wittenberg was now to be found at the Augustinian monastery—where Gabriel Zwilling (1487–1558) held forth. He issued passionate challenges to the brethren in the same spirit as Luther's reforms—or with even *more* energy, if that were possible. Luther himself claimed to be without fear. He repeated that he viewed Melanchthon as his successor.[29] "Even should I perish,

---

25. MBW 140.
26. Cf. MBW 139.2.
27. The MBW records *no* letters from Melanchthon to Luther before 1527. This is a curious omission, and one can only conclude that none of these epistles survived the exigencies of time.
28. MBW 141. WABR 2:346–52, Nr. 413.
29. MBW 141.

nothing will pass away from the Gospel, in which you now surpass me. You are Elisha who succeeds Elijah with a double portion of the Spirit, which may the Lord Jesus mercifully bestow on you. Amen."[30]

Melanchthon, for his part, was worried about Luther—especially about his health. In early July he expressed his concerns to Spalatin.[31] Due to Luther's great importance for both church and theology, it would be a tragic turn of events if anything happened to him. Melanchthon sought advice from doctors in Wittenberg on Luther's digestive troubles. He wrote to Spalatin, "Our Elijah is not yet with us, but we wait and hope for him. My longing for him tortures me grievously."[32]

Luther heard of Melanchthon's efforts, and, displeased, wrote to chastise him for being entirely too flustered. He told Melanchthon in no uncertain terms that he was being too faint-hearted and that he overvalued Luther. Luther was dispensable! Philipp should stop worrying. Nevertheless, he asked for Melanchthon's prayers for his loneliness and physical ails.[33]

Melanchthon did not take Luther's advice. He continued to be concerned about his colleague. In August, he wrote that Luther was expected daily in Wittenberg. In September, he began campaigning to Spalatin to exercise his influence to bring Luther back. Melanchthon was convinced that it was essential for Luther to return immediately.[34] He could no longer be dispensed with.[35] Melanchthon longed for his presence.[36]

September, 1521, brought further developments. Three people died of the plague in Wittenberg.[37] Luther was burned in effigy

---

30. MBWT 141:48–50. See 2 Kings 2:9-14.
31. MBW 150.
32. MBW 145. Trans. Manschreck, 70.
33. MBW 151. WABR 2:356–61, Nr. 418. See also MBW 158. WABR 2:373–77, Nr. 425.
34. MBW 163.
35. MBW 168.
36. MBW 169.

in Worms. This prompted Melanchthon to compare Luther to the legend of the phoenix.[38] Justus Jonas was made a licentiate in theology by Karlstadt, and a month later earned his doctor of divinity. At the end of September, Melanchthon reported being extremely busy.[39]

During this time, Melanchthon energetically focused on supporting Luther in print. He wrote a foreword for Luther's *On Good Works*,[40] and expressed outrage at the theology faculty of Paris's recent condemnation of Luther. In October, he fired off a vigorous tract called, *Against the Furious Decree of the "So-Called" Theologians of Paris*.[41] In it, Melanchthon used biting words and a sustained argument to attack the Paris theologians. He defended scriptural authority over tradition, and argued that the early fathers were more valuable than the Aristotelian scholastics. Luther actually *upheld* biblical truth. This foolishness from the Paris theologians was a case in point proving the lesser value of church councils, in comparison with Scripture.

When the authorities in Paris saw Melanchthon's tract, they had it burned. When Luther read it at the Wartburg, he was delighted, and happily set about translating it into German himself.[42]

Charles's Preoccupation

These months also proved extremely demanding for Charles V. However, it was Francis I and Suleiman—not Luther—who drew his attention. These distractions gave the Wittenberg movement

---

37. MBW 168.
38. MBW 167.
39. MBW 169.
40. Martin Luther, *De bonis operibus liber, denuo recognitus* (Wittenberg: Johannes Grunenberg, 1521). Melanchthon's foreword can be found in MBW 199.
41. *Adversus furiosum Parrisiensium Theologastrorum decretum Philippi Melanchthonis pro Luthero apologia*. MSA 1:141–62. Cf. MBW 146–47.
42. WABR 2:365, Nr. 420. See also WABR 2:397.27–28, Nr. 435.

breathing room to continue its growth relatively unmolested. Later, in his memoirs, Charles blamed Francis for distracting him from stamping out the Lutheran heresy when it was still relatively nascent. Due to Francis's actions, Charles was obligated to leave the German lands in 1521, and he was not in a position to return to take up again the Lutheran question until the Diet of Augsburg in 1530—nine years later.

But just what was Francis up to? Some have labeled the result of his actions "the Italian Wars" (1521–26). With Charles now the official Emperor, Francis found himself in a geopolitical tight spot. France was bordered by German territories to the east and Spanish territories to the south—both controlled by Charles. Likewise, he had heard rumors of Charles trying to make nice with both Henry VIII and Pope Leo X. Francis might have felt as if he were in a vice. The word "encirclement" might have come to mind. Moreover, personal rivalry with Charles (to whom he had lost the election as Emperor) and the prospect of glory and riches may have also contributed to Francis's decision-making. It was time for preemptive action. Hence, on April 22, only four days after Luther's defense at Worms, Francis took the initiative and declared war on Charles. A French army invaded Navarre, and surrogates of Francis simultaneously invaded Friesland, Groningen, Overijssel, and Luxemburg. That must have been interesting news in Worms. It certainly would have focused the mind of the young emperor.

Equally distressing (perhaps even more so) was the news that arrived in late summer of a massive Ottoman army, swinging ponderously up from Anatolia to smash into the European outpost of Belgrade. Despite a spirited defense, the Turks expertly undermined the city walls, employed heavy bombardment from their artillery, and easily took the softened city. A resulting outcry and wave of Christian fervor swept Europe. This was *exactly* the sort of thing Pope

Leo X had been warning about when he preached a crusade three years earlier. But just as the call to crusade fell on deaf ears then, so calls to action fell on deaf ears now. Charles was not in a position to act—Francis was the more immediate threat, and Belgrade was too far away. However, the prospect of conflict in North Africa and the Mediterranean must have entered his mind. Indeed, the Ottomans laid siege to the citadel of the Knights Hospitallers on the island of Rhodes in 1522. Six months later, after a tough and costly fight, the Christians were driven out, and the expansionist Muslim empire had a new and convenient base in the eastern Mediterranean from which to further project their power. As important as the issue of Luther and evangelical theology was, it could not remain at the top of Charles's list of priorities during the 1520s in the face of these wider existential geopolitical threats.

Loci Communes: A Theological Textbook

Due to Charles's preoccupation with Francis (and to some extent, with Suleiman), the evangelical movement experienced a temporary respite. It proved to be a time for consolidating their teaching, and for putting bounds on some of the first excesses. Melanchthon was involved in both aspects—beginning most significantly with his theological textbook, *The Commonplaces (Loci communes)*. It was an attempt to gather evangelical doctrine together in one convenient, concise book.[43]

---

43. Melanchthon's *Loci communes* served as a kind of gathering place for evangelical theology, early in the Reformation. Similarly, one modern scholar has employed these Latin words to describe the cozy confines of the Gryffindor common room at Harry Potter's famous Hogwarts school: "Postmeridiano tempore Harrius et Vislii beate vivebant inter se pugna furenti globorum nivalium in campo certantes. Tum frigidi, madentes, anhelantes ad ignem loci communis Gryffindorensis redierunt." J. K. Rowling, *Harrius Potter et Philosophi Lapis*, trans. Peter Needham (New York: Bloomsbury, 1997), 164.

While the *Loci communes* would play a significant role on the stage of the Reformation, it first grew out of Melanchthon's theological teaching responsibilities at Wittenberg. Now that Melanchthon could teach theology, the normal next step toward receiving a doctorate involved teaching Peter Lombard's *Sentences*. This would have made Melanchthon a *Sententiarus*. However, he did not acquire this title—his disgust with the scholastic thinker was too great.[44] He lectured on Romans instead.

Melanchthon taught Paul's letter to the Romans in the summer semester of 1519, and then in both the summer and winter semesters of 1520. He considered Romans to be "the acme of holy writ."[45] He viewed it as the key to the whole Bible. Further, current commentaries on it were wholly inadequate,[46] and no suitable Greek edition of the text was readily available. As a result, Melanchthon produced his own Greek edition of Romans,[47] and began to work out how best to present the theology of this epistle to his students.

From his readings of Agricola on rhetoric and Erasmus's paraphrase of Romans, Melanchthon had become impressed with the *loci* method. This is the idea of collecting a simple outline of common theological topics that one finds in Scripture. Indeed, Melanchthon even wrote a foreword to an edition of Erasmus's paraphrase of Romans, in which he praised the *loci* method.[48] Hence, it was not surprising that Melanchthon wrote to Johannes Heß, confiding that his teaching notes on Romans were growing out of these common theological topics—*loci*.[49]

---

44. Scheible, *Melanchthon*, 34.
45. CR 1:128.
46. MBW 84.
47. CR 1:521. MBW 142.
48. May, 1520. MBW 94a. Foreword to *Textausgabe: Epistola Pauli ad Romanos Erasmo interprete* (Wittenberg: Melchior Lotter, 1520).
49. April 27, 1520. MBW 84.

Meanwhile, as Melanchthon lectured on Romans, his students took copious notes. Soon, they began publishing what they had gleaned—even without his permission.[50] First came the *Theologica Institutio*,[51] which was appended by the *Summa*.[52] Later that year, a more expanded set of notes known as the *Capita* appeared.[53] These three documents represented Melanchthon's developing thoughts as he prepared to write the *Loci*.[54] In them, he both explained Paul's teaching, and contrasted it with that of the philosophers and scholastic theologians. However, Melanchthon was displeased with the deficiencies of these documents and so began working on his own more complete work.

In 1520, Melanchthon produced two further writings based on Paul's letters to the Romans. In the *Declamatiuncula*,[55] Philipp delivered an oration at an academic feast in honor of the apostle Paul. Here he proclaimed Paul superior to all philosophers and theologians because he gave the true understanding of Christ and his benefits, and how believers are to order their lives in response. Melanchthon then

---

50. Definitively dating many of Melanchthon's writings from 1519–22 is a matter of some debate. For more information on this topic, see Bizer's editorial introductions in *Texte aus der Anfangszeit Melanchthons* (Neukirchen-Vluyn: Neukirchener Verlag, 1966). See also Barton and Maurer's articles: P. F. Barton, "Die exegetische Arbeit des jungen Melanchthon 1518/19 bis 1528/29: Probleme und Ansätze," ARG 54 (1963): 52–89. Wilhelm Maurer, "Zur Komposition der Loci Melanchthons von 1521. Ein Beitrag zur Frage Melanchthon und Luther," *Lutherjahrbuch* 25 (1958): 146–80.
51. *Theologica Institutio Philippi Melanchthonis in Epistolam Pauli ad Romanos.* ca. 1519. CR 21:49–60.
52. *Pauli ad Romanos Epistolae Summa.* ca. 1519. CR 21:56–60.
53. *Rerum theologicarum capita seu Loci fere sunt.* ca. 1519–20. The CR editors also place this work under the heading of *Lucubratiuncula Philippi Mel.* CR 21:11–46.
54. For an in-depth analysis of the chronology of these early works, see Rolf Schäfer, "Melanchthon's Interpretation of Romans 5:15: His Departure from the Augustinian Conception of Grace Compared to Luther's," in eds. Timothy J. Wengert and M. Patrick Graham, *Philipp Melanchthon (1497–1560) and the Commentary*, (Sheffield: Sheffield Academic Press, 1997), 88–90. Cf. Graybill, *Evangelical Free Will*, 82–83.
55. *Declamatiuncula in Divi Pauli doctrinam.* January 21, 1520. MSA 1:26–53. First published by Melchior Lotter in Wittenberg in 1520, and then in Augsburg. Melanchthon wrote a foreword for it in February, 1520 (MBW 75).

wrote another introductory work in which he exhorted students to study Paul.[56]

In the spring of 1521, as Luther went off to Worms, Melanchthon was hard at work on the *Loci communes*. He had even begun the process of getting this new book in print.[57] Nevertheless, he kept working on the document well into the summer, even during the challenging days while Luther was in the Wartburg. By August, Spalatin, for one, complained that the *Loci* was appearing much too slowly for his taste.[58] A few weeks later, Melanchthon sent the first part of the document to Spalatin and Luther.[59] On September 9, Luther sent back high praise from the Wartburg.[60] The completed work finally appeared in December—the first of several editions and innumerable printings.

The central themes Melanchthon dealt with in the *Loci communes* were sin, law, and grace. He gave a central place to the atonement of Jesus Christ, justification by faith, and the word of God (as opposed to Aristotle) as the chief source for theological knowledge. Based on the key book in the Bible (Romans), the *Loci communes* gave the central theological themes that students would need to know in their studies of the Bible. It was not so much a commentary or a systematic theology as a list of topics designed to assist the student of Scripture. As such, it provided the central emphases of the emerging evangelical theology.

Upon its publication, the *Loci communes* was immediately influential and widely read. It was assigned reading at Cambridge, and Queen Elizabeth I studied it closely—both for its doctrine and

---

56. *Adhortatio ad Paulinae doctrinae studium* (Wittenberg: Melchior Lotter, 1520). Melanchthon's foreword can be found in MBW 94.
57. MBW 135.
58. MBW 158. WABR 2:373–77, Nr. 425.
59. MBW 162–63.
60. MBW 165.

for its eloquence of language.[61] Erasmus praised it, even if he did not agree with everything in it.[62] It even sold well in Rome—until the authorities realized who had written it and immediately banned it. Spalatin translated the *Loci* into German and added a foreword. Justas Jonas likewise translated later editions. The *Loci* became a standard Lutheran theological textbook for more than a century. Later Lutherans such as Victor Strigel and Martin Chemnitz even wrote commentaries on it. Luther, not to be outdone in lavishing praise, named it worthy of immortality and inclusion in the canon.[63]

Roman Catholic reaction, naturally, was more muted. Eck and Johannes Cochlaeus attacked it with gusto. Cochlaeus called it "a new Koran, a pest, more dangerous than Luther's Babylon." It was "heretical, abominable, and putrid—produced by a Saxon beast in league with Satan."[64] Johann Campanus, writing more than a decade later, claimed that the *Loci* was full of historical inaccuracies, "gathered by an imperious, vanishing lightweight who had written putridly about many things."[65] Melanchthon, however, was determined to give as good as he got.

61. Manscreck, 83. T. W. Baldwin, *William Shakespeare's Small Latine and Lesse Greeke*, 2 vols. (Urbana, IL: University of Illinois, 1944), I, 259.
62. MBW 341. Sept. 6, 1524.
63. CR 10:303, 305, 293–313.
64. Quoted in Manschreck, 88.
65. CR 2:513. Cf. Manschreck, 88.

TAKING A STAND

The Passion of the Christ and the Antichrist

A page from the Passional. Woodcuts by
Lucas Cranach, text by Melanchthon.

Whereas the *Loci* was meant to be constructive for evangelical theology, Melanchthon's *Passional Christi und Antichristi* (1521) was meant to be destructive of Roman Catholic theology. This book contained a series of woodcuts made by Lucas Cranach. Each depicted a scene from the life of Christ on one side, along with a scene from the life of the Pope on the other. The purpose was to present the most dramatic contrast possible, showing how the Pope was violating both the commands and the Spirit of Christ. It was a powerful propaganda tool—and so bold that many thought Luther had authored the text.[66] But it was Melanchthon who had done it. He was no quiet reformer.

---

66. MBW 141 shows, though, that Melanchthon—and not Luther—was the author.

13

Bounding the Fire

1521–1522

Substance and words—Philipp.
Words without substance—Erasmus.
Substance without words—Luther.
Neither substance nor words—Karlstadt.
  —Martin Luther[1]

Within limits, fire is a great servant of humanity. Beyond them, it is a destroyer. Which would it be, then—this flame that Luther had kindled? Would it be the refiner's fire he intended for the purification of western Christianity, or would it become an uncontrolled inferno? While Luther and Melanchthon sought to bring careful biblical boundaries to this new evangelical movement, they soon found themselves contending not just with Roman Catholics, but also with incendiary figures emerging from within the evangelical camp itself.

---

1. *Luther's Works, American Edition*, 54:245, Nr. 3618. WATR 3:460–461:38–40, 1–3, Nr. 3619.

Karlstadt and Zwilling: Zeal for the Bible

Some of the young men in Wittenberg—as in any age—were looking for trouble. In February, 1520 (more than a year before Luther departed for Worms), fighting broke out between Leucorea University students and journeymen studying art at Lucas Cranach's Wittenberg academy.[2] As a result, Luther preached, warning both sides, and the city banned the carrying of weapons. The city council also imposed a 9 p.m. curfew. The upshot of this incident was a classic town-and-gown situation—the art students and citizens of Wittenberg found the Leucorea students with their aristocratic backgrounds to be obnoxious.

The antagonism continued, and a few months later, in mid-July, 1520, more fights broke out. Melanchthon reported on it to Spalatin and downplayed the issue. He advised official restraint.[3] Instead, a police squad led by Hans von Dolzig came and arrested the ringleaders. The civil government sent a clear message that the disturbing of the peace would not be tolerated. But some of the students showed a clear willingness to do just that. It wouldn't take much to egg them on to new exploits in the near future.

With Luther, the key figure of this nascent Reformation, gone at the Wartburg in 1521, what would become of the movement in Wittenberg? Some looked to Melanchthon for leadership. Luther himself, for example, thought Melanchthon should receive a call to preach in Wittenberg.[4] However, he was already over-extended with heavy teaching duties (increased during Luther's absence), writing projects, and growing family responsibilities. Others, however, hastened to the fore. The chair of the theology faculty and head deacon at the Castle Church, Andreas Bodenstein von Karlstadt,

---

2. Scheible, *Melanchthon*, 60.
3. MBW 100. July 14, 1520.
4. WABR 2:387–89, Nr. 429.

raised his voice with enthusiasm. Likewise, at the other end of town, Gabriel Zwilling (1487–1558), the head of the Augustinian chapter, began a vigorous course of evangelical preaching. Far from simply allowing the embers of Luther's movement to smolder, Karlstadt and Zwilling actively fanned the flames. They pushed for increasingly-radical changes.

In June, 1521, Karlstadt proposed an academic disputation on clerical celibacy. He maintained that all priests should marry, and that those already living with concubines *must* marry. Monks and nuns, too, should be allowed to marry. Some found Karlstadt's arguments to be a reasonable exegesis of Scripture. As a result, Jacob Seidler, a pastor in Meissen, got married just a few weeks later,[5] as did another minister in Mansfeld. Bartholomew Bernhard of Feldkirch followed suit at about the same time. Melanchthon, in fact, wrote a defense on Bernhard's behalf. In it, he gave a scriptural justification for clerical marriage. His work was translated into German as *Priests May Take Wives*.[6] It was widely read and likely saved Bernhard from execution.[7] All these newly married ministers, however, did end up in prison.[8] Jacob Seidler—unfortunately under the jurisdiction of Duke Georg—did *not* escape execution.[9]

In the midst of this controversy, Melanchthon and Luther began corresponding about the proper relationship between the civil authorities (the power of the sword) and the gospel.[10] Melanchthon, too, observing that Karlstadt's motives in his preaching agenda might

---

5. CR 1:418–20.
6. See CR 1:421–40. See also MBW 200, where Melanchthon also expresses support for clerical marriage.
7. CR 1:440–2.
8. CR 1:418, 422.
9. CR 1:419–21.
10. E.g., MBW 151. Unfortunately, none of Melanchthon's letters to Luther prior to 1527 have survived. WABR 2:356–61, Nr. 418. See also Bernhard Lohse, *Martin Luther's Theology: Its Systematic Development*, ed. and trans. Roy A. Harrisville (Edinburgh: T & T Clark, 1999), 149.

not be restricted solely to the glory of God, reproved his colleague for envy and pride.[11] But his admonition had little effect.

While the Christian community of faith is often resistant to sudden changes, Karlstadt and Zwilling called for just that. They wanted the immediate implementation of practical reforms implicit in the new evangelical theology. Luther agreed with the changes in principle. On August 1, he promised Melanchthon that "I will never again celebrate a private mass in eternity."[12] However, Luther thought Karlstadt and Zwilling were moving too quickly in implementing their agenda. By autumn, however, their preaching was having an effect.

On September 29, a mass was held in the City Church with communion served in both kinds. This went against a very long tradition of denying the cup to the laity (out of fear that parishioners might blasphemously spill the transubstantiated blood of Christ). This was a major shift in protocol. Melanchthon attended the service and participated in the sacrament.[13] Change was in the air.

A few days later, on October 5, a small group of mendicant monks arrived in Wittenberg. They began getting harassed, with some even throwing rocks and dirt at them. When they tried to preach, people heckled them. When they sought to consecrate holy water, a few hotheads overturned their container.[14] After these incidents, however, the public disorder died down for the next two months.

---

11. MBW 157. WABR 2:370–72.
12. MBW 157. WABR 2:372, Nr. 424.
13. Some sources claim that Melanchthon actually *served* communion at this service. However, judging by the fact that Melanchthon had rejected ordination (for example, when offered it along with a benefice by Duke Ulrich in Württemberg a few years earlier) it is unlikely that he would have officiated. Cf. Scheible, *Melanchthon,* 63.
14. See Scheible, 66; and Mullett, 136.

The Augustinian monastery in Wittenberg. Gabriel Zwilling lived and preached here. Luther also lived here (while not at the Wartburg), and it later became his family home. Photo by Gregory Graybill.

Meanwhile, in October, Zwilling led the Augustinian monks to abolish private masses and serve communion in both kinds. Masses now required the presence of a congregation, preaching, and the availability of both communion bread and wine for all present.[15] Melanchthon, who had already signalled his endorsement of these changes, wrote a letter to the general vicar of the Augustinian Order, Wenzeslaus Linck, in support. Linck was a friend of Luther's, and had been the prior of the Wittenberg chapter until 1516. Melanchthon encouraged him to validate the abolition of private masses and the practice of communion in both kinds.[16] Zwilling, however, did not stop there—he also led the Augustinians to give up their distinctive

---

15. CR 1:456–8, WA 8:398–409. Cf. Scheible, *Melanchthon*, 63.
16. MBW 173.

monastic dress, to renounce begging, and to prepare for even more changes to come.

While Melanchthon (and Luther, from afar) offered cautious support of these things, the Elector Friedrich was not so sure. It was one thing to give a careful reading of Scripture and then say that private masses should not be said. It was something else altogether to say this when it meant overturning a long tradition now tangled into an intricate web of financial endowments. A good percentage of the priests' income, in fact, came from endowments set up in people's last wills and testaments for clergy to say numerous private masses on behalf of the deceased to speed them through purgatory. A sudden theological change undermining this whole system would create a massive administrative headache for the elector. Accordingly, he tried to slow things down. On October 12, he ordered a halt to the changes in the mass and decreed that a committee be established to study the issues—including both private masses and the practice of giving the cup to the laity in communion. The next day, the Augustinians halted the mass. To make up for it, Zwilling preached for two hours straight.

The elector's committee was comprised of key officials and theology professors from the University of Wittenberg: Melanchthon, provost Justas Jonas, Karlstadt, Tilemann Plettener (prorector), Hieronymous Schurff (jurist), Nikolaus von Amsdorf (logic professor and canon), and Johannes Dölsch (dean of the theology faculty). They met immediately, and about a week later, on October 20, they sent their report to the elector.[17] In short, they were in full agreement with the Augustinians. In the minds of too many people, the mass had become a good work thought to merit salvation. The forms had become short and streamlined for efficiency—for "mass" production, if you will[18]—as if sheer numbers

---

17. MBW 174.

mattered. This was, however, a great sin. Therefore, the private mass ought to be abolished, and the cup given to the laity. However, the changes *should* be introduced slowly and only after ample instruction. Also, private masses, if not subject to the above-mentioned abuses, might be permitted as expressions of heartfelt personal piety on the part of the priests. But in the end, the gospel must stand above human rules and institutions. The changes in the mass, though disruptive to existing structures, needed to go forward.

The Elector Friedrich received this report and issued a swift but thoughtful response: please reconsider.[19] The committee should seek further opinions, for the abolition of the private mass would have serious financial consequences and may even lead to civil unrest. This had to be avoided.[20] When the committee received the elector's response, they duly took a reasonable period for further deliberation.

During this time, the evangelical theology continued to make inroads outside of Wittenberg itself. On October 20, 1521, Wolfgang Capito came to visit Wittenberg. He had a long talk with Justas Jonas and Melanchthon about Luther. They also discussed free will, the authority of the pope, and the centrality of the Scriptures. Capito likewise showed himself an able student of Hebrew.[21]

At this time, Zwilling—despite the Elector Friedrich's concerns—ascended the pulpit and passionately exhorted the people to stop participating in the mass. By October 23, most of the Augustinian monks had heeded his advice. About this time, Melanchthon confided to Spalatin that he was concerned about Luther. Adding a mildly apocalyptic tone to these events, Melanchthon reported in this same letter that the plague had cropped up in the area.[22] In an era where sudden death and short lives were

---

18. Pardon the pun.
19. MBW 177.
20. Cf. Scheible, *Melanchthon*, 65.
21. MBW 175.

normal, this reinforced the importance of the spiritual issues at stake. It was more than a month before these reports of the plague began to subside.²³

Next, on October 31, Wittenberg showed itself already prepared to start celebrating the anniversary of Luther's nailing of the *Ninety-Five Theses* to the Castle Church door. Justus Jonas (who lived across the street from the Castle Church) preached, decrying indulgences as rubbish. On the next day, All Saints, Jonas again preached—this time against prayers and private masses for the dead. No matter what the administrative and financial inconveniences, the simple fact of the matter was that donated masses should not be performed for the dead, for it was a blasphemy and danger to the soul to do so.²⁴ Jonas himself pledged never again to say a private mass.

A local prior, though, Konrad Helt, defended the tradition of the private mass. The elector, too, pointed out that because the private masses were endowed expressly for that purpose, that if the priests stopped saying them, then they surely could not keep drawing their stipends with a good conscience.

November saw more changes afoot. On November 12, thirteen monks left the Augustinian cloister. Preaching in the City Church shifted to Georg Mohr, whom Melanchthon considered to be accomplished. Luther, from the Wartburg, penned his *Abuse of the Mass*, in which he called for reforms—though inaugurated gradually.²⁵ Three other tracts Luther had written, however, did *not* appear in print, despite his best efforts. He had sent *On Monastic Vows*, *On the Abolition of Private Masses*, and *Against the Idol of Halle* to Spalatin for publication. Spalatin, however, demurred and just sat on

22. MBW 179.
23. MBW 184.
24. See Scheible, *Melanchthon*, 66.
25. Cf. Mullett, 136.

them. Miffed about this, and eager now to get a feel for events in Wittenberg himself,[26] Luther decided to make a secret visit to town at the start of December.

Luther's Clandestine Visit

Luther arrived in Wittenberg at Nikolaus von Amsdorf's house on the evening of December 3. He appeared dressed as a knight, complete with sword and beard. Melanchthon and a small group of colleagues met him there. As they sat inside discussing the state of affairs in Wittenberg, events outside were moving swiftly forward without them.

That night in the City Church, rocks were thrown during worship, priests were dragged away from the altars, and service books were hacked with knives. The next day, the Franciscan monastery was attacked and vandalized. A revolutionary temper simmered among the people. Hearing the reports of these events, Luther sought to address the situation with a call for calm. He penned *A Sincere Admonition by Martin Luther to All to Guard Against Insurrection and Rebellion*,[27] in which he argued that preaching, prayer, and the proper authorities were the only legitimate avenues for change. Violence and lawlessness were not permitted, and those who broke the peace should be punished by the civil authorities.

Apart from excesses such as the events of December 3–4, however, Luther remained generally pleased with the progress in Wittenberg. On December 5, he encouraged it to continue. Meanwhile, Melanchthon and his theological colleagues shared their correspondence with Luther from the Elector Friedrich, in which he had appointed a special commission to study the issue of changes to the mass, and had then asked them to reconsider once they sent

26. WABR 2:409–11.
27. WA 8:676–86.

him their official report at the end of October. Now, emboldened by Luther to remain steadfast, they sent a new report to the elector on about December 6, essentially repeating their earlier stance.[28]

Luther disguised as the knight "Junker Georg."

Luther sought to hasten the ongoing reforms. He insisted that Spalatin publish his three tracts, and threatened to write worse ones if he refused.[29] Spalatin relented (but nevertheless still withheld *Against the Idol of Halle* simply because he viewed it as unwisely incendiary on a political level). Luther further suggested that the elector sell his vast collection of relics and give the money to the poor. He then left town on December 10 and returned to the Wartburg, where he began the monumental task of translating the New Testament into German.

28. MBW 185–6.
29. WABR 2:409–10, Nr. 443.

Christmas Turmoil

In the minds of Karlstadt and Zwilling, Luther's calls for restraint paled next to his enthusiasm for accelerated reforms. They energetically continued their fiery calls for swift change. Karlstadt urged that begging be outlawed, with assistance for the poor coming instead from a common chest. He made a case that prostitutes should be banned from the city. Regarding church, he began to talk about removing the images of saints from worship spaces. Organs, trumpets, and flutes, moreover, belonged in the theater, and not the church.[30]

From his study of the Gospels, Karlstadt soon hit on a striking new observation. He noticed that Christ and the original twelve disciples had no formal education.[31] Likewise, he reasoned, Christians should follow that example and abandon all higher learning. Zwilling agreed, noting that Jesus said, "Do not call anyone teacher, because you have one teacher."[32] Karlstadt, in his passion for this new simplicity, began asking startled uneducated townsmen to interpret Bible passages for him.[33] More radically, he began telling his students to drop out of the university and to go learn a tradecraft. A large number of students *did* begin to leave the university in response. Karlstadt then began to make a case for dissolving the university altogether.

Melanchthon, who had earlier warned Karlstadt about his motives, now worked strongly to oppose this new rush to attack education itself. Melanchthon regarded Karlstadt's attacks on higher learning as "a new sophistry more foolish and impious than the old."[34]

---

30. Barge *Karlstadt* I, 368–9. See also Bainton, 208.
31. He did not seem to consider the apostle Paul, however, who had an outstanding education at the highest levels.
32. Matthew 23:8.
33. Cf. Manschreck, 76.
34. MBW 248. Trans. Manschreck, 97.

Melanchthon and Amsdorf, working together, managed to halt the momentum for dissolving the university. For Melanchthon, learning and piety went together. It was the lack (or misapplication) of higher learning that had led to errors in the church in the first place. *You shall love the Lord your God with all your mind.*[35]

On the mass, though, Melanchthon and Karlstadt stood in general agreement. The elector was the one dragging his feet here, in deference to vested interests in the church and town. When the committee of the theology faculty appointed by the elector sent their report in early December on changes in the mass, they knew the elector would not like it. But they wrote that if their positions caused offense, then so did Christ. However, though the professors held a strong view, not all the church officials in town supported it. Therefore, Friedrich decided not to make any hasty moves until everyone could come to agreement.

Karlstadt disagreed with that approach. In mid-December, he announced that he would serve communion in both kinds on New Year's Day, 1522. The elector warned against it. No changes would be made to the mass without unanimous support. But Karlstadt decided to go ahead with it anyway—a week earlier, in fact, just to make sure he got it in.

Christmas Eve set the tone of unrest. That Saturday night saw rioting in Wittenberg, including the smashing of lamps in the church, people yelling at priests, the interruption of worship with boisterous drinking songs, and the heckling of priests. But the next day—Christmas Day—would be Karlstadt's moment.

Karlstadt was determined to hold a public, evangelical mass for Christmas, no matter what the elector said. He picked his moment well. Christmas Day fell on a Sunday in 1521, and about two

---

35. Matt. 22:37. Mark 12:30. Luke 10:27.

thousand people (out of a population of around 2,500) showed up for worship at the Castle Church.[36] Karlstadt officiated without vestments, in street clothes. He preached that confession and absolution were not necessary prior to taking the Lord's Supper. Faith alone was required. He consecrated the elements in German rather than Latin, and proceeded to celebrate communion in both kinds—by inviting the people to serve themselves from the altar.

As if this wasn't enough of a stir, the very next day Karlstadt invited Melanchthon, Jonas, and a few other colleagues to ride in a wagon with him south across the Elbe River and then about seven miles further to the village of Seegrehna. Karlstadt led them—bundled in their furs—to the home of a country aristocrat named von Mochau. The professors watched with no small amount of surprise as Karlstadt concluded an official engagement to marry von Mochau's daughter, Anna, age fifteen. The wedding date was officially set for January 19, only about three weeks later.

The little party of professors bumped back into Wittenberg that evening, and early the next morning, Melanchthon penned a letter to Spalatin expressing his unease over the situation in Wittenberg.[37] Meanwhile, that very day, a former Wittenberg student named Thomas Müntzer arrived in town, in the company of three self-proclaimed prophets recently expelled from the city of Zwickau near the border with Bohemia. They were about to make Karlstadt and Zwilling's reform agenda seem downright pedestrian.

---

36. Whereas in the English-speaking world Christmas and Easter are the two most attended worship services in the year, my experience in Germany suggests that Christmas alone is the single most important religious holiday there (at least, today). The sanctuary of the Ruit village church on December 24, 2012, was full to overflowing. But I was surprised to find it nearly empty on Easter morning, 2013, with those few attending wearing clothing more informal than usual (jeans and sweatshirts, for some). This experience makes me think that Karlstadt perhaps chose the most significant and well-attended worship service possible to try out his new evangelical changes—the Christmas *Gottesdienst*.

37. MBW 191.

Karlstadt and Zwilling, however, were by no means finished. On January 6, 1522, Zwilling presided over the disbanding of the Augustinian congregation in Wittenberg. At about this time, the Augustinian monks also held a provincial convention and agreed to stop private masses, cloistral confinement, and anything else that was not really Christian. All were free to leave the monastery, if they so wished.[38]

More dramatically, a few days later Karlstadt and Zwilling, out of zeal to stamp out private masses, led an energized group of young men in destroying the side altars at the convent church. Somebody also had the bright idea of igniting the supply of oil used for extreme unction. Moreover, Zwilling and Karlstadt now spoke (and wrote) with one voice on the dangers of tolerating art of various kinds in the context of worship. They argued that this violated the commandment against making graven images, and that such things created great spiritual dangers of leading people astray from the living God to idols of human creation. God was only to be worshiped in spirit and in truth.[39] Karlstadt and Zwilling therefore made common cause to spearhead an aggressive program of iconoclasm. They led groups that vigorously worked to remove or destroy images—on gravestones, on the outside of churches, and inside the sanctuaries as well. In response, the university faculty and town council sought to reform the mass to head off any further incidents. This now included the use of German, instead of exclusively Latin.[40]

A scant few days later, Karlstadt was off to marry the teenager Anna von Mochau. Shortly after the nuptials, he was again at work, this time encouraging the Wittenberg city council to pursue an ambitious unified set of religious and social reforms. Even Justas

---

38. WABR 2:471–73, 478–79.
39. John 4:24.
40. CR 1:540–41.

Jonas—not otherwise considered overly radical—got into the act by getting engaged himself. On February 9, 1522,[41] he married Katharina Falk.

Seeking Restraint

The fall and winter of 1521–22 saw extraordinary changes in Wittenberg. Priests, monks, and nuns began to get married (even to each other). Monks stopped using the tonsure. Wine was given to the laity in communion. Some priests began celebrating mass in plain clothes, without vestments. German began to replace Latin in the mass. A lively movement began to remove or destroy images. Meat began to be eaten on feast days. Finally, endowments for private masses began to be withdrawn. Was it all biblically justified? Karlstadt and Zwilling certainly thought so. Others were not so sure. Duke Georg (ever hostile to Luther) registered a protest of all these actions at Wittenberg. The imperial diet was meeting at Nuremberg, and Georg convinced the estates to send an official message of concern to the Elector Friedrich and the Bishop of Meissen: "We have heard the priests celebrate mass in lay habit, omitting essential portions. They consecrate the holy sacrament in German. The recipients are not required to have made prior confession. They take the elements into their own hands and of both kinds. The blood of our Lord is served not in a chalice but a mug. The sacrament is given to children. Priests are dragged from the altars by force. Priests and monks marry, and the common people are incited to frivolity and offense."[42]

Elector Friedrich, by all accounts a man of faith, was ever bold to stand for Luther and the evangelical cause when he thought it was right. But Duke Georg's last sentence struck home: "the common people are incited to frivolity and offense." This accusation held a

---

41. Bainton (p. 19) claims the wedding was on February 26.
42. Pallas, ARG V, 238–40. Cf. Bainton, 209.

grain of truth. Restraint was in order. When the Bishop of Meissen asked Friedrich to permit a visitation of the churches in his domains, he agreed—however, he did not promise to make any specific changes. Things did, however, need to settle down.

14

Old Testament Dreams

1522

Beloved, do not believe every spirit, but test the spirits, whether they are of God; because many false prophets have gone out into the world.
—1 John 4:1

The arrival of Thomas Müntzer and the Zwickau prophets on December 27, 1521, did anything but produce a calming effect in Wittenberg. Melanchthon, who went to bed on December 26 pondering the day's cold wagon trip to Seegrehna and Karlstadt's engagement, awoke on the 27th to confront an entirely new situation.

Zwickau, located near the Bohemian border more than a hundred miles south of Wittenberg, had a reputation for religious strife going back half a century. Freshly expelled by the Zwickau city council, Müntzer and the three self-proclaimed prophets were convinced that there was no better destination for them than Wittenberg. Melanchthon, for one, was not so sure about this.

Thomas Müntzer was not new to Wittenberg. He studied at the university there in 1518, where Luther was one of his professors. Luther had even recommended him for the call to preach in Zwickau in 1520. Müntzer assumed the role of town preacher there in August, 1520.[1] He proved himself to be well-spoken from the pulpit—but radical.

Thomas Müntzer (1490–1525).

In Zwickau, Müntzer met a weaver named Nicholas Storch, who claimed to be a genuine prophet with a direct connection with the Holy Spirit. He even claimed to predict the future.[2] The two were broadly in agreement, and when Müntzer was dismissed from his preaching post in April, 1521, it allowed Storch greater latitude in reaching more people with his own proclamations. Marcus Stübner,[3]

1. See OER, "Zwickau prophets."
2. It is difficult to get an accurate assessment of Storch, due to the agenda of vilification of most contemporary and later sources.
3. Sometimes referred to as Marcus Thomae.

another former student from Wittenberg, claimed a similar divine revelation. A blacksmith, Thomas Drechsel, did as well—though not to the same extent as Storch and Stübner. When unrest began to blossom in Zwickau, and with it, pressure from the authorities, it was only natural that Müntzer and Stübner would suggest heading back to their *alma mater*, Wittenberg.

When the Zwickau prophets arrived in town on Tuesday morning, two days after Christmas, they immediately began preaching. With all the reforms happening in town recently through the efforts of Karlstadt and Zwilling, the people were open to change. As Luther had observed in December, a revolutionary spirit was in the air. The Zwickau prophets were adding accelerant to a fire the elector had hoped to keep within bounds.

The most radical teaching of the Zwickau prophets was their claim to receive direct revelation from God and the angel Gabriel apart from Scripture. This was precisely the authority claimed by Old Testament prophets—but was it true that God was now speaking through these fugitives from Zwickau? If so, how could anyone tell? Hearing this new preaching, some immediately went to find local theology professors to help them make sense of it. Amsdorf and Melanchthon were summoned to the scene.

One of the key doctrines advocated by the Zwickau prophets was putting an end to infant baptism. Where was such a practice ever specifically commanded? Furthermore, how was a notion of vicarious faith even possible? They made a sustained case that sounded reasonable to many. They insisted as well that Luther would agree with them.[4]

A second key doctrine took a much more radical form—and in pursuing it, Thomas Müntzer would meet torture and death just

---

4. MBW 203.

three years later. The Zwickau prophets advocated the immediate establishment of God's political kingdom on earth. The ungodly should be slaughtered, either at the hands of the Turks (whom God used to afflict the wicked), or even at their own hands. The current political rulers should soon be overthrown, and Storch himself confidently expected to rule as a sovereign.

Testing the Spirits

Amsdorf and Melanchthon interviewed the Zwickau prophets on the day they appeared in Wittenberg.[5] After their interviews, the two professors sent immediate reports to Spalatin, the elector, and Luther.[6] It was an urgent matter because many people in town were giving these newcomers serious consideration.

Melanchthon confessed to the elector that though the prophets had made an impression on him, he was leery of them, and he suggested consulting Luther: "For there are in them spirits of some sort with many apparent arguments—but of what kind, no one can easily judge apart from Martin. . . . We must be vigilant lest we oppose the Spirit of God, and also lest we be possessed by the Devil."[7] In a separate letter to Spalatin (also written on December 27), Melanchthon warned to take the Zwickau prophets seriously, that Luther should definitely be consulted, and that he himself was somewhat flummoxed by the whole situation.[8]

---

5. Both wrote reports to Spalatin and the elector immediately. Melanchthon certainly did so on this very day. Cf. MBW 192–93, 201–22.
6. We have no extant letter from Melanchthon to Luther on this date to verify this assertion. However, *all* letters from Melanchthon to Luther prior to 1527 have been lost, and it is reasonable to assume that Melanchthon would have written to Luther right away, especially considering his insistence that Luther be consulted. Likewise, Luther's letter in response on January 13, 1522 (MBW 205; WABR 2:424–28, Nr. 450; LW 48:364–72, Nr. 112) shows that he had already received a full report of the events of December 27, 1521.
7. MBW 192.
8. MBW 193.

Four days later, on New Year's Eve, the elector summoned Melanchthon and Amsdorf to come meet with him at the nearby village of Prettin to discuss the situation.[9] There, Melanchthon gave further details on his interviews with the prophets.[10]

He had talked first with Stübner—whom he knew from the young man's relatively recent student days in town. In this interview, Stübner demonstrated an accurate knowledge of Scripture, and at first he had said nothing about visions.[11] In the end, all three of the men answered Melanchthon's questions deftly, leaving him unable to pin them down on an obvious error. Melanchthon then stressed to the elector that the arguments of the Zwickau prophets on infant baptism required a very careful theological response, and that Luther needed to give it. Augustine himself had struggled to teach well on this issue, and so it was not a matter to be taken lightly. Further, Melanchthon was aware that the elector was concerned about growing unrest in Wittenberg. It was indeed worrying that these visitors had left tumult behind them in Zwickau. However, peace should be maintained in this case through spiritual weapons, rather than by force.

The elector, it turned out, still did not wish to risk bringing Luther back to Wittenberg while he remained under the imperial ban. If Luther came, then Friedrich could not guarantee protection for him from the emperor. Moreover, as a layman himself, the elector had no wish to arbitrate theological disputes. Because Melanchthon and Amsdorf were for instruction and against violence, then they were free to instruct, and the Zwickau prophets would be spared arrest for the time being. In fact, Amsdorf would be given an official call to preach in Wittenberg starting on February 14. However, in light of the fallout from the Leipzig Disputation a couple years earlier, the

9. MBW 195.
10. MBW 201–04.
11. MBW 202.

elector ruled out any public academic disputations. The Wittenberg theologians would have to render their judgment on the Zwickau prophets—but out of the public eye, so as not to encourage any more undue tumult.[12]

Finally, even though the elector was just a layman unqualified to assess theological disputes, he did have an opinion. While it was true that God sometimes did extraordinary things through ordinary people, it was clear that these "prophets" were yielding bad fruit. Because of their results, he was convinced that these Zwickau prophets were seducers.[13]

Melanchthon responded by assenting to the Elector Friedrich's wishes. He would refrain from disputing on infant baptism. Besides, he noted, this issue seemed to be chiefly Stübner's concern, and Storch (who dominated the preaching) did not say much about it. Melanchthon expressed understanding for why Luther could not come to Wittenberg and assured the elector that he and his colleagues would do everything in their power to keep the peace in Wittenberg and to dampen the enthusiasms of these new prophets without having to resort to judicial interference.[14] Melanchthon and Amsdorf returned to Wittenberg on January 2, determined to keep a sharp eye on the Zwickau prophets.

Meanwhile, a week and a half later, Luther finally weighed in on the situation from afar:[15]

> Coming now to the prophets. . . . In the first place they bear witness of themselves and are not to be listened to at once, but according to John's advice (1 John 4:1), the spirits must be proved. If you are not able to prove them, you have the advice of Gamaliel to postpone judgment (Acts 5:38). Hitherto I have heard of nothing said or done by

---

12. MBW 203.
13. MBW 203.
14. MBW 204.
15. MBW 205. WABR 2:424–28, Nr. 450. Jan. 13, 1522.

them which Satan could not emulate. Do you, in my place, search out whether they can prove their calling? For God never sent anyone who was not either called by men or attested by miracles, not even his own Son. . . .

But now to discover their private spirit, inquire whether they have experienced those spiritual straitenings [*spirituales illas angustias*], that divine birth and death and infernal torture. If you find that their experiences have been smooth, bland, devout (as they say) and ceremonious, do not approve them even though they say they have been caught up to the third heaven, because they have not the sign of the Son of Man.[16]

It is interesting that Luther's advice on discernment was not to compare what the prophets said and did with Scripture alone, but rather to inquire if they had experienced spiritual sufferings—*Anfechtungen*—like Luther himself had. Nevertheless, Luther goes on in his letter to make a sustained biblical case for the awesomeness and majesty of God (e.g., he is a consuming fire) and that anyone who claims to have direct experience of God should not reflect a blithe breeziness about the whole affair. Luther then went on to begin chewing over the whole issue of infant baptism.

In a separate letter to Spalatin, Luther concurred that he should not yet return to Wittenberg. "I am sure we can restrain these firebrands without the sword. I hope the Prince will not imbrue his hands in their blood. I see no reason why on their account I should come home."[17]

Despite Luther's chastening, Melanchthon was already at work "testing the spirits" by the time his colleague's letter arrived from the Wartburg. He agreed with Friedrich that he did not like the chaos that seemed to follow this trio, but he also did not yet have the clarity to denounce them outright. Too many of their arguments sounded

---

16. MBWT 205:10–18, 23–27. Trans. Manschreck, 79–80.
17. WABR 2:444, Nr. 452. (Jan. 17, 1522). Trans. Bainton, 209.

convincing. So Melanchthon invited Stübner, the most educated of the three Zwickau prophets, into his home. There, he observed him carefully.

"Testing the spirits" with Stübner was challenging, for he knew Scripture well and employed it effectively in his arguments. However, an incident one afternoon convinced Melanchthon that this prophet was not genuine. Stübner, who had always denied purgatory, took a nap. When he awoke, he excitedly asked Melanchthon what he thought of John Chrysostom. Melanchthon replied that he liked him, but thought him too wordy. Stübner then claimed to have just had a vision of Chrysostom suffering in purgatory. Spotting the inconsistency with Stübner's previous position, Melanchthon laughed.[18]

Melanchthon: Boldness and Caution

In navigating the challenging days of Luther's absence, Melanchthon made many bold moves. He also expressed distress, and at times proceeded with such caution that it is common even today for some historians to impugn Melanchthon's character.[19] A careful analysis of Melanchthon's actions in context, however, reveal a talented young proponent of the Reformation, overextended with work, surrounded by impetuous and bellicose older colleagues, seeking the truth of God's will in the midst of a host of competing claims.

On several counts in 1521–22, Melanchthon proved himself a daring partisan for the evangelical theology. The text and illustrations of the *Passional Christi und Antichristi*, for example, were anything but meek. Likewise, the late summer and early fall of 1521 saw much controversy over the mass in Wittenberg. Melanchthon, afraid

---

18. Cam., *Vita*, 51–52.
19. For example, see Michael Rogness, *Philipp Melanchthon: Reformer without Honor* (Minneapolis: Augsburg, 1969). The title says it all.

that people's very salvations were at stake, published sixty-five propositions on the mass.[20] He made a strong case that the mass should be altered so that it might not be perceived as a good work meriting the forgiveness of sins. Christ was not being re-sacrificed on the altar. Justification was by faith and not by the "work" of the mass.

In December, Melanchthon sent a sharp message to Archbishop Albrecht von Mainz regarding relics and indulgences.[21] The archbishop responded, denying that he deserved such a reproach, and claiming that he actually did honor the gospel.[22] Nevertheless, Melanchthon had thrown down the gauntlet to one of the highest officials in the church. Then, in that same month, he led the counter-charge against Karlstadt's anti-education campaign and enthusiasm for dissolving the Leucoria University. Sometime after this, Melanchthon received a letter from Nicholas Gerbel—his friend from his Pforzheim days. Gerbel asserted Melanchthon had become such a polarizing figure himself that Gerbel could get into trouble just for maintaining contact with him.[23]

Early in the New Year, Melanchthon went on to write a position paper on the mass as well as the use of images in worship.[24] There he maintained that thinking of the mass as a sacrifice contradicted the spirit of righteousness, but that the ceremonies could be maintained as *adiaphora* (non-essentials). In that line, communion in both kinds was dispensable. Images of the saints, however, were nothing. Idols were nothing. No location was intrinsically more holy than another, for the Holy Spirit was not bound by time and place. In the end, Melanchthon recommended moderation, but he clearly supported the abolition of images.

---

20. MSA 1:163–7. Melanchthon sent a copy to Spalatin on Nov. 7, 1521. MBW 180.
21. MBW 189. Dec. 11, 1521.
22. MBW 190.
23. MBW 194. Dec. 27, 1521.
24. MBW 206.

In sum, in matters of controversy where Melanchthon was convinced of the correct theological position, he was unflinching in advocating what he believed to be truth. However, sometimes Melanchthon became disheartened and overwhelmed. Luther chastised him at least twice in this regard, and because Melanchthon's critics so often use Luther's words here as jumping off point, it will be helpful to consider them—first on their own, and then in their full context.

In July, 1521, with controversies on clerical celibacy and the mass just starting up, Luther commented to Spalatin, "I see that they do not need me anymore [in Wittenberg], except Philipp; he gives in too easily to his moods, and bears the cross more impatiently than is fitting for a disciple, especially such a great teacher of teachers."[25] Later, in the immediate wake of the arrival of the Zwickau prophets, Luther wrote to Melanchthon, "Coming now to the prophets, let me first say that I do not approve your irresolution [*timiditatem*], especially since you are more richly endowed with the Spirit and with learning than I am."[26] This followed on Melanchthon's refusal of the Wittenberg city council's invitation to take over preaching at the City Church in October, 1521.[27] Some see this, too, as a sign of timidity.

Nevertheless, Justas Jonas had also opposed the invitation for Melanchthon to preach, based on the fact that he was not ordained. Melanchthon agreed with this argument and also felt it important for the elector to take the lead on keeping the peace in Wittenberg. As a compromise on the preaching question, Luther suggested that each week Melanchthon should explain the Sunday Gospel passage in German in the lecture hall.[28] This plan never materialized, but

---

25. July 15, 1521. LW 48:269. WABR 2:364.10–13.
26. Jan. 13, 1522. MBWT 205:10–11. LW 48:364–72, Nr. 112. WABR 2:424–28, Nr. 450.
27. Scheible, *Melanchthon*, 62. Cf. WABR 2:387–89, Nr. 429.
28. Scheible, *Melanchthon*, 62.

Melanchthon did end up doing regular Sunday morning lectures in Latin on the key biblical texts used in worship for those foreign students unable to follow along in German.[29]

Why else might Melanchthon have declined the offer to preach? One must look to other known factors. Perhaps Melanchthon was cautious about the gravity of the situation and did not want to do anything precipitously—he no doubt remembered the vigorous quashing of the Poor Conrad rebellion in Württemberg. He also had sharp memories of the siege of Bretten. Moreover, the imperial ban remained in effect. Nevertheless, people were fired up and ready for action. Melanchthon knew this was a violent world, and he saw others rushing to the fore—each (with the exception of Luther, he thought), tumbling into errors of various kinds. Probably more importantly, Melanchthon did not sense a genuine call to be a preacher. He was a deeply religious man, not prone to be opportunistic. He had already turned down Duke Ulrich of Württemberg's offer of ordination and a benefice.

Returning now to Luther's two remarks, one must keep their context in mind. In July, 1521, a dramatic series of events was still in motion. Luther had been condemned in a papal bull and was under the imperial ban. He was now hidden in the Wartburg, and Karlstadt was spearheading a feverish rate of change in Wittenberg. Melanchthon was twenty-four years old—probably the youngest faculty member at Wittenberg. He was under a great deal of pressure. Likewise, when Melanchthon almost certainly wrote his report to Luther on the Zwickau prophets on December 27, 1521, he had just seen rioting on Christmas Eve, Karlstadt's provocatively evangelical service for two thousand in the Castle Church on Christmas Day, the wagon trip to Seegrehna on December 26 for Karlstadt's engagement

---

29. That is, *plattdeutsch*.

to a fifteen-year-old girl, and then the arrival of Müntzer and the Zwickau prophets promptly the next morning. It was no wonder his head was spinning.

Despite these various considerations, some may still ask, "Why didn't Philipp do more?" Surely, some argue, he could have taken stronger steps to stem the excesses of Karlstadt and Zwilling. Surely he could have more effectively opposed the Zwickau prophets once he became convinced of their falsity. These questions, however, are sheer speculation. All one can do in response is point out further factors of Melanchthon's context in 1521–22 that may well have applied.

Regarding the Zwickau prophets, one must remember that this was an age in which most people believed strongly in spiritual realities. Unlike what is often the case today, professors and students of the Bible kept no ironic and urbane distance between the material they were studying and their own souls. On a popular level, witch burning was not uncommon—Melanchthon himself had witnessed one as a child in the marketplace of Bretten, just outside his front door. If the Holy Spirit therefore decided to move and inspire new prophets for an age in the midst of momentous change—then that prospect would have been taken very seriously. Claims of divine prophetic inspiration would not necessarily have been dismissed out of hand, as they would be in the modern world. Melanchthon's cautious approach was appropriate for his age.

Similarly, much of modern scholarship views the subject of iconoclasm with varying levels of abhorrence. It is often seen as the willfully ignorant destruction of artistic cultural treasures. Karlstadt and Zwilling's endeavors on these counts therefore usually come across as somewhat unhinged to the modern reader. But if one seeks to grapple with a sixteenth-century mindset and the seriousness with which some took these theological issues, then opposition to the use of religious art in worship starts to make more sense. For many in this age, the world of the Bible was as real as their present experiences. Hence, when they heard about the powerful narratives of Exodus, Deuteronomy, Samuel, Kings, Chronicles, Ezra, and the prophets, they could not help but be imbued with an overriding concern to "remove the high places," "cut down the Asherah poles," and live in total obedience to a God jealous for his own glory, who tolerates no false worship of idols. Karlstadt and Zwilling thought to imitate the zeal of Old Testament prophets and the godliest kings of Judah. Melanchthon, as a man of deep personal piety who was willing to take bold steps for the gospel when necessary, was concerned to get the issues right. He wanted to give God all due honor. He also did not want to be led astray by radical spirits. He was all for evangelical change, but where exactly was that fine line between judicious speed and undue haste?

The obvious absence of Luther, too, made the situation in Wittenberg more complex. He was not easily replaced, and the void he left ended up being filled by at least three individuals. Luther's role in Wittenberg was many-sided—he was a professor with a public ministry and a classroom presence. He was a monk of the Augustinian Order, and a public preacher. As much as Luther wanted Melanchthon to step in as his deputy, it was impossible to do so—especially considering Philipp's refusal to preach. Instead, Philipp mostly filled in by assuming much of Luther's theological lecturing load. It was Karlstadt who pushed himself forward to take Luther's more public professorial and preaching roles. Likewise, Zwilling sought to stand in for Luther's intellectual leadership of the Augustinian Order, as well as his influence in preaching. Melanchthon, therefore, could never wield the same influence as Luther in Wittenberg, no matter how highly Martin praised him.

During this tumultuous period in Wittenberg, one must also remember that while Karlstadt, Zwilling, and Luther were all unmarried,[30] Melanchthon was a newlywed with a growing household. His attentions were divided, and it was likely in the crucial month of December, 1521, that Katharina informed her husband that she was pregnant. Their daughter, Anna, would be born on August 24, 1522.

Melanchthon, who always valued friends as well, was getting to know Joachim Camerarius, who moved to Wittenberg in 1521, matriculating in September. Camerarius would become one of Melanchthon's most significant lifelong friends. His crest is painted on the wall of Melanchthon's study in Wittenberg, and Camerarius—who outlived Melanchthon by fourteen years—sought to write the definitive biography of his friend.[31] Space for family and friends was a necessity for Melanchthon.

Besides time with family and friends, Melanchthon was also pursuing a heavy publishing and teaching schedule during 1521–22. The *Loci communes* appeared in its final first edition in December, 1521. In that same month, Melanchthon began to help Luther with his German translation of the New Testament.[32] He also produced a Greek text edition of Arat's *Phaenomena*, which Melanchthon found useful for linguistics, natural history, and astronomy.[33] In addition, he issued a Greek edition of Plutarch's *Sermo convivialis primus*.[34]

---

30. Karlstadt married on January 19, 1522.
31. It is this close friendship that makes Timothy Wengert skeptical of the reliability of Camerarius's biography. See, "'With Friends Like This. . .': The Biography of Philipp Melanchthon by Joachim Camerarius," in *The Rhetorics of Life-Writing in Early Modern Europe: Forms of Biography from Cassandra Fedele to Louis XIV*, eds. Thomas F. Mayer and D. R. Woolf (Ann Arbor: University of Michigan Press, 1995), 115–32.
32. In January, Luther expressed his desire to come back to Wittenberg so that he could be nearer to his collaborators in translation. MBW 205.
33. Wittenberg: Melchior Lotter, 1521. Foreword in MBW 196.
34. Wittenberg: Melchior Lotter, 1521. Foreword in MBW 198.

The crest of Joachim Camerarius, as painted on the wall of Melanchthon's study in Wittenberg. Photo by Gregory Graybill.

When it came to teaching, Melanchthon bore an extra burden in Luther's absence. While he was only paid to teach linguistics in the philosophy department, he was nevertheless very active with theological lecturing. Besides his Sunday morning Latin gospel explanations, he also gave formal lectures on 1 and 2 Corinthians and the Gospel of John (beginning in February, 1522).

To tie this all together then, one may observe that while some have criticized Melanchthon for not taking on a greater leadership role in Luther's absence, one can also see that he was stretched in many directions. With an increased teaching load, ambitious publishing agenda, and a growing family, he was already extremely pressed. Taking on a preaching role would have meant curtailing one of these other areas of his life. Meanwhile, aggressive unmarried senior colleagues were already stepping forward to preach messages with which Melanchthon often agreed. But perhaps he could have been more forceful. Then again, those who tried to be forceful ended up with unbalanced results—e.g., Karlstadt, Zwilling, the Zwickau prophets, and Müntzer (a few years later). One gets the impression that this talented twenty-four-year old suddenly felt slightly out of his depth in Luther's absence during 1521–22. It was certainly a growing experience for him. He had no desire to be the head of a popular movement—his heart was in the lecture hall and the library. Melanchthon would do what he could for the evangelical cause, but it was Luther's role to preach, and the Elector Friedrich's job to keep the peace.

Official Actions

In February, 1522, the Elector Friedrich began taking clear action to stem the disorderly spirit that seemed to be infusing Wittenberg. On February 3, he sent a letter to Melanchthon asking him to tell Zwilling to refrain from preaching any further sedition.[35] On February 5, Melanchthon replied that he had spoken often with Zwilling and Karlstadt, asking them to be more restrained. But like a broken dam, they kept gushing forth, and Melanchthon could not hold back the water. He hoped that they would avoid such errors in the future.[36]

On February 13, the elector decided to employ less private channels in the pursuit of restraint. He summoned the officials of

---

35. MBW 208.
36. MBW 209.

the university, and told them that they had gone too far too fast. He required them to refrain from destroying images; he said that begging would be allowed; and he ordered that the mass be retained in its essentials. Karlstadt, though, would have to stop preaching altogether. Showing that Duke Georg's official complaint had had an effect on him, Friedrich said, "We have gone too fast. The common man has been incited to frivolity, and no one has been edified. We should have consideration for the weak."[37] The committee from the university answered agreeably to the elector's decisions and inquired further about the acceptable details of the mass.[38]

While the elector was satisfied that he had taken reasonable steps to ensure the continued peace of Wittenberg, the city council was not convinced. Melanchthon wanted to speed up the printing of Luther's Advent postils and also issue the German New Testament as soon as possible. These books could broadcast Luther's influence and help calm things down.[39] The city council, though, thought they had a better idea—bringing in Luther himself. Acting apart from the elector, they sent a letter to Luther inviting him to return. When he received it, Luther considered it to be a providential summons from God.[40] He was soon on his way.

Luther's Return

The Wartburg lay about 160 miles southwest of Wittenberg. Luther, upon receiving the city council's invitation, boldly set out on March 1 straight across Duke Georg's territory. He remained disguised as the knight "Junker Georg." Stopping at an inn outside Jena, he even discussed the controversial Martin Luther with two Swiss students.[41]

---

37. MBW 211. Cf. Pallas, ARG, VI, 238–9. (Nos. 3 and 4).
38. MBW 213–15.
39. MBW 218.
40. WABR 2:453–70.

Luther understood that he came at the invitation of the city council, and *not* of the elector. The elector knew that Luther risked grave physical danger by coming. If Luther appeared publicly in Wittenberg, then the elector had no plausible deniability of the knowledge of Martin's whereabouts. Accordingly, Luther faced the danger of extradition orders coming either from the Imperial Diet of Nuremberg, or from the emperor himself. Likewise, though Ulrich von Hutten and Franz von Sickingen had offered Luther some measure of protection, Hutten was currently ill, and von Sickingen was more than occupied at the moment with an assault on Trier. Well aware of these things, but determined to place his safety in the hands of God, Luther wrote Friedrich the day before he entered Wittenberg, saying, "I would have you know that I come to Wittenberg with a higher protection than that of Your Grace."[42] He arrived on March 6, still dressed as a knight, and carrying his sword. The next day he thought better of his overly bold words to the elector, and offered a more conciliatory follow-up missive: "In my absence, Satan has fallen upon my flock and committed ravages which I cannot still by writing, but only in person."[43]

Luther arrived in Wittenberg at the beginning of Lent, and he almost immediately ascended the pulpit to deliver one of his most influential series of sermons from March 9–16, 1522.[44] Over eight days, he stressed patience, love, and consideration for the weak. He condemned violence and rioting. Papal tyranny on the one hand and radicalism on the other were *both* to be rejected. One should not violate the word of God, and no one should abuse their freedom

---

41. For a detailed account of the scene, see Preserved Smith, *The Life and Letters of Martin Luther* (London: John Murray, 1911), 141–43; and E. G. Rupp and Benjamin Drewery, eds., *Martin Luther* (London: Edward Arnold, 1980), 82–86. Cf. Mullett, 139–40.
42. WABR 2:455, Nr. 455. March 5, 1522. Trans. Bainton, 212.
43. WABR 2:460.36–41.
44. These sermons are usually called the *Invocavit Sermons*, based on the first word of the celebration of the mass for the first Sunday in Lent. *Luther's Works*, 51:67–100. WA 10(iii).1–64.

in such a way that others were harmed. Evangelical freedom had to be paired with love and restraint. During this week of sermons, Melanchthon wrote that Luther's main purpose in returning was to correct a false understanding of evangelical freedom in the minds of the Wittenbergers.[45]

The sermons were highly effective, and the formerly charged atmosphere of the town became noticeably calmer. These sermons also reestablished Luther's preeminence in town, at the expense of Karlstadt and Zwilling, each of whom now pursued a different path.

Both Karlstadt and Zwilling left town soon after Luther's arrival. Karlstadt, though, continued in his radicalism, whereas a chastened Zwilling became more moderate. Indeed, even at the height of the unrest, Melanchthon had never expressed as much disapproval for Zwilling as for Karlstadt. Melanchthon even warmly recommended Zwilling for a preaching position to Hektor Pömer in Nuremberg.[46] Luther, too, recommended Zwilling for a preaching post in Altenburg, and when Zwilling departed to take it up, merely warned him to proceed cautiously.[47] Years later, Luther spoke highly of Zwilling as an apt teacher and advocate for the Gospels. He grouped Zwilling together with the eminent Spalatin and Bugenhagen, openly wondering how these men could ever be replaced once they died.[48]

Karlstadt, by contrast, remained unbowed and anything but contrite. In disgust, he left town and took up a pastorate in the nearby village of Orlamünde. Almost a year later—in January, 1523—Melanchthon was still expressing worry that Karlstadt, out

---

45. MBW 220. Interestingly, it was during this week as well that Wolfgang Capito again visited (on March 14). After this visit, he began to incline toward the evangelical cause much more strongly.
46. Feb. 1, 1522. MBW 207.
47. Zwilling would move on to Torgau in 1523.
48. WATR 5:642, Nr. 6399.

of sheer vindictiveness, would yet cause harm for the cause of the gospel.[49] In Orlamünde, Karlstadt adopted the life of a peasant, later disputed with Luther on the Eucharist, and, in time, found himself ordered out of Saxony—a pariah in northern Europe. At one point, he (surprisingly) found refuge in the very home of Martin Luther.

Luther statue (in foreground), with the City Church (Stiftskirche) in the background. Photo taken in Wittenberg, by Gregory Graybill.

---

49. MBW 257.

OLD TESTAMENT DREAMS

The pulpit from which Luther preached (now housed in the Luther House). Photo taken in Wittenberg, by Gregory Graybill.

Turning next to the Zwickau prophets, Luther finally allowed Stübner, Drechsel, Storch, and a convert named Marcus Cellarius[50] the meeting with him that they so desired. These men laid out their views in detail, but Luther rejected them.[51] The prophets departed in anger, leaving little further historical trace after their sojourn in Wittenberg. Thomas Müntzer, however, continued to ponder matters of life, theology, and the kingdom of God. He wrote to Melanchthon on about March 27, 1522, expressing basic agreement with the Wittenberg theology—especially with its anti-Roman emphases and permission for priests to marry. On the mass, however, Luther wrongly protected the weak. A return to full apostolic practice should be made, in spite of the weak.[52] Müntzer's disregard for the weak, though, provided a foreshadowing of his later attempt to institute the kingdom of God through strength. It would not turn out well.

Back in Wittenberg, Luther returned to wearing his Augustinian habit and resumed life in the cloister. He would retain his monastic habit for three years after his excommunication. More substantially, with Luther back in town, some of the changes to the mass were retained, and others were removed for the sake of those "weak" ones who were not quite ready for them. The abolition of private masses and the renunciation of the idea of Christ as sacrificed anew in the mass were the most significant enduring alterations. Regarding indulgences, Luther continued to seek the removal of the relics from the Castle Church. However, some local priests opposed this move vociferously, thus thoroughly irritating Luther. In response, he asked

---

50. *Marcus* Cellarius should be distinguished from *Martin* Cellarius—Melanchthon's former student from Tübingen who had taught at Ingolstadt, and then come to Wittenberg in 1521. Cf. MBW 66.
51. Cam, *Vita*, 51–2. See also a letter from Hieronymus Schurf to Elector Friedrich of March 15, 1522, in Enders 3:306–07, Nr 493.
52. MBW 223.

the elector to remove the relics by force. The elector replied by returning Luther's recent sermons to him—let the gospel alone effect the change, rather than relying on government force.

In regions further south, Johannes Reuchlin died in Stuttgart on June 30, 1522. Melanchthon received confirmation of this news in September via a letter from Brassicanus,[53] who was going to Ingolstadt to take over Reuchlin's chair. It wasn't until October, 1523, though, when Melanchthon would discover that although Reuchlin had promised Philipp his extensive library, he had changed his mind at the end and set up a foundation instead in Pforzheim.[54]

The summer of 1522 arrived in Wittenberg as something of a respite from the recent strife and controversy. Luther was back. The rioting was hopefully now just a memory. Life was moving along in an orderly fashion. Far to the southeast, however, Turkish fleets arrived to assault the Knights Hospitallers in Rhodes. To the west, Henry VIII, in alliance with Charles V, invaded France. In the south, Charles and Francis fought over Italy. In the north, Christian II, despite his Bloodbath, found himself deposed. The fires in Wittenberg were contained for the moment—but elsewhere, they burned with abandon.

---

53. MBW 235.
54. MBW 294.

15

Homecoming

1522–1524

Wir haben hier keine bleibende Stadt, sondern wir suchen die zukünftige.
We have here no lasting city, but we look for the one that is to come.
—Hebrews 13:14[1]

While the unrest in Wittenberg began to subside in the spring of 1522 upon Luther's return, elsewhere events continued to develop rapidly. During Lent in Zurich, Huldrych Zwingli, pastor of the *Grossmünster*, defended a man who ate sausages on a Friday and served them to his workers.[2] Thus began a movement for reform in Switzerland. Melanchthon, though, with the excesses of the recent events in Wittenberg still freshly in mind, proved critical of Zwingli's actions. He wrote that Zwingli erred in that the sausage affair violated

---

1. This was the theme verse for the evangelical church in 2013 while I lived in Bretten. I was fortunate to preach on it as well in the Ruit and Rinklingen congregations of Bretten in that year.
2. *Von Erkiesen und Freiheit der Speisen.* CR 88:88–136.

a *civil* law rather than an ecclesiastical one. Zwingli thereby demonstrated that he did not understand the doctrine of the two kingdoms adequately. Melanchthon acknowledged that he understood Zwingli's thinking, but would avoid the extreme approach.[3] He advised his correspondent, Michael Hummelberg, to avoid such measures in Ravensburg. Hummelberg promptly voiced his agreement[4]—but then a few weeks later wrote again to recommend more of Zwingli's writings.[5] The Swiss Reform movement was already showing a dynamism that would come to rival Wittenberg's.

Huldrych Zwingli (1484–1531).

3. MBW 229, July 16, 1522—to Michael Hummelberg in Ravensburg.
4. MBW 232.
5. MBW 234.

Melanchthon remained concerned, though. Was Zwingli moving too quickly, like Karlstadt and Zwilling had done in Wittenberg? At the end of 1523, Philipp was displeased to hear reports of unrest in Constance, and he worried about Zwingli taking action against images.[6] A couple months later, he wrote to his friend Oecolampadius in Basel, admonishing him to teach the unadulterated gospel, and to be discerning about the growing opposition to images in Zurich.

Tumult Abroad

Meanwhile, the Italian Wars between Habsburg and Valois continued. On April 27, 1522, at the Battle of Bicocca near the strategic city of Milan, the imperial and papal armies inflicted a resounding a defeat on a combined French and Venetian force. The Swiss mercenaries employed by the French were unable to withstand Spanish-Imperial harquebus fire. With this action, Milan, then Genoa—and with it, Lombardy—fell under the control of Charles V, at the expense of Francis I.

About six weeks later, the plague erupted in Rome. It spread steadily, building to a peak of around 150 fatalities per day. With bodies stacked in the streets, tens of thousands of Romans fled—a few bringing plague with them, to infect Florence and other regions. Meanwhile, in that same month of June, 1522, Charles V visited Henry VIII to sign the Treaty of Windsor, pledging a joint invasion of France. The next month, the English army duly attacked Brittany and Picardy from Calais, burning and looting the countryside. This ongoing war with Francis clearly left Charles little time for further initiatives on the Luther question.

During these summer months, Melanchthon's friend from Tübingen, Ambrosius Blarer, made the decision to leave the

---

6. MBW 303.

monastery for evangelical reasons. Facing attack over his choice, he wrote to Melanchthon for advice.[7] Philipp responded with approval over his exit from the monastery and sought to encourage Blarer's conscience. He advised, according to Luther's example, not to discard the monastic habit just yet, so as to avoid offense. Showing concern for the possible fracturing of the evangelical movement, he also sharply rejected the term "Lutheran" for certain fanatics who were going far beyond what Luther would approve. Surely the Wittenberg unrest and the Zwickau prophets were at the forefront of his mind. Finally, Melanchthon reminded Blarer that to confess Christ is to carry the cross.[8]

A few months hence, Ferdinand Magellan's battered ship, the *Vittoria*, limped into harbor in Spain, thus completing the circumnavigation of the world. But while Charles's explorers made spectacular discoveries to the west; in the east, the Ottomans continued their expansion into Europe. After their defeat at Rhodes, Charles V eventually allowed the Knights Hospitallers to reestablish themselves on Malta—but the Ottomans would pursue them there as well.

Closer to home for Melanchthon, the so-called Knights' Revolt—Franz von Sickingen's doomed assault on Trier—got people's attention in Wittenberg. Von Sickingen, seeking to elevate the role of the knight at the cost of the Roman Catholic potentates of the German lands, worked with Ulrich von Hutten (despite his illness) and a number of nobles from the upper Rhineland to gather a sizable army. Appointed commander, he flew the imperial flag—without permission. Von Sickingen led the army in September against the Archbishop of Trier, Richard Greiffenklau von Vollraths. The city of Trier, though, rallied to the archbishop, and when the Landgrave of

---

7. MBW 231.
8. MBW 236.

Hesse Philipp I and Count Palatine Louis V also showed up to help Greiffenklau, von Sickingen was forced to fall back to his stout *Burg* (Castle) Nanstein in Landstuhl.

Franz von Sickingen (1481–1523).

In the second half of October, trouble over the "intercession of the saints" cropped up in Erfurt, about 125 miles southwest from Wittenberg. Luther, Jakob Propst, Johannes Agricola, Wolfgang Stein, and Melanchthon formed a delegation to attempt mediation. Spending time in Weimar and Erfurt, they proved unable to bring resolution to the problem, despite Luther's preaching on faith, works, and the two kingdoms.[9]

On October 22, 1522, von Sickingen was placed under the imperial ban for his actions in Trier. In retaliation, he laid waste to the city of Kaiserslautern.

---

9. WA 10.iii:352–375. Cf. Manschreck, 81. MBW 240 (Melanchthon's report to Spalatin on the affair).

Around New Year's, 1523, Melanchthon began to complain to Camerarius of both public and private misfortunes. The events surrounding von Sickingen were grievous to him. The evangelical cause would not win the day through military intervention. He was convinced that von Sickingen's military initiatives were inflicting great damage on the evangelical reputation.[10]

A few weeks later, with future armed conflict looking like a real possibility, the Elector Friedrich asked Melanchthon for a theological opinion on it. Philipp responded with an analysis of the rights of resistance of Christian princes. In sum, the belligerents need a just cause, and the prince should only go to war with the consent of the people. There should be no war for the sake of the gospel. The kings of the Israelites in the Old Testament had direct commands from God to engage in warfare. But these commands did not apply to Christian rulers today.[11] Turning next to the rights of resistance of Christian subjects, Melanchthon taught that Christians must expect to suffer much, and that it was an open question as to whether a Christian could employ force to defend their neighbor—such actions were properly the prince's duty.[12] A month later, Luther contributed a similar work, *On Civil Authority*.[13] Further unrest in April in Breslau (Wroclaw) garnered Melanchthon's disapproval.[14] In the wake of the recent Wittenberg unrest, and in light of unfolding events in central Europe, the use of military force was proving to be a live issue for Melanchthon and Luther.

At about this time, the Swabian League joined with Louis V and Philipp I to besiege von Sickingen at his Castle Nanstein in late spring, 1523. The use of artillery by the attackers proved decisive,

---

10. MBW 255. Melanchthon further condemned von Sickingen in MBW 256–57.
11. MBW 263.
12. MBW 264.
13. *Von weltlicher Obrigkeit*. WA 11:229–81.
14. MBW 275.

and von Sickingen was killed in the action. When Hutten, who was not with von Sickingen, heard the news, he fled to an island in Lake Zurich, where he, too, died just a few months later in August, at the age of thirty-five. These events turned out to be the last gasp for the influence of knights in central Europe. After von Sickingen, these once powerful figures now faded to memory.

Ulrich von Hutten (1488–1523).

As spring moved into the summer of 1523, the first stirrings of theological controversy surrounding Andreas Osiander (1498–1552) in Nuremberg began to be heard.[15] While Melanchthon remained generally supportive of this self-proclaimed follower of Luther in 1523, later decades would see John Calvin devoting significant space in his *Institutes of the Christian Religion* to contesting with Osiander on the issue of justification and just how one receives the

15. MBW 271, 279.

righteousness of God. In the meantime, July 1, 1523, marked the burning of the first evangelical martyrs in Brussels.

Tiptoeing around Erasmus

While some of the first evangelicals died for their faith in Brussels, Melanchthon began to look south, to Basel, where he feared that the great humanist Erasmus might be starting to develop unfavorable attitudes toward the Wittenberg reformers. The recent publication of a work by Hutten (though listing Melanchthon and Luther on the title page), made critical statements about Erasmus.[16] Both the arguments and their attribution to himself brought Melanchthon distress. He had, after all, just published a tract praising both Luther and Erasmus the previous year.[17]

In July, Melanchthon wrote repeatedly of his disapproval of Hutten's writing.[18] He was convinced that it would harm evangelicals,[19] and he was outraged that his own name appeared on it.[20] Melanchthon disbelieved a report of Hutten's death at first,[21] but remained focused on the key issue of Erasmus's possible alienation. Melanchthon retained a great respect for the famous humanist and still likely considered him a valuable ally for the evangelical cause. In September, he wrote Oecolampadius in Basel, anxious to convey to Erasmus that Wittenberg had nothing to do with Hutten's attack on him.[22] Hummelberg, far to the south in Ravensburg, wrote to Melanchthon at the end of November that his views on Hutten's work and reassurances to Erasmus had indeed found their way to

---

16. *Expostulatio.* Ulrich von Hutten, *Opera quae reperiri potuerunt omnia,* ed. Eduard Böcking, 5 vols. (Leipzig: 1859–1870): 2:180–248.
17. *P. Melanchthonis de Erasmo et Luthero Elogion.* CR 20:699–704.
18. MBW 279, 286–89.
19. MBW 287.
20. MBW 288.
21. MBW 287.
22. MBW 292.

Basel, but that some evangelical scholars were actually disappointed by Melanchthon's stance against Hutten.[23] Perhaps they sensed something that Melanchthon only feared—that Erasmus was inclining more to the Roman Catholic fold than to that of the evangelicals.

Papal Changes

The Roman Catholic fold itself was seeing changes in these years. In December, 1521, Leo X died suddenly of malaria. Hadrian VI, the former tutor of Charles V and an experienced inquisitor, was soon elected to take his place. His high moral reputation and the confidence in which Charles held him were very attractive to the conclave of cardinals. Born in Utrecht, he was the last non-Italian pope elected until John Paul II in the twentieth century. Ascetic and pious, Hadrian VI prioritized slowing the Reformation through reforming the central administration, thus planting the seeds of the Counter Reformation. He sought to purge nonbelievers from the *curia*, to distribute benefices based on merit and spiritual discernment rather than patronage, and to impose economic austerity measures to deal with the large debts left by his more sumptuous predecessor, Leo X. Nevertheless, at the Diet of Nuremberg, his representative insisted that Luther should be punished and the Edict of Worms carried out.[24]

Seeing a humble attitude in the new pope, the Elector Friedrich asked Melanchthon to write him on his behalf. In this letter of January, 1523,[25] the elector stressed that he had been seeking a just resolution to the Luther case for four years, and that he had high

---

23. MBW 297.
24. The Elector Friedrich took this position seriously (along with the emperor's views), and in August, 1523, wrote Melanchthon and a couple other faculty members asking them to talk with Luther to warn him his preaching may be putting him in trouble with the imperial mandate. MBW 284–284a. They reported back that Luther would continue preaching against endowed private masses, but that he would be careful not to incite the people. MBW 285.
25. MBW 261.

hopes of an amicable working relationship with the new pope. Cardinal Cajetan, as Luther's initial interviewer at the Diet of Augsburg in 1518, for example, might be employed as an agent to limit the indulgence controversy. The elector went on to defend his own actions, arguing that he had kept his promises, and that he had only protected Luther because the universities who condemned him (Louvaine and Cologne), did so without scriptural proof. Likewise, even Leo X's papal bull, *Exurge Domine*, did not employ scriptural justifications, and it was abused by Aleander and Eck.[26] The elector closed by stressing his genuine impartiality and love for the Church. He asked that Hadrian keep this case in mind.

Pope Hadrian VI (1459–1523, r. 1522–23).

26. The elector may have excised these criticisms of *Exsurge Domine* from the final draft. Cf. MBW 262.

HOMECOMING

Pope Clement VII (1479–1534, r. 1523–34).

Directly addressing the issue of Luther, however, was not at the top of Hadrian's agenda. Muslim swords and artillery were more pressing. Therefore, in addition to reforming the *curia*, Hadrian VI prioritized uniting Christian Europe to fight these invasions from the East. He was keenly aware of the destruction wrought on Belgrade the year before, the siege of Rhodes, and the danger in which Hungary lay. Hadrian's recognition of the dire situation was not matched by his diplomacy, however. Though striving to be neutral between Charles V and Francis I, he ended up earning the hostility of both. In a series of missteps, his diplomatic efforts to unite Christendom against the Turks came to naught. Finally, in the summer of 1523, he fell sick and died.

In November, after a fifty-day conclave, the cardinals selected Charles V's pick to be the next pope—Giulio de Medici, Leo X's cousin. Raised by his Florentine uncle, Lorenzo the Magnificent, de

Medici took the papal name of Clement VII. According to the *Oxford Dictionary of Popes,* "His election was widely acclaimed, but it soon became evident that, excellent as second-in-command, he lacked the character and capacity for supreme office at a time of crisis."[27]

Pressures at Wittenberg

Back in Wittenberg, the unrest fomented by Karlstadt and the Zwickau prophets had subsided, but friends, family, and publishing kept Melanchthon on the move. In the summer of 1522,[28] his friend Camerarius contracted a serious illness that lingered into the winter,[29] when Joachim's mother also died. In January, 1523, Camerarius was still struggling to cope with these dual challenges.[30] At the same time, Melanchthon worked hard to maintain his epistolary friendship with Oecolampadius (despite a long silence),[31] and sought to support Wenzeslaus Linck by attending his wedding.

Regarding his own marriage, September 20, 1522, was a day of joy for Philipp and Katharina—their daughter Anna was born. Melanchthon's younger sister, also named Anna, now lived in Heilbronn. Luther once called little Anna, "Melanchthon's elegant daughter." The young professor held a lifelong tender affection for his daughter. Melanchthon was often seen holding a book in one hand and rocking the cradle with the other, and he showed distress when reporting an accident in 1524 in which Anna hurt herself.[32]

Of course, Anna's birth brought strains as well as joys. This new arrival meant that Melanchthon had increased needs for both family

---

27. J. N. D. Kelly and M. J. Walsh, eds., *The Oxford Dictionary of Popes* (Oxford: Oxford University Press, 2010), 262.
28. MBW 233.
29. MBW 240, 243.
30. MBW 257.
31. MBW 278.
32. MBW 312.

time and funds. His current pay and workload, however, both militated against it. Moreover, Melanchthon showed some irritation at the possibility of the curtailment of his time for study. In 1523, he (jokingly?) warned Hieronymus Baumgartner against the yoke of marriage.[33] Obviously, the "yoke" still chafed.

In the academic realm, Melanchthon continued publishing at a torrid pace. One of his more significant achievements lay in assisting Luther with his German translation of the Bible. In March, 1522, he reported working with Luther on the project,[34] and he began looking for a map of the Holy Land to include with it.[35] Eventually, he published Jerome's.[36] In May, Melanchthon spoke of the New Testament going to press.[37] In the meantime, he began making detailed inquiries about translation questions revolving around crops and coinage.[38] The New Testament in German finally appeared in September, 1522—hence its famous "September Testament" moniker. By January, 1523, the Pentateuch was ready, though it was costing a great deal of time and effort.[39] Then in late April, when Luther came down with a fever, the publication of the Old Testament had to be delayed.[40] The Bible translation project proceeded steadily, however.

In other biblical studies, Melanchthon had been teaching on Romans and Corinthians for the past couple of years. Luther, impressed with Melanchthon's commentaries, urged his colleague to publish them. Philipp declined on the basis that they were not yet of sufficient quality. Luther, losing patience, stole them and published them anyway, complete with an introduction pinning the blame

---

33. MBW 286.
34. MBW 224.
35. MBW 219.
36. *Hieremiae prophetae Threni* (Wittenberg: Josef Klug, 1524). In the foreword (MBW 252) Melanchthon condemned the idea that the Bible could be studied without auxiliary sciences.
37. MBW 226.
38. MBW 225 (crops), and MBW 226, 226a, 227 (coinage).
39. MBW 257.
40. MBW 276.

entirely on Melanchthon, and threatening to steal and publish more from him. Luther claimed that no one had written better on Paul than Melanchthon.[41] Despite some errors (over which Melanchthon laughed), this book received a wide reading, and, along with the *Loci*, made Melanchthon a famous expositor of the Bible.

Speaking of the *Loci*, Melanchthon periodically returned to this work throughout his career to refine, reshape, and—to some extent—to rewrite it. In the late spring of 1522, however, the changes he made were relatively minor—revisions on the freedom of the will and the freedom of a Christian.[42]

Further theological writings included a tract on the difference between worldly and Christian righteousness,[43] annotations on the Gospels of Matthew[44] and John[45] (again pilfered by Luther[46]), exegesis on Genesis,[47] a foreword for Luther's commentary on Galatians,[48] a foreword for Bugenhagen's commentary on the Psalms,[49] an exhortation for children to study Christ as the model of piety,[50] a Hebrew edition of the book of Jeremiah,[51] and more.[52]

---

41. MBW 230—Luther's preface, dated July 29, 1522. Cf. Manschreck, 92–93. *Annotationes Philippi Melanchthonis in Epistolas Pauli ad Rhomanos et Corinthios* (Nuremberg: Stuchs, 1522). In an interesting side note, Melanchthon told Heß that although he did not discuss the conversion of the Jews in his commentary on Romans 11, he did believe in their inclusion at the end times. March 25, 1522—MBW 222. See also *Annotationes in priorem Epistulam Pauli ad Corinthios* (MSA 4:16–84), and *Annotationes in posteriorem Epistulam Pauli ad Corinthios* (MSA 4.85–132).
42. MBW 227–8. Cf. Graybill, *Evangelical Free Will*, 83–97, 111–13.
43. *Unterschidt zwischen weltlicher und Christlicher Fromkeyt*. MSA 1:171–175. See also *Themata ad sextam feriam discutienda*. MSA 1:163–67.
44. Cf. CR 14:543–1042.
45. *Annotationes in Iohannem* (Nürnberg, 1523). Cf. CR 14:1047–1220. For detailed information on the printings of Melanchthon's lectures on Matthew and John (among others), see appendices 2 and 3 in Timothy Wengert, *Philip Melanchthon's Annotations in Johannem in Relation to Its Predecessors and Contemporaries* (Geneva: Droz, 1987), 255–63.
46. CR 14:1043. Cf. Manschreck, 93.
47. CR 13:761–92. Notes on Exodus 20 can also be found in Suppl. V, 1, 3ff.
48. MBW 283.
49. MBW 299.
50. *Enchiridion elementorum puerilium* (Wittenberg, 1523). Foreword in MBW 298. *Handbüchlein, wie man die Kinder zu der Geschrift und lere halten soll* (Nürnberg, 1524).
51. *Hieremiae prophetae Threni* (Wittenberg: Josef Klug, 1524). Foreword in MBW 309.

In addition to his theological and biblical output, Melanchthon by no means neglected the realm of philosophy and linguistics. He translated Homer,[53] revised a Greek lexicon for Thomas Anshelm,[54] wrote about the necessity of studying the arts,[55] and issued an edition of one of Cicero's commentators.[56] "Prolix" is a barely adequate descriptor for Philipp Melanchthon. We await the new edition of Melanchthon's *Opera Omnia* (underway now in Germany and internationally) to fully sort out the vast thicket that is Philipp's literary residue.

An Unmanageable Teaching Load

Melanchthon's copious writings were matched by an onerous teaching load. When Luther had gone to Worms and then the Wartburg, Melanchthon had picked up much of the slack in offering theology courses at Wittenberg. He did this without giving up his original full-time position as a professor of Greek. Naturally, when Luther returned to Wittenberg, Melanchthon was more than ready to hand all the theological and biblical lecturing back to him. Luther, though, argued that Melanchthon taught so well and to such good effect that it would be a complete waste of his talents to give up lecturing on the Bible and theology. Melanchthon quickly pointed out that he was hired to teach *Greek*. He was not paid to teach theology. By adding those theological lectures, his workload doubled, without any extra pay.[57] Further, this came at a time when

---

52. E.g., *Theologicae Hypotiposes Philip. Melan.* (Basel, 1522), and *Epitome renovatae ecclesiasticae doctrinae ad ill. Prin. Hessorum* (Wittenberg, 1524).
53. MBW 233.
54. MBW 240, 246.
55. *Necessarias esse ad omne studiorum genus artes dicendi* = *[Encomion eloquentiae]* (Hagenau: Johannes Setzer, 1523). MSA 3:43–62. Foreword in MBW 277.
56. Q. Asconius Pedianus, *Fragmentum commentariorum in orationes aliquot M. Tullii Ciceronis* (Hagenau: Johannes Setzer, 1524[?]). Foreword in MBW 313. He also wrote a foreword to *Der Ausgabe der Annalen des [Lambert von Hersfeld]* (Tübingen: Ulrich Mohrart, August, 1525). MBW 304.

his growing family demanded more of his time and more funds to support.

Luther proposed a solution: Melanchthon should give up teaching Greek grammar and instead just teach theology. Philipp had a unique talent for theology. Greek grammar, on the other hand, could be taught just as well by a number of capable young men in Wittenberg. In July, 1522, Luther expressed his frustration on this to Spalatin: "How I wish you would see that Philipp be relieved from grammar, that he may devote himself to theology! It is utterly shameful, as I wrote some time ago, that he should receive one hundred gulden for teaching grammar, when his theological lectures are beyond price. There are plenty of masters who can teach grammar as well as Philipp, who, because of him, are forced to be idle."[58]

Melanchthon, though, was passionate about his Greek studies. He was excited to see the progress of his students—some were already bringing Homer into polished Latin verse. Melanchthon told Spalatin in September, 1522, that he knew Luther wanted to have his Greek duties transferred to someone else. But what *he* (Melanchthon) preferred was to give up teaching theology! He wrote, "I hear that Dr. Martin wants me to commit the Greek teaching to another. This I do not wish to do. I would rather discontinue theology. Hitherto, my work was only a substitute for that of Martin, when he was absent, or otherwise engaged. I see the need of many earnest teachers of the classics, which at present not less than in the age of sophistry are neglected."[59]

Besides, these humanistic and linguistic studies provided prerequisite knowledge for the proper pursuit of theology. Greek and Latin were vital building blocks for the study of theology.[60] To

---

57. Cf. MBW 342.
58. WABR 2:573–74, Nr. 515. Trans. Richard, 109.
59. MBW 237. Trans. Manschreck, 96.
60. MBW 248.

approach ministry without the source languages was like "trying to fly without feathers."[61]

Melanchthon faithfully continued his assigned theological teaching duties, but at every reasonable opportunity, he petitioned for a reduction in his teaching load. On March 12, 1523, he wrote to Spalatin, noting that he had just finished his lectures on John's Gospel the day before. Now, in light of the ample theological faculty available (and his own inadequacy), he asked Spalatin that his teaching load for introductory theology courses be reduced. He suggested that Spalatin, Luther, and Amsdorf could decide together how to proceed.[62] He then repeated this same request two days later.[63]

A year down the road, the issue remained. In March, 1524, Luther now wrote to the Elector Friedrich himself, asking him to direct Melanchthon to lecture on the Bible instead of on Greek, seeing that Philipp had a special gift for it—even more than himself. Besides, a good number of other people were fully competent to teach Greek. Luther concluded by asking the elector to stipulate that Melanchthon's salary should now be for the purpose of teaching theology rather than Greek—and further, that salary definitely ought to be raised in any case.[64]

Melanchthon, for his part, still held back at the thought of giving up Greek, even though it might actually be easier to teach eager theology students than sleepy Greek pupils trying to work their way through drills.[65] But he was glad of Luther's advocacy for a raise for him, and valued his friendship.[66] In the end, the Elector Friedrich

---

61. MBW 252.
62. MBW 268.
63. MBW 270.
64. WABR 3:258–59, Nr. 723.
65. MBW 342.
66. MBW 382.

never took action on Melanchthon's teaching situation. Nothing changed until after Friedrich's death in 1525.

The Need to Reform the University

Indeed, Melanchthon's workload *increased* rather than decreased. After finishing his exegesis of John's Gospel in March, 1523, he then devoted himself to the reform of the arts faculty, serving as the rector of the university, starting on October 18, 1523.[67]

Melanchthon had been pushing for reforms at the university for the past few years. In 1522, he and Amsdorf had collaborated on the idea of assigning a tutor to every student. Despite their energetic advocacy, the idea went nowhere, due to the arrogance of many students, the failure of the city council to forbid undeclared students, and the laziness of the masters—that is, the graduate students who would be responsible for the actual tutoring.[68]

Nevertheless, in early 1523, Melanchthon continued to stress to Spalatin the need for university reforms.[69] In February, he reiterated the need to resurrect humanist studies more thoroughly in Wittenberg. The university was well-attended, and these studies (to which the Holy Spirit gives success), were essential for both theologians and non-theologians. As a not-so-subtle dig, Melanchthon opined that there were now truer Lutherans in Freiburg than in Wittenberg![70]

As the spring of 1523 moved into summer, Melanchthon continued his campaign. He wrote several letters to Spalatin pushing for change and providing specific proposals for university reform based on an agenda that put humanism and theology at the center.

---

67. Scheible, *Melanchthon*, 61. MBW vol. 10, *Itinerar*, p. 311.
68. MBW 249. Cf. MBW 251.
69. MBW 259–60.
70. MBW 265.

Additionally, the university should be broken into colleges[71] to provide better communities of support for the students, along with dedicated preceptors.[72] With all these suggestions, so steadfastly advanced, it is not surprising that Melanchthon soon found himself assuming an administrative role.

Ill Health

But despite his prodigious abilities, Melanchthon proved unable to sustain the steadily increasing loads in the various parts of his life. The stresses of family, writing, teaching, and administration proved to be excessive—especially in these momentous days of the early Reformation. At times, he gave way to pessimism. In November, 1522, he wrote to Spalatin, "Oh, that with pious hearts we might recognize the divine goodness and show our gratitude by better manners! If I mistake not, Christ is about to avenge the contempt of the Gospel by new darkness. He is blinding the minds of those who, under cover of the name of Christ, are now confounding things divine and human, sacred and profane. In a word, I fear that this light, which a little while ago appeared in the world, will be taken from us."[73] Physical illness followed.

Melanchthon had never enjoyed an especially strong constitution, and as a boy at university, his mother had worried about him. Part of the decision to leave Heidelberg had come as a result of his poor health there. Luther now sometimes expressed concern about Melanchthon's wellbeing in Wittenberg. One of his first remarks upon meeting him, after all, had been, "I fear that his delicate constitution may not bear the mode of life in this country."[74]

---

71. This idea would have followed the pattern of Oxford and Cambridge.
72. MBW 272, 279, 282.
73. MBW 247. Trans. Richard. CR 1:547 gives the date as Feb. 6, 1522, but the MBW lists it as Nov. 20, 1522.
74. WABR 1:192.19–20. Nr. 88.

Likewise, he had pushed Philipp to get married partly out of hopes that a wife would provide better care for Melanchthon than he was prone to do for himself. Despite the marriage, though, Melanchthon now complained to Spalatin of heart pains.[75]

Philipp's strenuous workload was taking a toll on his fragile health. Already thin when he arrived in Wittenberg, he grew thinner. He became subject to unrelenting insomnia. Because he only allowed himself a few hours for sleep each night, insomnia left him without many reserves.[76] In January, 1524, he turned down an invitation to write a commentary on Cicero due to overstress and poor health.[77] In February, he continued to complain of an inability to sleep.[78] By the end of March, something needed to give.

In poor health and having trouble meeting his responsibilities, Melanchthon took the initiative on April 4, 1524, of writing to the elector via Spalatin to ask for time off.[79] He felt compelled to take a rest. He asked for a leave of absence as soon as possible, to last for five or six weeks. He wanted to get out of town, and go back to see his home and family, in Bretten. He had been away for six years.

Spalatin wrote back a few days later with the permission for a leave of absence. The elector sent gifts for Melanchthon's mother as well.[80] Luther was supportive of the trip: "Go, brother Philipp, go in God's name. Our Lord did not always preach and teach; sometimes he went aside to visit friends and relatives. I demand only one thing of you: that you come back again. I will include you in my prayers day and night. And now, go!"[81]

---

75. Jan. 24, 1523. MBW 259.
76. Scheible also talks about Melanchthon's insomnia (*Melanchthon*, 74).
77. MBW 308.
78. MBW 312.
79. MBW 316.
80. This letter is not extant, but Melanchthon is clearly responding to such a missive in his April 12, 1524, letter in MBW 317.

HOMECOMING

Melanchthon did just that. On April 12, he thanked Spalatin and the elector for both the leave and the gifts for his mother.[82] On the 16th, he wrote to Hieronymus Baumgartner telling him of his plans—he would go to Bretten, accompanied by Camerarius. Joachim would then journey onward to Basel to see Erasmus (and to emphasize to him that Wittenberg took great offence with Hutten's work and that they had nothing to do with it).[83] Three days later, Melanchthon was on his way. Interestingly, we have no indication about whether or not he took his wife and toddler with him.

A Rest in Bretten

Unlike Luther's disappearance into the Wartburg, Melanchthon's vacation was no clandestine affair. He rode south out of Wittenberg on the morning of Tuesday, April 19, 1524,[84] accompanied by four fellow travelers. Camerarius, age twenty-three, was Melanchthon's primary companion.[85] He planned to travel with Philipp to Bretten, and then ride on to Basel to visit Erasmus. Two younger students—Franz Burchard of Weimar (1503–60), and Johannes Silberborner of Worms (died 1574) would go with him. Burchard later rose to some prominence as vice-chancellor of Saxony. Wilhelm Nesen (b. 1493), though about a decade older than the other students, was also studying at Wittenberg. He had already received a notable humanist education at Basel, Louvain, and Paris, and was a part of Erasmus's circle. Formerly, he held a lucrative position as the head of a Latin school in Frankfurt am Main. But he became convinced by the ideas of the Reformation in 1523 and had given up his position

---

81. This quotation should be taken as provisional. It comes from Manschreck, p. 97—though he provides no original source. Moreover, the MBW provides *no* letters from Luther to Melanchthon in 1523–24.
82. MBW 317.
83. MBW 319.
84. Cf. Scheible, *Melanchthon*, 74–78. See also Camerarius (Strobel, ed.), 88, and CR 11:930.
85. MBW 319.

309

to come to Wittenberg to learn more. Now he was making a trip to Frankfurt to take care of some old business. Showing the transience of life, though, Nesen would not survive the year. But for now, the spring sun shone, and while the five travelers were somewhat awkward horsemen, they made pleasant progress.[86]

On the first day, they covered the forty-five miles to Leipzig. There, Melanchthon and Camerarius arrived just in time to visit the Greek professor Peter Mosellanus on his deathbed.[87] The next day, they attended a mass, and Melanchthon wrote his friend Johannes Heß to ask that he mediate a conflict.[88] While Melanchthon's body had left Wittenberg, his mind was still racing with cares and concerns.

The next morning they departed Leipzig and made it the eighty miles to Weimar by the following day. There the town council asked to meet with Melanchthon. They inquired of him about the proper relationship between the law of Christ and civil laws. Melanchthon also met with Jacob Strauss in Eisenach further down the road to discuss a question about interest payments. This issue hinted at some of the unrest among the peasantry that would soon break out into a broad open armed conflict in the German lands. Strauss did not appreciate what Melanchthon had to say.[89] Clearly, the stresses of Melanchthon's work followed him onto vacation.

On Tuesday, April 26, the small company rode into the city of Fulda, over a hundred miles southwest of Weimar. There, the humanist Johannes Crotus Rubianus and Adam Krafft (later the

---

86. MBW 317.
87. MBW 320. They also visited with Heinrich Stromer von Auerbach. See Allen 5:450.41.
88. MBW 320.
89. MBW 321. Scheible, *Melanchthon*, 74–5. The issue was obviously important, because Luther, too, wrote to Strauß in Eisenach on April 25, 1524. WABR 3:275–78, Nr. 733.

Reformer of Hesse) entertained Melanchthon at an elegant meal.[90] They were able to confirm the death of Hutten.

By Friday, April 29, the party had covered the remaining sixty-five miles to Frankfurt am Main.[91] The next day they visited here with Nesen's friend, the canon, humanist, and former secretary to Wolfgang Capito, Ludwig Carinus (ca. 1496–1569). Carinus was now running the Frankfurt Latin school in Nesen's stead. Indeed, it must have been a lively conversation—two heads of the Latin school in an important city, talking with Melanchthon about the education of children in Latin, Greek, and classical learning. Camerarius, taking it all in, would go on to help (with Melanchthon) found the *gymnasium* model of education when he agreed to head up a new school in Nuremberg in 1526. This model is still largely in use in modern Germany. Thus, it is likely that a conversation on the road to Bretten helped shape the future educations of millions of German citizens.

Nesen stayed on in Frankfurt, and on Sunday, May 1, the rest of the party set out to cover the last eighty-five miles to Bretten. Though they would pass by near Heidelberg, they did not stop there. Perhaps Melanchthon still rued the ill treatment he had received there, and did not wish to revisit the place.

On Tuesday, May 3, after twelve days of travel, Melanchthon, Camerarius, and the two students from Wittenberg finally sighted Bretten. Melanchthon reportedly dismounted, kissed the ground, and said, "O my homeland! How I thank you, Lord, that I may enter it again!"[92]

---

90. Cam, *Vita,* 89–91.
91. Cam., *Vita,* 91.
92. Mühlhaupt, 36. Cf. Manschreck, 98. Mühlhaupt hints that the scene might actually be apocryphal, though. In any case, Melanchthon was surely glad to see his hometown. See also Pauli, 22.

May 3, 1524: Melanchthon sees Bretten again. The painting is located in the Gedächtnishalle of the Melanchthon House, in Bretten. Photo by Gregory Graybill.

Upon entering Bretten, the land and buildings were familiar, but readjusting to family relationships would prove a little more challenging. First off, Philipp's mother was still irritated about his marriage.[93] He had done it on short notice, and he had married a foreigner—a *Landfremde*. (One must remember that the unity of

---

93. Cam., *Vita*, 5. Mühlhaupt, 36.

modern Germany is a recent phenomenon—in Melanchthon's time, Wittenberg was as a foreign country to Bretten, even if people *did* still speak German there.)

Philipp, for his part, had to adjust to the fact that his mother had remarried for the second time soon after his own marriage.[94] He had to learn to deal with a second stepfather. Moreover, this man—Melchior Hechel—was the owner of the Krone guesthouse, across the street from Melanchthon's childhood home. So now Philipp's mother lived with Hechel in the Krone, and his younger brother, Georg, now lived in the old family home. Georg, by the way, also showed an affinity for the Hechel family—he had married Melchior Hechel's daughter, Anna, who now lived across the street in the old Reuter-Schwartzerdt home, rather than *her* childhood home of the Krone! Anna, then, was both Melanchthon's stepsister *and* sister-in-law.[95]

While Melanchthon was left to process these changes, Camerarius, Burchard, and Silberborner said their goodbyes and continued south toward Basel and a visit with Erasmus. Melanchthon, though eager to be at peace with Erasmus, did not, in the end, give Camerarius any letter to take to the great humanist.[96] Instead, he went for a subtler method, writing to Conrad Pellikan in Basel, in which he gave his friendly opinion of Erasmus. He knew that this would get back to Erasmus. Thus he finished his letter in his room at the Krone and gave it to Camerarius to hand deliver.[97] Camerarius also carried a

---

94. Manschreck, p. 98, incorrectly presents the details of Barbara's marriages. Cf. Scheible, *Melanchthon*, 75; and Mühlhaut, 36. Their accounts synchronize with the information in the MBW.
95. So we have an Anna Schwartzerdt, who was Melanchthon's sister; an Anna Schwartzerdt, who was Melanchthon's sister-in-law *and* stepsister, and an Anna Melanchthon, who was his daughter.
96. At least, there is none extant.
97. MBW lists the date of this letter as the beginning of May (with a question mark). However, I think it likely that Melanchthon would have written this letter and given it to his friend to hand deliver in Basel. We have no definitive evidence either way.

peace-making letter from Luther, written the day before the party left Wittenberg, addressed directly to Erasmus in Basel.[98]

The sign for the Hotel Krone in present-day Bretten. Photo by Gregory Graybill.

Once Melanchthon's friend and students left, another family issue needed to be worked out—while Melanchthon adhered to the new (or old, depending on one's perspective) evangelical theology, his mother still clung to the Roman Catholic Church. How would they relate to each other in matters of faith? She was a pious woman—Philipp's upbringing under her was part of the reason he took his own faith so seriously. Melanchthon, however, considered himself a reformer of the church—someone faithfully seeking restoration from within. In the end, neither Philipp nor his mother reproached the other for their approach to the Christian faith.

---

98. April 18(?), 1524. WABR 3:268–71, Nr. 729.

HOMECOMING

After a couple days at home in Bretten, three travelers arrived at the Krone seeking the famous professor from Wittenberg. They likely watered their horses at the fountain in the *Marktplatz* right outside the Krone and took out rooms at the very guesthouse where Melanchthon was staying. Word of his travels had indeed gotten around.

The three travelers turned out to be professors from Heidelberg, and at least one was quite well known to Melanchthon—his friend Simon Grynaeus, who had studied at Pforzheim with him and who had visited Wittenberg just the year before. Now he was a professor of Greek at Heidelberg, and he brought with him the like-minded dean Martin Frecht (1494–1556)—later the Reformer of Ulm—and the older professor of Latin Hermann von dem Busche (1468–1534). They were all committed humanists, intellectual allies of Melanchthon, and friends of the Reformation.

The purpose of this unexpected visit was to present Melanchthon with an expensive silver goblet to honor his academic achievements. Jesus once said, "A prophet is not without honor except in his own country and in his own house."[99] Nevertheless, these dignified outsiders with their costly trophy demonstrated to the townsmen inclined to scoff at the frail boy from Bretten that he was, in fact, the real deal. Philipp duly sent a letter of thanks on the same day.[100] Perhaps warming to Heidelberg once again (or at least to like-minded connections there), Melanchthon would stop in at the university on his return trip to Wittenberg a few weeks hence.

The rest of the weekend remained quiet, but then on about Tuesday, May 10, another traveler turned up at the Krone. This one probably impressed Philipp's pious Catholic mother more than more than the other three—Cardinal Lorenzo Campeggio's private

---

99. Matthew 13:57.
100. MBW 323.

secretary, Friedrich Nausea (1496–1552). Nausea, age twenty-eight, was a highly capable man. He would go on to serve as the bishop of Vienna for more than a decade. Educated under Johannes Cochlaeus, he was opposed to the Lutheran movement, but at the same time, he held a lifelong passion to try to reunite Catholics and evangelicals—and it was for this very purpose that he now sought out Melanchthon in Bretten.

Philipp spoke with Nausea at length, and it soon became clear that Nausea came on a special mission from Cardinal Campeggio, who earnestly wished to rescue Melanchthon from the evangelical camp and safely return him to the Roman Catholic fold. Nausea sought to entice Melanchthon away from Luther, calling him a disturber of the peace, and he promised Melanchthon a place of prominence in the Roman Church should he return.

Following the interview, Melanchthon chose to respond formally in writing. Vacation or not—this had to be dealt with. If he said nothing, the rumors alone of his meeting with a Catholic representative in Bretten could be damaging. So Melanchthon wrote Cardinal Campeggio in Stuttgart[101]—and then published his reply in both German and Latin. In sum, he turned him down. For Luther, he wrote, the problem was not essentially about ceremonies—instead, it was about human and divine righteousness. The observation of traditions did not add anything to this. Melanchthon wanted to keep many traditions for the sake of peace, but the current state of the Roman Catholic mass and the requirements for clerical celibacy were full of destructive errors. Peace would return to the land when the authorities would start providing genuine learned preachers, instead of pursuing the Lutherans:

People are mistaken when they think that Luther simply wants to

---

101. MBW 324.

abolish public traditions. . . . Luther does not fight for external things, he knows something greater, namely, the difference between human righteousness and the righteousness of God. He goes back to the Scriptures in order to know with certainty just how the conscience can be fortified against the gates of hell and to know the real nature of penance. Keeping human rites and traditions do not make one righteous before God, but for the sake of love and peace they may be kept if piety is not shamed. . . . I, too, wish ceremonies to be kept so long as they do not lead any astray. However, in the mass and in celibacy there is too much corruption. . . . It is abominable to think that the essence of religion consists either in despising or in observing ceremonies![102]

Finally, with an eye to Erasmus and the recent publication from Hutten (as well as more radical tracts now surfacing), Melanchthon said that Luther was not to blame for everyone writing or speaking in his name.[103]

Melanchthon stood fast: "When I have ascertained that a thing is true, I embrace and defend it without fear or favor of any mortal and without regard for profit or honor; neither will I separate myself from those who first taught and now defend these things. As hitherto I have defended the pure doctrine without strife and abuse, so shall I continue to exhort all who in this matter of common interest wish for peace and safety, to heal the wounds which can no longer be concealed, and to restrain the rage of those who with hostile hands do not cease to tear open the wounds. If they will not do this, let them look out lest they themselves be the first to fall."[104]

Despite Melanchthon's strongly worded response, the very attempt by the Catholic party to woo Melanchthon showed they thought that he could be won. In future years, fellow evangelicals would sometimes think the same thing—and become suspicious.

---

102. MBW 324. Trans. Manschreck, 99.
103. MBW 324.
104. Cam. *Vita*, 97. Trans. Manschreck, 99.

Melanchthon stayed in Bretten through Pentecost, and only near the end of the month began to make preparations to travel back to Wittenberg. This would be Melanchthon's only true vacation in Bretten—limited just to his hometown—for the remainder of his life.

Melanchthon was happy in Bretten—and so it is a fitting place to say our farewells for the time being. As the limitations of space and time compel our narrative to a close, we shall leave Melanchthon where we first met him—in the familial confines of his beloved hometown. Here he first became convinced of the reality of the risen Lord Jesus Christ. Here he followed the example of his parents' strong faith. Here, perhaps from his grandfather's firm commitment to regular worship attendance, he began to value the church, despite all its problems. He once said, "You are not to act in so brutish and impertinent a manner as to think it does not matter if I do not go to church, for it is nothing but popery and superstition. No, but it is barbarism to neglect these privileges. There is no more beautiful sight than orderly and holy assemblies, in which men are instructed of God, and where they unite in prayer and thanksgiving. We have here a type of eternal life, where we shall sit in the presence of God and his Son, and hear the Son of God instructing us in reference to the greatest wonders."[105]

Here in Bretten, Melanchthon learned that piety and education can go together. He would always value it thus.[106] Then, as his fame grew, he warned of the dangers of the applause of the crowd.[107] God can test one through success, as well as failure. His greatest desire, in the midst of it all, was to see the glory of the gospel of Jesus Christ grow.[108] Nothing was more important than to see God glorified, and

---

105. Quoted in Ledderhose, 333—unfortunately with no original citation.
106. E.g., in MBW 274, and in Melanchthon's strong opposition to Karlstadt's anti-education initiatives in Wittenberg in 1522.
107. MBW 295. Nov. 18, 1523.
108. MBW 290a—August, 1523.

to proclaim the message of salvation—of the forgiveness of sins by God's grace through faith in the crucified and now risen Lord Jesus Christ. Academic trophies paled by comparison.

Grapes in Ruit, Bretten, at Herr und Frau Jaschke's house. Photo by Gregory Graybill.

As I write these words, it is September, 2013. This valley, the Kraichgau, in which Bretten sits, is a temperate land, with rolling green hills. Church bells mark the quarter hours. In these pleasant evenings of golden light and deep blue skies studded with the glimmering contrails of distant jets, I wander among the fields and gardens outside Bretten with my wife, dog, and baby daughter. The border collie cavorts along the path with her ball, and the baby leans from her stroller to grasp purple clover flowers. We pass grapes hanging in thick clusters, corn standing at attention, gourds round and full, tomatoes in their spiral cages, and above all, trees laden—no, bursting—with fruit. Apples, mirabellas, nectarines, plums, and pears crowd their boughs in such a cornucopia that those who live here can never eat it all. And so, fruit falls untasted, returning to the fruitful land from which it sprung.

A year after his time at home in Bretten, Melanchthon himself reflected on these things:[109] "Whenever a weary spirit comes upon me, nothing gives me more refreshment and recovery than the memory of home. I see myself there wandering through the fields and gardens, then going down to the stream. I silently contemplate the riches of nature, and the industry of my farm town people. I admire the wisdom of those who have gone before, who have so diligently established and adorned the fields and the town. If I now rejoice in the grace of the place, so I rest myself still more in the idea of home to which it is bound."

---

109. CR 11:72. Mühlhaupt, 37.

16

Epilogue

> Then I took the little book out of the angel's hand and ate it, and it was as sweet as honey in my mouth. But when I had eaten it, my stomach became bitter.
> —Revelation 10:10

Despite the peace of home, life did not become simpler after 1524. Charles and Francis continued their war over Italy. The Zwickau prophets had left Wittenberg, but Thomas Müntzer took up some of their most radical ideas about trying to institute the kingdom of God by force. The peasants of the land rose up in a massive rebellion—and by the time it was put down, a hundred thousand people lay dead.

Erasmus did not hold his peace with the evangelical camp, despite Luther and Melanchthon's efforts. He attacked Luther on the freedom of the will. When Luther vigorously defended the bondage of the will, the rupture became permanent. Melanchthon, who so respected Erasmus's scholarship, stood on Luther's side in this doctrinal dispute.[1]

---

1. See Graybill, *Evangelical Free Will*, 125–31.

Elector Friedrich the Wise died. Luther married the former nun Katharine von Bora and they lived in the Augustinian monastery at the east end of town.² Casper Cruciger left town, and Nicholas von Amsdorf began to air criticisms of Melanchthon. Philipp himself finally received a raise, and (with the encouragement of Camerarius) also provided key advice to Nuremberg in starting a *gymnasium*—a seminal development that affects German education to this day. The *gymnasium* provided a natural bridge between grammar school and university studies. Camerarius became the first rector.³

In 1525, much of the French nobility was wiped out at the Battle of Pavia.

There, Charles V took Francis I prisoner. Cannons and rifles (or at least, harquebuses) proved key to the victory, and they would thenceforth become standard features of European warfare. At about the same time, Charles unsuccessfully petitioned the Shah of Persia (of the Safavid Dynasty) to attack their Turkish neighbors. The Ottomans, meanwhile, continued their drive through eastern Europe. In Hungary, in 1526, Suleiman's armies struck a massive blow against Christian forces at the battle of Mohács. Twenty-three thousand Christian soldiers were killed in the action. The two thousand taken prisoner were systematically decapitated before the sultan. The sultan then allowed his troops to loot and burn the cities of Buda and Pest. The news of this spread quickly. Even in Wittenberg, Elector John the Constant began construction of a large rampart around the town.

The imperial Diet of Speyer convened at this time, as well. The emperor encouraged all princes to enforce the Edict of Worms. However, he tacitly allowed Lutheran princes to continue with Lutheran practices in their territories. With conquering Muslim

---

2. His marriage is now reenacted in an annual summer festival in Wittenberg: *Luthers Hochzeit*.
3. For further information see the school's current website: www.melanchthon-gymnasium.de.

armies advancing from the east, it made sense to foster a greater degree of Christian unity.

In Saxony, the elector approved systematic visitation and evaluation of the various congregations scattered over the countryside. Melanchthon and Luther took the lead on this, writing the *Visitation Articles*[4] as a baseline against which to measure local theology and ethics.

The year 1527 saw a remarkable breakdown in Christian unity between Charles V and Pope Clement VII. Charles actually attacked Rome itself with his forces and plundered the city. It was the worst sack of Rome in nearly a thousand years. Cardinal Cajetan, who had interviewed Luther at Augsburg, was dragged through the streets and paraded on the shoulders of *landesknechts*. Horses were stabled in the Sistine Chapel. Even the pope was captured, but he was later allowed to escape. To add insult to injury, the plague broke out afresh in the city. European nobles found these developments distasteful, regardless of their opinions on faith.

In matters further afield, Charles honored Hernán Cortés for his conquest of Mexico, and approved Francisco Pizarro's planned annexation of Peru. The work of the conquistadors would soon flood the treasuries of the Habsburgs with gold and silver, creating an oversupply of funds and substantial European inflation.

During these years, evangelical theology advanced in some places, and was suppressed in others. Melanchthon contributed through commentaries on Colossians,[5] as well as the Schwabach[6] and Marburg

---

4. *Articuli de quibus egerunt per Visitatores in regione Saxoniae.* 1527. CR 26.7–28. *Vnterricht der Visitatorn an die Pfarhern ym Kurfurstenthum zu Sachssen.* 1528. CR 26.49–96. MSA 1.215–71. Another, even more recent, scholarly edition can be found in vol. 3 of Hans-Ulrich Delius, ed., *Martin Luther: Studienausgabe* (Berlin: Evangelische Verlagsanstalt, 1979–99), pp. 402–62.
5. *Scholia in Epistolam Pauli ad Colossenses.* MSA 4:209–303. See also Philipp Melanchthon, *Paul's Letter to the Colossians*, trans. D. C. Parker (Sheffield: Almond, 1989).
6. *Articuli XVII Suobacenses. Artickel vom Churchfürst von Sachssen des glawuns halb.* WA 30/3:81–91 (here titled more simply as *Schwabacher Artikel*). CR 26.151–60. WA 30/3.81–91. The Schwabach

Articles.[7] At Marburg, Luther and Melanchthon met with Zwingli and Oecolampadius, agreeing on most areas of doctrine, but differing on the real presence of Christ in the Lord's Supper. In that same year of 1529, the Second Diet of Speyer brought about a formal reinstatement of the Edict of Worms. This elicited protests from the Lutherans, giving birth to the title, "Protestant." At about the same time, the so-called "Peace of the Ladies" finally ended the Italian Wars between the Habsburgs and the Valois in the west, while the Ottoman armies laid siege to Vienna itself.

1530s

The 1530s brought the immensely significant imperial Diet of Augsburg. Melanchthon wrote the *Augsburg Confession*[8] for this gathering, and the Protestant princes were united in supporting it. A finely-crafted piece of theology, this document is still used in the Lutheran Church to this day. Charles, though, called upon the Protestants to recant their errors and accept the Roman Catholic doctrines expressed in the *Confutation of the Augsburg Confession*.[9] He was not willing to use force, however, in light of the continued Ottoman threat. In the following months, Melanchthon responded

---

Articles may also be found in English translation, in trans. William R. Russel, "The Schwabach Articles," in Robert Kolb and James A. Nestingen, eds., *Sources and Contexts of the Book of Concord* (Minneapolis: Fortress Press, 2001), 83–87.

7. *Articuli XV Marpurgenses*. WA 30/3:160–171 (there titled, *Die Marburger Artikel*). CR 26.121–128. For an English translation, see trans. Russell, (in Kolb and Nestingen), 88–92.

8. *Confessio Augustana*. BSLK 33–137 (This has the German and Latin in parallel columns). Another source for the Latin text is CR 26:263–336. In German, the title is *Confessio odder Bekanntnus des Glaubens etlicher Fürsten und Stedte: Uberantwort Keiserlicher Maiestat zu Augspurg*, and it can be found (in addition to BSLK) in CR 26:537–688. In modern English translation, see BoC 27–105 (Tapp. 23–96). See also TRE 4.616–28.

9. The *Responsio Pontifica seu Confutatio Confessionis Augustanae* can be found in CR 27:82–183. To read it in English, see trans. Mark D. Tranvik, "The Confutation of the Augsburg Confession," in *Sources and Contexts of the Book of Concord* ed. Robert Kolb and James A. Nestingen (Minneapolis: Fortress Press, 2001), 106–39. See also Herbert Immenkötter, ed., *Die Confutatio der Confessio Augustana vom 3. August 1530* (Münster: Aschendorff, 1979).

to the *Confutation* with his thoroughgoing *Apology to the Augsburg Confession*.[10] The Protestants, seeing Charles's immovable position and the external geopolitical restraints that solely prevented him from employing force, decided to join their own strength. In March, 1531, they ratified the Schmalkaldic League for mutual self-defense. Elsewhere, Zwingli went so far as to engage in battle. He died in action at Kappel on October 11, 1531.

In 1532, Suleiman, hoping to prove himself an Islamic Alexander the Great, led another Ottoman invasion of Europe. He had his eye on Vienna and beyond. In light of this threat, the Protestants and Catholics concluded a formal peace accord. Francis, though, seeing an opportunity to harm his Habsburg nemesis, made his own pact—with the Turks. The Ottoman forces ravaged lower Austria, but Charles did not rise to the provocation, and refused to sally forth from the relative safety south of the Alps. Suleiman was disappointed not to have the climactic battle between Islam and Christianity that he was sure would prove the superiority of his own faith. Now overextended, he withdrew his armies and began to turn his attention to the far eastern frontier of his empire, where the Shi'ite threat of Persia loomed.

In Wittenberg, Justas Jonas was now rector of the university. Melanchthon continued teaching and writing, producing such books a *Summary of Ethics*[11] and a *Commentary on Romans*.[12] In 1533–35, he issued an updated version of his *Loci communes*.[13] Here he began

---

10. While the *Apologiae confessionis Augustanae* can be found in CR 27 and 28, the newer edition in BSLK 139–404 is better. This source prints the Latin and German texts in parallel columns. See Christian Peters's *Apologia Confessionis Augustanae: Untersuchungen zur Textgeschichte einer lutherischen Bekenntnisschrift (1530–1584)* (Stuttgart: Calwer Verlag, 1997).
11. *Epitome ethices,* in ed. Heineck. This work can be found translated into English in Keen, 203–38.
12. *Commentarii in Epistolam Pauli ad Romanos.* MSA 5:25–371.
13. Melanchthon lectured on the *Loci communes* in 1533, and students copied down his lectures and published them. These notes can be found in CR 21:253–332, and in most cases are nearly

to demonstrate shifting thoughts on both the freedom of the will and the Lord's Supper. His fame continued to increase and within a year, he received invitations from not only his former university at Tübingen, but also from the Kings of France and England. He declined all these invitations, and the University of Tübingen would eventually enlist Brenz in 1537 to reform the university and oversee the reformation of the Württemberg churches.

In the summer of 1533, plague struck Constantinople, killing around fifty thousand people. In the Mediterranean, Barbarossa expanded a Muslim pirate port from Algiers to Tunis, thereby creating an Islamic harbor less than a hundred miles from Sicily. This made European leaders nervous, but as Suleiman launched an invasion of Persia, western leaders became more absorbed by the actions of King Henry VIII of England and his rupture from the Roman Catholic Church. Charles V, though, would not be distracted. He saw Suleiman's absence from eastern Europe as the perfect moment for a counter-offensive. Launching a last crusade, Charles advanced by land to shore up the defense of Vienna, while simultaneously engaging Muslim naval elements in the eastern Mediterranean. Charles's naval expedition, led by Andrea Doria, resulted in the successful capture of Tunis, along with eighty-four pirate ships—although Barbarossa himself escaped.

All these military activities prevented Charles from paying much attention to the Lutheran lands in northern Germany. In this, the Wittenberg theologians enjoyed a providential respite. During this time, Luther's complete German translation of the Bible appeared in 1534, with Melanchthon's close collaboration. This was also the year that Paul III became pope, and Ignatius Loyola founded the Jesuits.

---

identical to the 1535 edition of the *Loci* that Melanchthon himself published, which can be found in CR 21:347–558.

EPILOGUE

In this moment of transition and relative calm, Melanchthon seized the opportunity to meet with Bucer at Cassel in December, 1534, to discuss union between the Lutheran and Reformed camps on an understanding of the Lord's Supper. Success could unite great numbers of German-speaking churches—serving both an ecumenical good and geopolitical expediency. A union would strengthen the Protestant political position in relation to Charles and the Holy Roman Empire. These initial discussions bore fruit in 1536 with the Wittenberg Concord. Bucer and Capito came to Wittenberg and found agreement with Luther and Melanchthon on the Lord's Supper. It did not prove lasting, but for the time being, it was an encouragement to everyone involved.

Also in 1536, Elector John the Constant built a new house for Melanchthon—it is the house that still stands on the site in Wittenberg today. The university shared in the costs, and the physician Augustine Schurff oversaw the work, along with Melanchthon's brother-in-law, Hieronymus Krapp. The new house provided a gracious accommodation for Melanchthon's large family and frequent visitors. Final work on the home was completed in 1539.[14]

Meanwhile, word had finally emerged of Francis's alliance with Suleiman, which caused great scandal throughout Europe. Charles V engaged in a fresh war with Francis, invading Provence in 1536. Henry VIII proved an erstwhile ally for the Holy Roman Empire against Francis, for the emperor was deeply offended by Henry's divorce of Charles's aunt, Catherine of Aragon. With these many political distractions, Charles petitioned Pope Paul III to call a general council to deal with the Protestant problem.

The year 1536 brought the death of Erasmus, as well as a new theological controversy for Melanchthon. Conrad Cordatus deeply

---

14. More recent renovations were underway as of 2013.

disapproved of Melanchthon's evolving teachings on justification and the freedom of the will.[15] Melanchthon's new evangelical doctrine of free will drew repeated attention from various theologians over the following decades.

A few years later, in 1539, Melanchthon provided key input in reorganizing the nearby Leipzig University. At the same time, a more thoroughgoing reformation was evidenced in Wittenberg with the establishment of a consistory comprised of theologians and jurists from the university. However, all that was overshadowed by the scandal of the bigamy of Philipp of Hesse. Melanchthon and Luther initially cited examples of polygamy from the Old Testament in support of their ally, but Catholic partisans mocked the Protestants for this incident.

1540s

Adding to Melanchthon's stress, he became grievously ill in Weimar on the way to a colloquy in Hagenau. Luther came and prayed at his friend's bedside. Philipp anticipated death but recovered. In the same year, he revised the *Augsburg Confession* (known as the *Variata*[16]), and also wrote a new commentary on Romans.[17] Karlstadt died at about this time.

The year 1541 marked perhaps the last great push for concord between the Protestant and Catholic parties. Melanchthon and Cardinal Gasparo Contarini were key players in the talks at the Diet of Regensburg (or Ratisbon). Though both sides strained to find common ground, the resulting language meant different things

---

15. See Graybill, *Evangelical Free Will*, 224–7.
16. CR 26:350ff.
17. *Commentarii in Epistolam Pauli ad Romanos*, 1540. CR 15:495–796. For an English translation, see *Commentary on Romans*, trans. Fred Kramer (St. Louis: Concordia, 1992).

to different players, and ultimately, both Catholics and Protestants rejected the so-called Regensburg Book.

Further east, the Turks officially annexed Hungary, while Charles and Francis went to war with each other one last time. Imperial diets followed in quick succession at Speyer and Nuremberg. After Charles managed to invade France itself from Lorraine, Charles and Francis finally ended hostilities once and for all at the Peace of Crépy in 1544. Francis I died three years later.

During these years, Melanchthon continued to be productive. He wrote a new textbook on rhetoric[18] and issued an updated edition of his *Loci communes*.[19] Archbishop Hermann of Cologne invited him to come to Bonn to help reform the church in the region. The Elector of Saxony agreed, and so Melanchthon departed to western German lands for several months. Philipp wrote a *Consultation*, describing the Lord's Supper in practical terms that did not please Luther and Amsdorf back in Wittenberg. Luther was opposed to what the "babbler" Bucer was teaching and disapproved of Melanchthon's words on the will and the Lord's Supper. Melanchthon was grieved by this tension with Luther, but their relationship ultimately endured. Luther continued to attack the views of Zwingli and Oecolampadius (both now long since dead), but affirmed unity with Melanchthon.

In 1545, Martin Chemnitz came to study in Wittenberg. He would go on to be one of the most influential Lutheran theologians of his generation. He sat at the feet of both Luther and Melanchthon. In that same year, Spalatin died. Further south, the Council of Trent began—in which the Roman Catholic Church would formalize its

---

18. *Elementorum rhetorices libri duo*. CR 13:413–506. The text can also be found both in the original Latin, and in parallel English translation, in Sister Mary Joan La Fontaine's useful unpublished dissertation, *A Critical Translation of Philipp Melanchthon's 'Elementorum Rhetorices Libri Duo.' (Latin Text)* (Ann Arbor: University of Michigan, 1968).
19. The original Latin text for the *Loci communes* of 1543 may be found in CR 21:601–1106. The Latin text of the *Loci* of 1559, found in MSA 2/1–2/2, is identical with that of 1543 except for minor variations in punctuation, spelling, and capitalization.

distinctive teachings on justification, and cement the rupture with the Protestants.

A year later, in 1546, Martin Luther died. Melanchthon gave the eulogy, comparing Luther to Isaiah, John the Baptist, Paul, and Augustine.[20] At this time, job offers flooded in to Melanchthon from all sides. In the end, though, he decided to stay in Wittenberg.

Politically, with a chastened papacy, the death of Francis I, and the preoccupation of the Ottomans with Persia, Charles V finally had an opportunity to turn his full attention to the Protestant princes in the northern German lands. Charles placed John Friedrich (the Duke of Saxony) and Philipp Landgrave of Hesse under the imperial ban. Philipp of Hesse went to Bavaria and attacked Charles as he was still gathering his forces, and the Saxon Duke Maurice conquered Zwickau. The Schmalkaldic War was underway. In Wittenberg, the spire of the City Church itself was melted down to make cannons.[21] The university was closed, and Melanchthon fled with his family to Zerbst. In the end, although Charles could not change the religious convictions of the Protestants, he was able to defeat them militarily in the decisive battle of Mühlberg. John Friedrich and Philipp of Hesse were taken captive and displayed outside the walls of the besieged city of Wittenberg. Although the city surrendered, John Friedrich continued to be a prisoner until 1552.

An imperial diet followed in 1548 in Augsburg, resulting in the Augsburg Interim. Charles asked the Lutherans to remain within the Catholic Church pending its reform (as seen to be underway through the Council of Trent). The doctrinal agreement sought the temporary unity of Catholics and Protestants. Many Protestants refused to abide by it, and so a new document, the Leipzig Interim, was promulgated later in 1548. Melanchthon sought to preserve

---

20. CR 11:726–34. English trans. in Richard, pp. 381–392.
21. Scheible, *Melanchthon*, 28.

what Protestant distinctives he could in the light of the Catholic political dominance. Some thought, though, that he conceded too much, theologically. The question then arose—what is essential to the Christian faith, and what is nonessential (or *adiaphora*)? Upon what must we insist, and where can we find the freedom to disagree? This has always been a live issue in Christianity, and 1548 was no different. Unfortunately, two parties within the Lutheran camp emerged—Gnesio-Lutherans ("real" Lutherans) who felt that Melanchthon had conceded too much in discussions with Catholic authorities, and Philippists, who thought that Melanchthon was correct. Matthias Flacius Illyricus proved to be an especially formidable adversary. The Adiaphoristic Controversy did not abate for at least four years.

1550s

In 1550, the Englishman Reginald Pole missed becoming pope by a single vote. It fell instead to the Italian Julius III—who had nearly been executed by Charles's forces during the sack of Rome twenty-three years earlier. He reconvened the Council of Trent upon his accession, and Melanchthon wrote *The Saxon Confession*[22] in hopes of influencing the proceedings. However, Julius III had to suspend the council again within a few months as Moritz of Saxony made bold to try to resurrect a league of Protestant princes to challenge Charles V once more. The Council of Trent would not convene again until 1562.

Closer to Melanchthon's home region, Brenz's *Württemberg Confession* of 1551 became the official confession of the Württemberg church—which included the town of Tübingen. But even further

---

22. Philipp Melanchthon, *Confessio Doctrinae Saxonicarum Ecclesiarum scripta Anno Domini MDLI ut Synodo Tridentinae exhiberetur*, MSA 6:80–167.

south in Geneva, sad events unfolded as John Calvin finally saw fit to disavow Melanchthon's innovations on the freedom of the will.

In 1551, controversy over the doctrine of predestination arose in Geneva, and John Calvin found himself having to defend his position over and against Melanchthon's, especially as articulated in the *Loci communes* of 1543. During the Bolsec controversy, Melanchthon's formulation of predestination from this document was used in opposition to Calvin's doctrine of predestination.[23] Word of this dispute found its way back to Melanchthon,[24] and Calvin prepared to defend himself.

In 1552, Calvin publicly distanced himself from Melanchthon on the doctrine of predestination.[25] He wrote a book titled, *On the Eternal Predestination of God*.[26] This book acted as both a completion of his reply to Pighius and also as a refutation of Bolsec. It distinguished Calvin's position from Melanchthon's, though it did not mention him by name. Calvin wrote to Melanchthon on November 28, 1552, to confirm this development. He began the letter by reiterating his friendship with Melanchthon. Calvin then went on gently to separate himself from Melanchthon on the doctrines of free will and predestination, and he referred him to *De aeterna praedestinatione Dei*.[27] However much Calvin respected Melanchthon and desired evangelical unity, he simply could not

---

23. For a detailed account of the Bolsec controversy, see P. Holtrop, *The Bolsec Controversy on Predestination from 1551 to 1555* (Lewiston, NY: Edwin Mellen, 1993). See also *Actes du Procès; Intenté par Calvin et les autres ministres de Genève a Jérome Bolsec de Paris*. 1551. CO 8:141–248.
24. Rumors of this controversy reached Melanchthon in 1552 as evidenced by two of his letters: Melanchthon (in Nuremberg), letter to Joachim Camerarius (in Leipzig), February 1, 1552. MBW 6322. CR 7:930–31, Nr. 5038. Melanchthon (in Nuremberg), letter to Caspar Peucer (en route to Wittenberg), February 1, 1552. MBW 6324. CR 7:931–32, Nr. 5040.
25. MacCulloch, *The Reformation*, 341.
26. *De aeterna Dei praedestinatione, qua in salutem alios ex hominibus elegit, alios suo exitio reliquit: item de providentia qua res humanas gubernat, consensus pastorum Genevensis ecclesiae, a Io. Calvino expositus*. CO 8.249–366. This work can be found in a modern English translation in John Calvin, *Concerning the Eternal Predestination of God*, trans. J. K. S. Reid (Louisville, KY: Westminster John Knox, 1961).

go along with Melanchthon's new doctrine of free will and predestination.[28]

In 1552, John Friedrich was finally released from captivity. He was joyfully met by his family on September 21 in Thuringia, at Saalfeld. In the Treaty of Passau of that same year, Moritz of Saxony negotiated a truce with Ferdinand and Maximilian, who represented Habsburg power. With renewed Ottoman threats, the Christian principalities began to gravitate toward the idea of confessional territorialism—which was eventually codified in the Peace of Augsburg in 1555 with its famous cachphrase, *cuius regio, eius religio* ("whoever's region—his religion"). In the near east, the Ottomans and the Safavids of Persia concluded their own treaty.

Back in Wittenberg, Melanchthon wrote *The Examination of Ordinands*[29] as a tool for discerning readiness for ministry among those called to the pastorate. Controversy continued over the exact nature of the Lord's Supper. At the city church, Johannes Bugenhagen continued to pastor, now at the age of seventy-two. Chemnitz moved back to Wittenberg as a guest of Melanchthon and joined the university faculty the following year. The Elector Moritz of Saxony died, and his successor, Elector August, transformed Luther's house into student housing, and improved the Leucorea University buildings. Melanchthon also wrote a philosophical work on the soul (*De anima*), and issued another update on his *Loci communes*.[30] Chemnitz began his university duties by lecturing on this

---

27. Cf. *Institutes* III.xxi.3, where Calvin criticized those who would "bury predestination," though without naming Melanchthon. Over the next few years, Calvin and Melanchthon would stay in contact, but apart from some gentle prodding on the part of Calvin in one letter in 1555, the two would not speak on the topic of free will and predestination again. The letter from 1555: Calvin (in Geneva), letter to Melanchthon (in Wittenberg), March 5, 1555. MBW 7:7424. CO 15:488–89, Nr. 2139.
28. The above paragraphs originally appeared in Graybill, *Evangelical Free Will*, 268–69.
29. *Examen eorum qui audiuntur ante ante ritum publicae ordinationis, qua commendatur eis ministerium evangelii*, and it can be found in CR 23:1–88.

very work, showing its celebrated status even during Melanchthon's own lifetime.

The following year, Melanchthon's house was updated to receive connection to the Wittenberg city water system. It still provides water in the garden today. The tranquility of the garden was beguiling, but outside its walls, controversies continued. Nikolaus Gallus took umbrage at Melanchthon's views of the will.[31] Nikolaus von Amsdorf also remained critical, even urging separation from Melanchthon. Philipp, however, continued his work, participating in 1557 on discussions at Worms and in Heidelberg on the reform of the university. But it was in this year that Philipp's wife, Katharina, died. Though he had entered his marriage with Katharina in an ungracious spirit, genuine love and affection had indeed sprung up between them over the years, and he mourned her passing.

In the following year, 1558, Charles V died of malarial fevers. Pius IV became pope a year later. During this time, Melanchthon remained theologically active, writing a *Response to the Bavarian Articles*[32] in which he defended evangelical doctrine against the charges of the Bavarian inquisition. Nevertheless, theological attacks on Melanchthon continued from both Catholics and various evangelicals.

1560

In early April, 1560, Philipp Schwartzerdt took a long carriage ride during unusually cold weather. When he arrived home, he soon fell

---

30. *Melanchthon on Christian Doctrine: Loci Communes, 1555,* trans. Clyde L. Manschreck (New York: Oxford University Press, 1965). *Heubtartikel Christlicher Lere: Melanchthons deutsche Fassung seiner Loci Theologici, nach dem Autograph und dem Originaldruck von 1553,* ed. Ralf Jennett and Johannes Schilling (Leipzig: Evangelische Verlagsanstalt, 2002).
31. See Graybill, *Evangelical Free Will,* 293–96.
32. *Responsiones Scriptae a Philippo Melanthone ad impios articulos Bavaricae inquisitionis.* 1558. MSA 6:285–364.

ill. By April 8, he was feverish. His eyes were sunken. Philipp's friends were concerned. He improved for a few days, but then pains returned in his side. On April 18, he called his grandchildren to his bedside and blessed them. On April 19, Philipp continued to weaken. He prayed aloud. His friends read Scripture to him. His prayers became silent, only his lips moving.

Philipp Melanchthon died at 7:00 p.m., on April 19, 1560, at the age of sixty-three.

While Melanchthon was no longer in a position to debate theology, this did not stop his critics from pronouncing a last word upon him. The chief of these was John Calvin, who now dropped his former restraint in order to serve the greater purpose of the public defense of the gospel, as he saw it. From the pulpit he condemned Melanchthon for his position on free will and predestination, calling him "evil-disposed," a "rustic," a practitioner of "villainous slander" (for equating a strong view of the determination of God with Stoicism), a "clown [who] babbles of free will," a man in error, a "troublecoast," "vile dog," "villain," and "troubler."[33] Melanchthon's final formulation of his doctrine of the will in justification was intolerable for Calvin.

For Melanchthon, the sweetness of the gospel message was accompanied by the bitterness of strife, division, and violence. Near the end of his life, he complained of the rage of theologians, though holding still to faith. In 1527, already weary, he noted, "Homer says that man tires of everything, except of war."[34] We are learning

---

33. John Calvin, "An Answer to certain slanders and blasphemies, wherewith certain evil disposed persons have gone about to bring the doctrine of God's everlasting Predestination into hatred," in *Sermons on Election and Reprobation*, ed. Ernie Springer, trans. Iohn Fielde (Audubon, NJ: Old Paths Publications, 1996), 305–17. The original text of this sermon may be found in John Calvin, *Traité de la prédestination éternelle de Dieu, par laquelle les uns sont éleuz à salut, les autres laissez en leur condemnation* (Geneva: 1560). This work was also republished in Geneva in 1562 as *Treze sermons traitans de l'élection gratuite de Dieu en Iacob, et de la réiection en Esau*.
34. Homer, *Iliad* 13:634.

by experience that this is only too true in the church. Repeatedly, and without good cause, new battles, new tumults are aroused by ambitious people. Nor is there any hope of peace, unless Christ restore it for us. Hence we should all in our prayers beseech him to cure the manifold evils of our times."[35] In 1554, he wrote, "The greatest part of humanity rages against the word of God, to their own destruction. Many are the Epicureans who are openly disdainful of God. Many are the worshipers of idols who are spellbound by demons, who, with monstrous madness contend against the Gospel. Many others are polluted by their evil desires and deeds. Despite such confusion in the human race, God nevertheless has begun saving those whom he himself truly honors by achieving their righteousness and salvation."[36]

The Melanchthon statue in Wittenberg (the City Church is in the background). Inscribed on the base are the words, Der Lehrer Deutschlands—the Teacher of Germany. Photo by Gregory Graybill.

---

35. MSA 4:210. Trans. D. C. Parker, in *Paul's Letter to the Colossians* (Sheffield: Almond, 1989), 27.
36. CR 15:1287–88.

EPILOGUE

Family and Faith

Philipp and Katharina's second child, Philipp, was born in 1525. Another son, Georg, arrived in 1527, but departed, to his parents' sorrow, in 1529. Magdalena was born in 1531. Melanchthon, the august professor, was often seen on the floor playing games with his children. He told them stories, bits of history, and invented puzzles for them to figure out. Above all, he and Katharina taught them faith in Jesus Christ, and a life rich with prayer. Further, if God did not answer prayer in the way they wished, they needed to remember that in the end, he would grant them something even better.[37]

Philipp routinely practiced his Christian faith when he rose before dawn to say his prayers. Throughout his life, he would teach the Christianity that was his own personal conviction as well as his public proclamation. It was a gospel of tremendous grace, glory to come, and costly discipleship, day by day. "The teacher of Germany," he ever sought to convey the will of God, which was "earnestly and sincerely to experience that God is angered by sinners, and to tremble fearfully before God's anger. Again, it is earnestly and sincerely to experience that God pardons sins for Christ's sake; that he defends those who have been received into grace, that he guides and keeps them by his Spirit; that he wishes them to be afflicted and their flesh put to death, but still consoles and helps them when they are upon their cross."[38] For after the cross comes the resurrection.[39]

If God is for us, who can be against us?
—Romans 8:31

Melanchthon's motto

---

37. MSA 1:226. Cf., Melanchthon, *Ich rufe zu dir*, ed. Martin H. Jung, 72.
38. MSA 4:217. Trans. D. C. Parker, 34–35.
39. Rom. 6:5.

Bibliography

Primary Sources

Calvin, John. *Ioannis Calvini opera quae supersunt omnia,* eds. Guilelmus Baum, et al., 59 vols. Brunsvigae: C. A. Schwetschke, 1863–1900.

Camerarius, Joachim. *Das Leben Philipp Melanchthons,* trans. Volker Werner. Leipzig: Evangelische Verlagsanstalt, 2010.

———. *De Philippi Melanchthonis ortu, totius vitae curriculo et morte, implicata rerum memorabilium temporis illius hominumque mentione atque indicio, cum expositionis serie cohaerentium narratio diligens et accurate Joach. Camerarii Pabep.* Lipsia: Impensis Valentini Voegelini, 1592. Also published in 1566 (see microfiche at Pittsburgh Theological Seminary library).

———. *De vita Philippi Melanchthonis, in qua conspicere licet Historiam Primae Reformationis Ecclesiae, multasue alias Res memorabiles seituque dignissimas.* Hagae-Comitum: Adriani Vlacq., 1655.

———. *De vita Philippi Melanchthonis narratio,* ed. Theodore Strobelius. Halle: Ioannis Iac. Gebaveri, 1777.

Capito, Wolfgang. *The Correspondence of Wolfgang Capito,* ed. and trans. Erika Rummel, with Milton Kooistra, 2 vols. Toronto: University of Toronto Press, 2005–09.

Cramer, Iohann Andreas. *Luther und Melanchthon, Zwey Oden* (Francfurth und Leipzig, 1773).

Erasmus, Desiderius. *Collected Works of Erasmus*, eds. Richard J. Schoeck and Beatrice Corrigan. Toronto: University of Toronto Press, 1974–.

———. *The Epistles of Erasmus from his Earliest Letters to his Fifty-First Year, Arranged in Order of Time*, ed. Francis Morgan Nichols, 2 vols. New York: Longmans, Green, and Co.: 1902–04.

———. *Opera omnia Desiderii Erasmi Roterodami*, ed. Joannes Clericus, 10 vols. Lugduni Batavorum: 1703–06.

———. *Opus epistolarum Des. Erasmi Roterodami*, ed. P. S. Allen, et. al., 12 vols. Oxonii: Typographeo Clarendoniano, 1906–58.

Hutten, Ulrich von. *Opera quae reperiri potuerunt omnia*, ed. Eduard Böcking, 5 vols. Leipzig: 1859–70.

Kalkoff, Paul, ed. *Die Depeschen des Nuntius vom Wormser Reichstage* 1521. Halle: Verein für Reformationsgeschichte, 1886.

Luther, Martin. *D. Martin Luthers Werke: Kritische Gesamtausgabe*, 111 vols. Weimar: H. Bölau, 1883–.

Melanchthon, Philipp. *Corpus Reformatorum: Philippi Melanthonis opera quae supersunt omnia*, eds. K. Bretschneider and H. Bindseil, 28 vols. Halle: Schwetschke, 1834–60.

———. *Ich rufe zu dir: Gebete des Reformators Philipp Melanchthon*, ed. Martin H. Jung, et al. Frankfurt am Main: Gemeinschaftswerk der Evang. Publizistik, 1996.

———. *Melanchthon: Selected Writings*, trans. Charles Leander Hill, eds. Elmer Ellsworth Flack and Lowell J. Satre (Minneapolis: Augsburg Publishing House, 1962).

———. *Melanchthons Briefwechsel: Kritische und kommentierte Gesamtausgabe*, ed. Heinz Scheible, 10 vols. Stuttgart: Frommann-Holzboog, 1977–. Available and searchable online at www.haw.uni-heidelberg.de/forschung/forschungsstellen/melanchthon/mbw-online.de.html.

———. *Melanchthons Briefwechsel: Texte*, ed. Heinz Scheible, 11 vols. Stuttgart: Frommann-Holzboog, 1977–.

———. *Melanchthons Werke in Auswahl [Studiensausgabe]*, ed. R. Stupperich, 7 vols. Gütersloh: Gerd Mohn, 1951–75.

Reuchlin, Johannes. *Briefwechsel*, ed. Matthias Dall'Asta and Gerald Dörner. Stuttgart: Frommann-Holzboog, 1999–.

Schwartzerdt, Georg. *1504: Die Chronik des Georg Schwartzerdt. Eine Stadt lebt ihre Geschichte.* Verlag Regionalkultur, 2000.

Wrede, Adolf, ed. *Deutsche Reichstagsakten unter Kaiser Karl V.* Gotha: Friedrich Andreas Perthes, 1896.

Secondary Sources

Bahn, Peter. *Das Brettener Hundle: Eine Spurensuch.* Karlsruhe: Lindemanns Bibliothek, 2011.

———. "Das Haus am Brettener Marktplatz—Biographische Notizen zu Herkunft und Familie Melanchthons," in ed. Peter Bahn, *Als ich ein Kind war. . . Bretten 1497—Alltag im* Spätmittelalter. Ubstadt-Weiher: Verl. Regionalkultur, 1997, 9–28.

Beuttenmüller, Otto, and Peter Bahn. *Nachfahren Philipp Melanchthons: Eine genealogische Sammlung.* Bretten: Druckerei Esser, 1997.

Beyschlag, Willibald. *Philipp Melanchthon und sein Antheil der deutschen Reformation.* Freiburg im Breisgau: Verlag von Paul Waekel, 1897.

Bietenholz, Peter G. and Thomas B. Deutscher, eds. *Contemporaries of Erasmus: A Biographical Register of the Renaissance and Reformation,* 3 vols. Toronto: University of Toronto Press, 1985–7.

Birnstein, Uwe. *Der Humanist: Was Philipp Melanchthon Europa lehrte.* Wichern Verlag, 2010.

Brennecke, Hanns Christof. "Philipp Melanchthon in seiner Zeit," in *Melanchthon: Zehn Vorträge*, eds. Hanns Christof Brennecke and Walter Sparn. Erlangen: Universitätsbund Erlangen-Nürnberg, 1998.

———, and Walter Sparn, eds. *Melanchthon: Zehn Vorträge.* Erlangen: Universitätsbund Erlangen-Nürnberg, 1998.

Brownworth, Lars. *Lost to the West: The Forgotten Byzantine Empire that Rescued Western Civilization*. New York: Crown, 2009.

Brüls, Alfons. *Die Entwicklung der Gotteslehre beim jungen Melanchthon, 1518–1535, Untersuchungen zur Kirchengeschichte*. Bielefeld: Luther-Verlag, 1975.

Cohrs, Ferdinand. *Philipp Melanchthon, Deutschlands Lehrer*. Halle: Verein für Reformationsgeschichte, 1897.

Corput, Abraham vande. *Het leven, ende dood, van den seer beroemden D. Philips Melanchthon: behelsende met eenen de gedenck-weerdighste saken soo in de kercke als politye voorgevallen, van het jaer 1520, tot den jare 1560, in Duytsch-Land, ende de aen-grensende provintien*. Voor Abraham Wolfganck, 1662.

Cox, Francis Augustus. *The Life of Philipp Melanchthon*. London: Gale and Fenner, 1817.

Czerwenka, Berhard, ed. *Philipp Melanchthon nach seinem Leben und Wirkenz*. Erlangen: Verlag von Theodor Bläsing, 1860.

Deane, David J. *Philipp Melanchthon: The Wittenberg Professor and Theologian of the Reformation*. London: S. W. Partridge, 1897.

Dingel, Irene, and Armin Kohnle, eds. *Philipp Melanchthon: Lehrer Deutschlands, Reformator Europas*. Leipzig: Evangelische Verlagsanstalt, 2011.

Ellinger, Georg. *Philipp Melanchthon: Ein Lebensbild*. Berlin: K. Gaertners Verlagsbuchhandlung, 1902.

Engelland, Hans. *Melanchthon, Glauben und Handeln*. Münich: C. Kaiser, 1931.

Feld, Helmut. "Die Tübinger Universitätstheologie im Urteil Melanchthons," in eds. Stefan Rhein, et al., *Philipp Melanchthon in Südwestdeutschland: Bildungsstationen eines Reformators*. Karlsruhe: Badische Landesbibliothek, 1997, 87–100.

Fraenkel, Peter, *Testimonia Patrum: The Function of the Patristic Argument in the Theology of Philipp Melanchthon* (Geneva: Droz, 1961).

Frank, Günter, "*Accingimur enim non vano conatu ad instauranda Aristotelica: Melanchthons Tübinger Plan einer neuen Aristoteles-Ausgabe,*" in ed. Franz Fuchs, *Der frühe Melanchthon und der Humanismus*. Wiesbaden: Harrassowitz, 2011, 51–72.

Fricke, Michael, and Matthias Heesch, eds. *Der Humanist als Reformator: Über Leben, Werk und Wirkung Philipp Melanchthons*. Leipzig: Evangelische Verlagsanstalt, 2011.

Galle, Friedrich. *Versuch einer Charakteristik Melanchthons als Theologen, und einer Entwicklung seines*. Halle: Johann Friedrich Lippert, 1840.

Göring, Christian Ernst Karl. *Philipp Melanchthons Leben und Wirken. In Fragen und Anfragen für Volk und Jugend*. Nürnberg: Ioh. Phil. Raw'sche Buchhandlung, 1860.

Graybill, Gregory B. *Evangelical Free Will: Philipp Melanchthon's Doctrinal Journey on the Origins of Faith*. Oxford: Oxford University Press, 2010.

———. "Captivity or Autonomy? Philipp Melanchthon's Theological Anthropology," *Inquiry* 54:5 (2011): 460–77.

Greschat, Martin. *Philipp Melanchthon: Theologe, Pädagoge und Humanist*. München: Gütersloher Verlagshaus, 2010.

Hannemann, Kurt. "Wendelin Gürrich der Ältere und der Jüngere (um 1495–1561): Lebenswege und Schicksale," in *Zeitschrift für die Geschichte des Oberrheins* 126 (1978): 145–221.

Hartfelder, Karl. *Melanchthoniana Paedagogica*. Leipzig, 1892.

———. *Philipp Melanchthon als Praeceptor Germaniae*. Nieuwkoop: B. de Graaf, 1964; reprint of 1889 edition.

Hehl, Werner. *Philipp Melanchthon: der Freund Martin Luthers*. Stuttgart: Luther Quell, 1982.

Heppe, H. *Philipp Melanchthon, Der Lehrer Deutschlands*. Marburg: Joh. Aug. Koch, 1860.

Herrmann, Johannes. "Theologische Selbstbehauptung und Politik: das Interim 1548 bis 1549," in eds. Günter Wartenberg and Matthias Zentner,

Philipp Melanchthon als Politiker zwischen Reich, Reichsständen und Konfessionsparteien. Wittenberg: Drei Kastanien, 1998, 167–82.

Hickman, J. T. "The Friendship of Melanchthon and Calvin," in *Westminster Theological Journal* 38 (1975–76): 152–65.

Hilderbrandt, Franz. *Melanchthon: Alien or Ally?* Cambridge: Cambridge University Press, 1946.

Hillerbrand, Hans. J., ed. *The Oxford Encyclopedia of the Reformation*, 4 vols. New York: Oxford University Press, 1996.

Horst, Jesse. *Leben und Wirken des Philipp Melanchthon.* Berlin: Frieling, 1998.

Jung, Martin H. *Philipp Melanchthon und seine Zeit.* Göttingen: Vandenhoeck & Ruprecht, 2010.

Jungk, William T. *Philipp Melanchthon, sein Leben und Wirken.* St. Louis: Eden Publishing House, 1896.

Kaiser, D. Paul. *Philipp Melanchthon, Deutschlands Lehrer.* Bielveld and Leipzig: Verlag von Velhagen & Klasing, 1896.

Keller, Rudolf. "Melanchthon—Leben, Werk, Bedeutung," in eds. Michael Fricke and Matthias Heesch, *Der Humanist als Reformator: Über Leben, Werk, und Wirkung Philipp Melanchthons.* Leipzig: Evangelische Verlagsanstalt, 2011, 11–21.

Kelly, J. N. D. and M. J. Walsh. *The Oxford Dictionary of Popes.* Oxford: Oxford University Press, 2010.

Köhler, Manfred. *Melanchthon und der Islam: ein Beitrag zur Klärung des Verhältnisses zwischen Christentum und Fremdreligionen in der Reformationszeit.* Leipzig: L. Klotz, 1938.

Kolb, Robert. "Philipp's Foes, but Followers Nonetheless: Late Humanism among the Gnesio-Lutherans," in *The Harvest of Humanism in Central Europe*, ed. Manfred P. Fleischer. St. Louis: Concordia, 1992, 159–77.

Keen, Ralph. "Melanchthon and His Roman Catholic Opponents," in *Lutheran Quarterly* 12 (1998): 419–29.

Kühlmann, Wilhelm. "Der Glanz Grühe. Melanchthons Erinnerungen an seine Heidelberger Studienzeit und an Rudolph Agricola," in ed. Franz Fuchs, *Der frühe Melanchthon und der Humanismus*. Wiesbaden: Harrassowitz, 2011, 35–50.

Kuropka, Nicole. *Melanchthon*. Tübingen: Mohr Siebeck, 2010.

———. *Philipp Melanchthon: Wissenschaft und Gesellschaft. Ein Gelehrter im Dienst der Kirche (1526–1532)*. Tübingen: Mohr Siebeck, 2002.

Kusukawa, Sachiko. *The Transformation of Natural Philosophy: The Case of Philipp Melanchthon*. Cambridge, UK: Cambridge University Press, 1995.

Ledderhose, Charles Frederick, trans. G. F. Krotel. *The Life of Philipp Melanchthon*. Philadelphia: Lindsay & Blakiston, 1855.

Lorenz, Sönke. "Melanchthon als Konventor der Tübinger Realistenburse," in ed. Franz Fuchs, *Der frühe Melanchthon und der Humanismus*. Wiesbaden: Harrassowitz, 2011, 73–94.

Maier, Hans. "Philipp Melanchthon: Praeceptor Germaniae," in eds. Günter Wartenberg and Matthias Zentner, *Philipp Melanchthon als Politiker zwischen Reich, Reichsständen und Konfessionsparteien*. Wittenberg: Drei Kastanien, 1998, 11–22.

Maltby, William. *The Reign of Charles V*. New York: Palgrave, 2002.

Manschreck, Clyde Leonard. *Melanchthon: The Quiet Reformer*. New York: Abingdon Press, 1958.

Martin, Petzoldt. "Politisches Handeln bei Luther und Melanchthon," in eds. Günter Wartenberg and Matthias Zentner, *Philipp Melanchthon als Politiker zwischen Reich, Reichsständen und Konfessionsparteien*. Wittenberg: Drei Kastanien, 1998, 23–36.

Matthes, Karl. *Philipp Melanchthon. Sein Leben und Wirken aus den Quellen dargestellt*. Altenburg: Julius Helbig, 1841.

Maurer, Wilhelm. *Der junge Melanchthon: zwischen Humanismus und Reformation*, 2 vols. Göttingen: Vandenhoeck & Ruprecht, 1967–69.

Maxcey, Carl E. *Bona Opera: A Study in the Development of the Doctrine in Philipp Melanchthon*. Nieuwkoop: B. De Graaf, 1980.

Mülhaupt, Erwin. *Heimaterinnerungen und Heimatbeziehungen Philipp Melanchthons*. Bretten: Melanchthonverein Bretten, 1983.

———. "Luther und Melanchthon: Die Geschichte einer Freundschaft," in *Luther im 20. Jahrhundert*. Göttingen: Vandenhoeck & Ruprecht, 1982, 121–34.

Müller, Nikolaus. *Georg Schwartzerdt, der Bruder Melanchthons und Schultheiß zu Bretten*. Leipzig: Verein für Reformationsgeschichte, 1908.

Mullett, Michael, ed. *Historical Dictionary of the Reformation and Counter-Reformation*. Lanham, MD: Scarecrow Press, 2010.

———. *Martin Luther*. New York: Routledge, 2004.

Mundhenk, Christine. "*Natus est Philippus in oppido Bretta*. Melanchthons Kindheit und Jugend in den Lebensbeschreibungen des 16. Jahrhunderts," in ed. Franz Fuchs, *Der frühe Melanchthon und der Humanismus*. Wiesbaden: Harrassowitz, 2011, 9–34.

Neuser, Wilhelm H. *Der Ansatz der Theologie Philipp Melanchthons*. Neukirchen Kr. Moers: Verlag der Buchhandlung des Erziehungsvereins, 1957.

Nitzelnadel, F. A. *Philipp Melanchthon, "Der Lehrer Deutschlands" und M. Luthers treuester Freund und Gehülfe bei den gesegneten Werke der Kirchenreformation*. Saalfeld: Verlag von Constanin Riese, 1860.

Oestmann, Günther. "Johannes Stoeffler, Melanchthons Lehrer in Tübingen," in eds. Stefan Rhein, et al., *Philipp Melanchthon in Südwestdeutschland: Bildungsstationen eines Reformators*. Karlsruhe: Badische Landesbibliothek, 1997, 75–86.

Pauli, Frank. *Philippus: Ein Lehrer für Deutschland; Spuren und Wirkungen Philipp Melanchthons*. Berlin: Wichern-Verlag, 1996.

Plitt, G. L. and T. Kolde. *Die Loci communes Philipp Melanchthonis in ihrer Urgestalt*, 4th ed. Leipzig: Deichert, 1925.

Pohlke, Reinhard. "Melanchthon und sein Griechischlehrer Georg Simler—zwei Vermittler des Griechischen in Deutschland," in eds. Stefan Rhein, et al., *Philipp Melanchthon in Südwestdeutschland: Bildungsstationen eines Reformators*. Karlsruhe: Badische Landesbibliothek, 1997, 39–62.

Posset, Franz. *The Real Luther: A Friar at Erfurt and Wittenberg: Exploring Luther's life with Melanchthon as Guide*. St. Louis: Concordia, 2011.

Probst, Veit. "Melanchthons Studienjahre in Heidelberg," in eds. Stefan Rhein, et al., *Philipp Melanchthon in Südwestdeutschland: Bildungsstationen eines Reformators*. Karlsruhe: Badische Landesbibliothek, 1997, 19–38.

Reichelt, Bettine. *Philipp Melanchthon: Weggefährte Luthers und Lehrer Deutschlands: Eine biographische Skizze mit Aussprüchen und Bildern*. Evangelische Verlagsanstalt, 2010.

Reston, James, Jr. *Defenders of the Faith: Charles V, Suleyman the Magnificent, and the Battle for Europe, 1520–36*. New York: Penguin, 2009.

Rhein, Stefan. "Buchdruck und Humanismus—Melanchthon als Korrektor in der Druckerei des Thomas Anshelm," in eds. Stefan Rhein, et al., *Philipp Melanchthon in Südwestdeutschland: Bildungsstationen eines Reformators*. Karlsruhe: Badische Landesbibliothek, 1997, 63–74.

———. "Katharina Melanchthon, geborene Krapp–Ein Frauenschicksal der Reformationszeit," in eds. Stefan Rhein and Johannes Weiß, *Melanchthon: neu entdeckt*. Stuttgart: Quell Verlag, 1997, 164–89.

———. ed. *Philipp Melanchthon. Biographien zur Reformation*. Drei Kastanien Verlag: Wittenberg, 1997.

Richard, James William. *Philipp Melanchthon, the Protestant Preceptor of Germany, 1497–1560*. New York: G. P. Putnam's Sons, 1898.

Rieger, Reinhold. "Ernst Troeltsch und Melanchthon," in eds. Günter Frank and Ulrich Köpf, *Melanchthon und die Neuzeit*. Stuttgart-Bad Cannstatt: Frommann-Holzboog, 2003, 167–86.

Rogness, Michael. *Philipp Melanchthon: Reformer without Honor*. Minneapolis: Augsburg, 1969.

Schaeffer, Rudolph. *Philipp Melanchthons Leben aus den Quellen dargestellt.* Gütersloh: C. Bertelsmann, 1894.

Schaff, Philip. *Saint Augustin, Melanchthon, Neander. Three Biographies.* London: James Nisbet, 1886.

Scheible, Heinz. "Das Augsburger Interim und die evangelischen Kirchen," in ed. Heinz Scheible, *Aufsätze zu Melanchthon.* Tübingen: Mohr Siebeck, 2010, 392–414.

———. "Das Melanchthonbild Karl Holls," in ed. Heinz Scheible, *Aufsätze zu Melanchthon* (Tübingen: Mohr Siebeck, 2010), 447–62.

———. "Der Catalogus testium veritatis: Flacius als Schüler Melanchthons," in ed. Heinz Scheible, *Aufsätze zu Melanchthon.* Tübingen: Mohr Siebeck, 2010, 415–30.

———. "Die Bedeutung der Unterscheidung von Gesetz und Evangelium für theologische Ethik und Praktische Theologie am Beispiel Melanchthon," in ed. Heinz Scheible, *Aufsätze zu Melanchthon.* Tübingen: Mohr Siebeck, 2010, 241–52.

———. "Die Universität Heidelberg und Luthers Disputation," in ed. Heinz Scheible, *Beiträge zur Kirchengeschichte Südwest-deutschlands.* Stuttgart: Kohlhammer, 2012, 29–48.

———. "Ein Irrtum Melanchthons: seine Warnung vor dem Fürstenkrieg 1551/2," in ed. Heinz Scheible, *Aufsätze zu Melanchthon.* Tübingen: Mohr Siebeck, 2010, 277–86.

———. "Luther and Melanchthon," *Lutheran Quarterly* 4 (1990): 317–39.

———. "Luther und Melanchthon," in eds. Gerhard May and Rolf Decot, *Melanchthon und die Reformation: Forschungsbeiträge.* Mainz: Philipp von Zabern, 1996, 139–52.

———. "Melanchthon als theologischer Gesprächspartner Luthers," in ed. Heinz Scheible, *Aufsätze zu Melanchthon.* Tübingen: Mohr Siebeck, 2010, 1–27.

———. *Melanchthon: Eine Biographie.* München: Verlag C. H. Beck, 1997.

———. "Melanchthon neben Luther," in eds. Gerhard May and Rolf Decot, *Melanchthon und die Reformation: Forschungsbeiträge*. Mainz: Philipp von Zabern, 1996, 153–70.

———. "Melanchthon rettet die Universität Wittenberg," in ed. Heinz Scheible, *Aufsätze zu Melanchthon*. Tübingen: Mohr Siebeck, 2010, 253–76. This article deals primarily with Melanchthon's role in relation to the university during and after the Schmalkaldic War, 1547–8.

———. "Melanchthon und Bucer," in eds. Gerhard May and Rolf Decot, *Melanchthon und die Reformation: Forschungsbeiträge*. Mainz: Philipp von Zabern, 1996, 245–71.

———. "Melanchthon und Frau Luther," in ed. Heinz Scheible, *Aufsätze zu Melanchthon*. Tübingen: Mohr Siebeck, 2010, 373–91. Many of Scheible's essays can be found in multiple sources. This is one such example. It can also be found in the *Lutherjahrbuch* (2001): 93–114.

———. "Melanchthon und Luther während des Augsburger Reichstags 1530," in eds. Gerhard May and Rolf Decot, *Melanchthon und die Reformation: Forschungsbeiträge*. Mainz: Philipp von Zabern, 1996, 198–221.

———. "Melanchthon und Osiander über die Rechtfertigung: Zwei Versuche, Wahrheit zu formulieren," in ed. Heinz Scheible, *Aufsätze zu Melanchthon*. Tübingen: Mohr Siebeck, 2010, 202–17.

———. "Melanchthon und seine Heimat," in ed. Heinz Scheible, *Beiträge zurn Kirchengeschichte Südwest-deutschlands*. Stuttgart: Kohlhammer, 2012, 201–22.

———. "Melanchthon zwischen Luther und Erasmus," in eds. Gerhard May and Rolf Decot, *Melanchthon und die Reformation: Forschungsbeiträge*. Mainz: Philipp von Zabern, 1996, 171–97.

———. "Melanchthons Abschiedbrief an seinen Schüler Jakob Runge," in ed. Heinz Scheible, *Beiträge zur Kirchengeschichte Südwest-deutschlands*, 359–72.

———. "Melanchthons Auseinandersetzung mit dem Reformkatholizismus," in eds. Gerhard May and Rolf Decot, *Melanchthon und die Reformation: Forschungsbeiträge*. Mainz: Philipp von Zabern, 1996, 222–44.

———. "Melanchthons Beziehung zu Leonhard Fuchs," in ed. Heinz Scheible, *Beiträge zur Kirchengeschichte Südwest-deutschlands*. Stuttgart: Kohlhammer, 2012, 329–49.

———. "Melanchthons Bildungsprogramm," in eds. Gerhard May and Rolf Decot, *Melanchthon und die Reformation: Forschungsbeiträge*. Mainz: Philipp von Zabern, 1996, 99–114.

———. "Melanchthons biographsiche Reden. Literarische Form und akademischer Unterricht," in eds. Gerhard May and Rolf Decot, *Melanchthon und die Reformation: Forschungsbeiträge*. Mainz: Philipp von Zabern, 1996, 115–38.

———. "Melanchthons Freundschaft mit Mattäus von Wallenrode," in ed. Heinz Scheible, *Aufsätze zu Melanchthon*. Tübingen: Mohr Siebeck, 2010, 317–27.

———. "Melanchthons Pforzheimer Schulzeit. Studien zur humanistischen Bildungselite," in ed. Hans-Peter Becht, *Pforzheim in der frühen Neuzeit: Beiträge zur Stadtgeschichte des 16. bis 18. Jahrhunderts*. Sigmaringen, Germany: Jan Thorbecke Verlag, 1989, 9–50.

———. "Melanchthons Verhältnis zu Johannes Setzer" in ed. Heinz Scheible, *Aufsätze zu Melanchthon*. Tübingen: Mohr Siebeck, 2010, 309–16.

———. "Melanchthons Werdegang," in ed. Heinz Scheible, *Aufsätze zu Melanchthon*. Tübingen: Mohr Siebeck, 2010, 28–45. This includes sections on Melanchthon's days in Bretten (29–30), Pforzheim (30–32), Heidelberg (32–6), Tübingen (36–43), and Wittenberg (43–5).

———. "Philipp Melanchthon, ein Theologe der Reformation," in ed. Heinz Scheible, *Beiträge zur Kirchengeschichte Südwest-deutschlands*. Stuttgart: Kohlhammer, 2012, 179–200.

———. "Reuchlins Einfluß auf Melanchthon," in ed. Heinz Scheible, *Beiträge zur Kirchengeschichte Südwest-deutschlands*. Stuttgart: Kohlhammer, 2012, 277–306.

———. "Von Meiningen nach Bretten. Melanchthon und Aquila über den Kirchenbann," in eds. Gerhard May and Rolf Decot, *Melanchthon und die Reformation: Forschungsbeiträge*. Mainz: Philipp von Zabern, 1996, 333–52.

———. "Wolfgang Musculus und Philipp Melanchthon," in ed. Heinz Scheible, *Beiträge zur Kirchengeschichte Südwest-deutschlands*. Stuttgart: Kohlhammer, 2012, 349–58.

Schmidt, Karl. *Philipp Melanchthon. Leben und ausgewählte Schriften*. Elberfeld: Verlag von R. L. Friderichs, 1861.

Sell, Karl. *Philipp Melanchthon und die deutsche Reformation bis 1531*. Halle: Verein für Reformationsgeschichte, 1897.

Smolinsky, Heribert. "Politik in der Kontroverse: Philipp Melanchthon und seine altgläubigen literarischen Gegner," eds. Günter Wartenberg and Matthias Zentner, *Philipp Melanchthon als Politiker zwischen Reich, Reichsständen und Konfessionsparteien*. Wittenberg: Drei Kastanien, 1998, 37–52.

Sotheby, S. Leigh. *Observations upon the Handwriting of Philipp Melanchthon, Illustrated with Facsimiles*. London: 1839.

Sperl, Adolf. *Melanchthon zwischen Humanismus und Reformation*. Münich: Chr. Kaiser Verlag, 1959.

Steinmetz, David. *Reformers in the Wings*. Philadelphia: Fortress, 2001.

Stuckwisch, D. Richard. *Philipp Melanchthon and the Lutheran Confession of Eucharistic Sacrifice*. Bynum, TX: Repristination Press, 2011.

Stump, Joseph. *Life of Philipp Melanchthon*. Reading, PA: Pilger Publishing House, 1897.

Stupperich, Robert. *Melanchthon*, trans. Robert H. Fisher. London: Lutterworth, 1965. Republished in 2006 under the title of *Melanchthon: The Enigma of the Reformation*.

———. *Philipp Melanchthon: Gelehrter und Politiker.* Verlag: Muster-Schmidt, 1996.

Urban, Georg. *Philipp Melanchthon: 1497–1560. Sein Leben.* Bretten: Melanchthonverein, 1960.

Vogt, Leo. *1504: Die Chronik des Georg Schwartzerdt. Eine Stadt lebt ihre Geschichte.* Esser Druck: 2010.

Wartenberg, Günter. "Melanchthon: Kursachsen und das Reich (nach 1547)," in eds. Günter Wartenberg and Matthias Zentner, *Philipp Melanchthon als Politiker zwischen Reich, Reichsständen und Konfessionsparteien.* Wittenberg: Drei Kastanien, 1998, 225–40.

Wengert, Timothy J. "Melanchthon and Luther/Luther and Melanchthon," in *Lutherjahrbuch* 66 (1999): 54–88.

———. "'With Friends Like This. . .': The Biography of Philipp Melanchthon by Joachim Camerarius," in eds. Thomas F. Mayer and D. R. Woolf, *The Rhetorics of Life-Writing in Early Modern Europe: Forms of Biography from Cassandra Fedele to Louis XIV.* Ann Arbor: University of Michigan Press, 1995, 115–32.

Wetzel, Richard. "Melanchthons Verdienst um Terenz unter besonderer Berücksichtigung 'seiner' Ausgaben des Dichters," in eds. Stefan Rhein, et al., *Philipp Melanchthon in Südwestdeutschland: Bildungsstationen eines Reformators.* Karlsruhe: Badische Landesbibliothek, 1997, 101–28.

Wilson, George. *Philipp Melanchthon. 1497–1560.* London: The Religious Tract Society, 1897.

Wischan, Frederick. *Philipp Melanchthon, der treue Freund Luthers: zum 400. Geburtstagsjubiläum unserm Volk.* Reading: Zu beziehen von A. Bartels, 1896.

Wohlfarth, Johan Friedrich Theodor. *Philipp Melanchthon. Zum Secular-Andenken an den 300 jährigen Todestag des großen Reformators.* Leipzig: Friedrich Fleischer, 1858.

Zeus, Marlis. *Johannes Reuchlin: Humanist mit Durchblick*. Karlsruhe: Helmesverlag, 2011.

Index of Names and Subjects

A Mighty Fortress (hymn), 2-3
ad fontes, 8, 117
Address to the Christian Nobility, 220-1
Adiaphora, 273, 331
Adiaphoristic Controversy, 331
Adrian/Hadrian VI (of Utrecht) (r. 1522-3), 22, 297-9
Adrianus, Mattäus, 168, 226
Agricola, Johannes, 181, 293
Agricola, Rudolf, 99, 124-5, 138, 243
Albrecht, Archbishop of Mainz, 273
Aleander, Girolamo, 218, 224, 236, 298
Alexander VI (r. 1492–1503), 12, 15, 16, *See also* Borgia family, Rodrigo
Altenburg, 283
Amberg Castle, 28-9

Amsdorf, Nicholas, 161, 181, 238, 254, 256, 260, 267-70, 306, 322, 329, 334
Anfechtungen, 271
Anshelm, Thomas, 87, 133-4, 136, 303
Aquinas, Thomas, 99, 105, 108, 111, 118, 172, 199
Aragon, 22
Aratus (Arat), 135, 227, 278
Aristophanes, 227
Aristotle, 84, 88, 90-1, 107-8, 125, 136-7, 169, 172, 174, 176, 187, 193, 245
Artillery, 7
Astrology, 44, 108, 121
Athenagoras, 169
Augsburg, 147-8, 170-3, 177, 241, 298, 324, 330; interim, 330; peace of, 333
Augsburg Confession, 324-5

355

Augustine, 198, 227, 330
Austria, 21-2, 172, 325

Babylonian Captivity of the Church, 221-2
baccalaureus biblicus degree, 193-4
Baden-Württemberg, 39
Barbaro, Ermolao, 93
Barbarossa, 9, 191, 326
Bavaria-Landshut, 62-5
Balkans, 9, 172
Baltic Sea, 44
baptism, infant, 269-71
Basel, 103, 123, 291, 296, 309
Bavarian-Palatinate War of Succession, 65, 101
Bebel, Heinrich, 122, 138
Belgrade, 241-2, 299
Bembo, 123
Bern, 83
Bernhard, Bartholomew, 251
Besigheim, 72
Bicocca, battle of, 291
Biel, Gabriel, 118, 132
Billican, Theobold, 102
Black Death, *see plague*
Blarer (Blaurer), Ambrosius, 119-20, 123, 133, 291-2
Bologna, 18
Bologna, Concordat of, 16
Bolsec controversy, 332

Bonaventure, 199
Bonn, 329
Borgia family, 11-12; Cesare, 12; Rodrigo, 11-12; *see also* Alexander VI
Böschenstein, Johannes, 168-9
Bourges, Pragmatic Sanction of, 13
Brandenburg, margrave of, 21
Brassican(us), Johannes, 122-3, 130, 138, 287
Breisgau, 70
Brenz, Johannes, 103-4, 155, 326, 331
Breslau (Wroclaw), 294
Bretten, 5, 32-3, 35-48, 53, 61-76, 116, 146-7, 276, 308-320; and the chubby pug gambit, 71-4; Peter and Paul Festival, 65; *Pfeifferturm*, 66; siege of, 62-74
Britain, 44-5
Brussels, 296
Bucer, Martin, 103-4, 155, 327, 329
Buda, 322
Bugenhagen, Johannes, 222, 226, 283, 302, 333
Bullinger, Heinrich, 83
Burchard, Franz, 309, 313
Burgundy, 18, 21-2

Byzantium, 7, *see also* Constantinople

Cajetan, Cardinal, 13n6, 147, 171-3, 216, 298, 323
Calixtus III (r. 1455-58), 11
Calvin, John, 96, 295, 332-3, 335
Cambridge University, 140, 245
Camerarius, Joachim, 58, 149, 278-9, 294, 300, 309, 311, 313, 322
Campanus, Johann, 246
Campeggio, Cardinal Lorenzo, 315-16
Capetian dynasty, 18
capitalism, 49
Capito, Wolfgang, 84, 137, 176, 255, 327
Capnio, *see* Reuchlin, Johannes
Carinus, Ludwig, 311
Castile, 22
Catherine of Aragon, 327
celibacy, clerical, 251, 274, 286, 316-17
Cellarius, Marcus, *see* Zwickau prophets
Cellarius, Martin, 188
Celtis, Conrad, 99-100
Charlemagne, 21
Charles, duke of Burgundy, 24

Charles V, 17-25, 189-92, 219, 221, 224, 229, 234-6, 238, 240-1, 287, 291-2, 299, 322-7
Chemnitz, Martin, 246, 329-31, 333-4
Christendom, 2
Christian II, 231-2, 238, 287
Christoph von Baden, Margrave, 31
Chrysostom, John, 84, 272
Cicero, 123, 125, 132, 303, 308
cities, 49
Clement VII (r. 1523-4), 13, 15, 17-18, 299-300, 323
Cochlaeus, Johannes, 246, 316
Coloniensis, Bartholomaeus, 135
Cologne, 83
Constance, 291; council of, 185
Constantine XI, 7
Constantinople, 7, 18, 151, 326
Contarini, Gasparo, 328-9
Cordatus, Conrad, 327-8
Cordus, Euricius, 209
Cortés, Hernán, 190, 323
Cranach, Lucas, the Elder, 158, 247, 250
Cranmer, Thomas, 85
Croke (Crocus), Richard, 150, 166
Cruciger, Caspar, 186, 322
crusades, 8, 20, 147, 171, 191, 215, 242, 326

de Medici, *see* Medici
de Vauldrey, Claude, 24-5
Demosthenes, 125, 227
Denmark, 44-5
dialectics, 108-9, 121, 125-6, 132, 170, 227
Diedelsheim, 64, 66-7
Dietrich, Leonhard, 113
Dölsch, Johannes, 254
Doria, Andrea, 326
Drechsel, Thomas, *see* Zwickau prophets
Duns Scotus, John, 118, 199
Dürer, Albrecht, 149

Eberhard the Bearded, Duke, 117-18
Eck, Johannes, 177, 179-89, 193-6, 216-9, 224, 246, 298
Ein feste Burg, *see A Mighty Fortress*
Einhart, Carius, 68
electors (of the Holy Roman Emperor), 21, 23, 27
Elizabeth I, 125, 245
Elsaß, 70
Emperor, Holy Roman, 1, 2, 189-91
Emser, Hieronymus, 219, 224, 230
England, 18

Erasmus, 80, 84, 139-40, 155, 174-6, 218, 243, 296-7, 309, 313, 317, 321, 327
Erb, Matthias, 84-5, 119, 249
Erfurt, 293
European Melanchthon Academy, 5, 39
Exsurge Domine (papal bull condemning Luther), 215-19, 222-4, 298

Falk, Katharina (wife of Justas Jonas), 263
Farel, Guillaume, 83
Feudalism, 1, 49
Fifth Lateran Council, *see* Lateran Council, Fifth
firearms, 28-30, 291, 294-5, 322
Flanders, 19
Florence, 19, 291
France, 17-21, 287
Francis, (pope), (r. 2013-), 16
Francis I, King of France, 16-19, 116, 189-91, 240-1, 287, 291, 299, 322, 325, 327
Frankfurt am Main, 309-11
Frecht, Martin, 315
Frederick of Saxony, *see* Friedrich of Saxony
Freedom of a Christian, 222
Freiburg, 306

Friedlieb, Franz, *see* Irenicus, Franciscus
Friedrich, Elector of Saxony, 17, 142, 147-8, 154, 158, 160-1, 169, 171, 190-1, 210, 218-19, 221, 224, 229, 232, 237, 254-5, 257, 260, 263-4, 268-70, 280-2, 294, 297, 305-06, 322
Fugger, Jakob, 172
Fulda, 310-11

Galen, 120
Gallus, Nikolaus, 334
Gansfort, Wessel, 128
Geiler, Johann, 88-9, 105, 107, 112
Geneva, 332-3
Genoa, 291
Georg, Duke of Pomerania, 98
Georg, Duke of Saxony, 180-89, 219, 238, 251, 263, 281
Gerbel, Nicholas, 79-80, 91, 273
Gerson, Jean, 128
Gnesio-Lutherans, 331
Gölshausen, 61, 64, 66-8
Greek language, 8, 90-2, 108, 123, 132-3, 135-7, 142-3, 167, 227, 303-5
Gregory VII, 14
Greiffenklau, Richard (von Vollraths), 292

Grenada, 8, 54
Grumbach, Chilian, 45
Grunenberg, Johannes, 169
Grynaeus, Simon, 81, 83-4, 119, 315
Günther, Peter, 107

Habsburg dynasty, 16, 18-25, 116, 323, 333
Hack, Friedrich, 67
Hadrian/Adrian VI (of Utrecht) (r. 1522-3), 22, 297-9
Hagenau, 136
Hagia Sophia, 7, 151
Haller, Berchtold, 81, 83
Hans Friedrich, Duke, Elector of Saxony, 31
Harquebus, *see firearms*
Harrer, Peter, 46
Hartmanni, Hartmannus, 102
Hassfurt, 44
Hebrew, 123, 130, 168, 255
Hechel, Anna, 45, 313
Hechel, Melchior, 45, 224, 313
Hedio, Caspar, 82, 84
Heidelberg: city, 25, 27-33, 39, 42-3, 46-7, 307, 311; disputation, 154-5; university, 86, 95-114, 118, 315
Heilbronn, 45
Helt, Konrad, 256

359

Helvetius, Conrad, 107-8
Henry IV, 14
Henry VIII, 84, 241, 287, 291, 326-7
Hermann, Archbishop of Cologne, 329
Hesiod, 123, 227
Heß, Johannes, 225, 310
Hilliard, Nicholas, 42
Hiltebrandt, Iohannes, 87, 94, 96, 106, 120, 133
Hochstratten, Jacob, 129-30
Holy League (of Julius II), 18
Holy Roman Emperor, *see* Emperor, Holy Roman
Holy Roman Empire, 16, 18, 21, 116-17 147, 327
Homer, 165, 303-04, 335
Horace, 55
Hospitallers (Knights of St. John), 8-9, 172, 191, 242, 292
humanism, 8, 52, 96, 98-101, 109-10, 112,133, 141-142, 174-5, 306, 315
Hummelberg, Michael, 290, 296
Hundred Years' War, 18
Hungary, 9, 21, 172, 299, 322
Huss, Jan, 185-6, 189
Hutten, Ulrich, *see* von Hutten
Hymnus in angelos, 169, 174

iconoclasm, 262, 273, 276-7, 281
Illyricus, Matthias Flacius, 331
indulgences, 12, 14, 151-3, 173, 185, 286, 298
Indus River, 9
Ingolstadt, 165, 177, 188, 194-7, 287
Inquisition, 11, 22, 62, 334
Innocent VIII (r. 1484–92), 11, 62
Invocavit sermons (by Luther), 282-3, 286-7
Irenicus, Franciscus, 91-2, 102, 119, 132, 134, 155
Isabella (wife of Charles V), 22
Italian Wars (1521-6), 241, 287, 291, 321, 324
Italy, 52

janissaries, 7
Jena, 281-2
Jerome, 198, 301
Jesuits, 326-7
Joachim, Elector of Brandenburg, 238
John Friedrich, Duke of Saxony, 330, 333
John Paul II (r. 1978-2005), 297
John the Constant, Elector, 322, 327
Jonas, Justas, 226, 233, 240, 246, 255-6, 262-3, 274, 325

INDEX OF NAMES AND SUBJECTS

Julius II (r. 1503–13), 12, 13, 15, 18, 116, 151-2
Julius III (r. 1550-1555), 331
Junker Jörg (Georg) (aka Luther), 237, 256-8, 281-2

Kaiserslautern, 293
Karlstadt, Andreas Bodenstein, 161, 176-7, 179-89, 218, 240, 249-57, 259-63, 267, 273, 275-8, 280-1, 283-4, 328
Käuffelin, Balthasar, 146
Kechel, Peter, 46
Kircher, Franz, *see* Stadian
knights, knighthood, 24, 31, 109, 294-5
Knights of St. John, *See* Hospitallers
Knights' Revolt, 292
Knittlingen, 39, 64, 67, 73
Koch, Johannes, 213-14
Koch, Konrad, *see* Wimpina, Konrad
Krafft, Adam, 310-11
Kraichgau Valley, 39, 54, 65, 319
Krapp family, 204-15;
  Hieronymus, 326; Katharina, *see* Melanchthon, Katharina
Krone ("crown") guesthouse/hotel, 38-9, 45, 55, 313-15
Kurfürsten, see electors

Kuropka, Nicole, 4

Landshut War, 65, 75-6, 101
Lang, Johannes, 181, 188
Laskaris, Konstantin, 91-2
Lateran Council, Fifth (1512-17), 13, 16, 116
Leipzig, 149-50, 160, 165, 176, 218, 310, 328; disputation, 180-6, 193, 269; interim, 330-1
Lemp, Jacob, 123, 141, 193
Leo X (r. 1513-21), 8, 13, 15-16, 18, 116, 171, 215, 229-30, 236, 241, 297-8
Letters of Eminent Men, 130-1
Letters of Obscure Men, 131, 170
Leucorea, *see* Wittenberg University
life expectancy, 49
Linck, Wenzeslaus, 253, 300
Livy, 132
Loci communes, 170, 231, 242-6, 278, 302, 325, 329, 332-3
loci method, 126, 229
logic, *see* dialectics
Lombard, Peter, 243
Lorenzo "the Magnificent," *see* Medici family
Lott, Hans, 67
Louis V, Count Palatine, 292-5
Louis IX, Duke of Bavaria, 62

361

Louis XI, 24
Louis XII, 18
Loyola, Ignatius, 326-7
Ludwig V, Count Palatine, Elector on the Rhine, 101
Lucian, 125, 169, 227
Luther, Martin, 1-3, 21, 101, 106, 112, 116-17, 128-9, 148, *passim*; *Anfechtungen*, 271; at the Wartburg, 237-40, 250, 281-2; as Junker Jörg (Georg), 237, 256-8, 281-2; *Invocavit* sermons, 282-3, 286-7; *Ninety-Five Theses*, 151-3, 256; secret visit to Wittenberg, 256-8

Machiavelli, Niccolo, 12
Magellan, Ferdinand, 190, 292
Malta, 292
Mandari, Fandius, *see* de Vauldrey, Claude
Mantuanus (Mantuan), Baptista, 55-6, 62, 111, 123
Marburg, 324
Margaret of Bavaria-Landshut, 62
Marignano, Battle of, 16, 18, 116
Martel, Charles, 20
martyrdom, 171, 231, 295-6
Mary of Burgundy, 24
mass in both kinds, 252-4, 260-1, 263

Maulbronn monastery, 64-7, 72-3
Maurice, Duke of Saxony, 330
Maurus, Bernhard, 133, 142, 146, 170
Maximilian I, Emperor, 16n1, 23-5, 31, 65, 75, 122, 130, 147, 171, 190
Medici family, 11-13, 18-19, 215; Catherine, 18; Giovanni, 12; Giuliano (Giulio), 11, 15, 299-300, *see also* Clement VII; Lorenzo "the Magnificent," 11, 12, 299-300
Megander, Kaspar, 82-3
Mehmed, 7
Melanchthon, Philipp, *passim*; children: Anna, 278, 300-01, 309; Georg, 337; Magdalena, 337; Philipp, 337; engagement, 204-9; marriage, 209-15; origin of name, 92-3; wife, 204-15, 238, 278, 300, 309, 334, 337
Melanchthon House (Bretten), 5, 39-40, 57, 312, *see also* European Melanchthon Academy
Melanchthon, Katharina, 204-15, 238, 278, 300, 334, 337
Mexico, 323
Michelangelo, 12, 215

INDEX OF NAMES AND SUBJECTS

Milan, 18-19, 116, 291
Miltitz, Charles, 173, 219
Möckmühl, 72
Mohács, battle of, 9, 322
Mohr, Georg, 256
Moors, 8
More, Thomas, 84
Moritz, Duke of Saxony, 331, 333
Mosellanus, Petrus (Peter), 150-1, 162, 166, 176, 310
Mühlberg, battle of, 330
Müller, Nikolaus, 39
Müntzer, Thomas, 261, 265-8, 280, 286, 321
Mycillus, Jacob, 35

Nanstein Castle, 293-4
Naples, 18-19, 22
Narr, Hänsel, 109
Nauclerus, Johannes, 134
Nausea, Friedrich, 316
Navarre, 241
Nazianzus, Gregory of, 227
Nebuchudnezzar, 10
Neckar River, 117
Nesen, Wilhelm, 309-11
Netherlands, 16, 22, 39, 79
New Testament in German, *see* "September Testament"
New World, Spanish explorations, 22

nominalism, 91, 118-19, 126, 132
Nördlingen, 102
Nuremberg, 29, 149, 263, 282-3, 295, 311; diet of, 263, 282-3, 297; *gymnasium*, 149, 311, 322

Oberes Reich, 68-9
Ockham, William, 105, 111, 118, 126, 132, 189, 199
Oecolampadius, Johannes, 84, 103, 105, 123-5, 137, 140, 160, 176, 187, 291, 296, 300, 324
Ölbronn, 64, 66-7
Origen, 227
Orlamünde, 283-4
Osiander, Andreas, 294-5
Osman (founder of the Ottomans), 7
Ottoman Empire, 8-10, 16, 21-2, 147, 172, 190, 241-2, 268, 292, 322, 324-5, 333
Ovid, 55

Palazzo S. Marco, 11
papacy, Renaissance, 10-17
Papal States, 11, 12, 14-15, 18
paradox, 91, 108
Paris, *see* Sorbonne
Passional, 247, 272
Passau, treaty of, 333
Paul II (r. 1464–71), 11

363

Paul III (r. 1534-1549), 326-7
Pavia, battle of, 19, 322
Pazzi affair, 11, 12
Peace of the Ladies, 324
Peasants' Revolt, 310, 321
pelican symbol, 41-2
Pellican, Conrad, 160
Persia, 8, 325-6
Peru, 323
Pest (city of), 322
Peter, the , 10
Pfefferkorn, Johannes, 129-31, 170, 216
Pforzheim, 35-6, 39, 45, 58, 76-94, 105, 287, 315
Pighius, 332
Philipp, Landgrave of Hesse, 292-5, 328, 330
Philipp the Upright, Count Palatine, Elector on the Rhine, 27-32, 39, 43, 62, 65-7, 70, 96, 101, 210; daughter Amalie, 98
Philippists, 331
philosophy, 4, 198-9, 333
phoenix symbol, 42, 240
Pindar, 165, 169
Pirckheimer, Willibald, 130-1, 137-9, 149, 176, 218
pirates, Barbary, 9, 191
Pisa, Council of, 13, 18
Pius II (r. 1458-64), 11

Pius III (r. 1503), 12
Pius IV (r. 1559-1565), 334
Pizarro, Francisco, 190, 323
plague (bubonic), 1, 54, 239, 255-6, 291, 323, 326, *see also* typhus
Platina, Bartolomeo, 11
Plato, 166, 169
Pleissenberg Castle, 180
Plutarch, 135, 165, 169, 175, 278
Poland, King of, 31
Pole, Reginald, 84, 331
Politan, 111
Poor Conrad Revolt, 116, 275
Prettin, 268
priesthood of all believers, 220-1
printing press, 49-51
Propst, Jakob, 293
"Protestant" (origin of title), 324
Purgatory, *see* indulgences

quadrivium, 107

Ratisbon, *see* Regensburg
Ravensburg, 290, 296
realism, 118-19, 132
Rechberg, 41, 64
Reconquista, 8
Reformation(s), 3
Regensburg Colloquy/diet, 102, 328-9

Reichstag: in Worms (1495), 24
Reuchlin, Elisabeth, 79, 146
Reuchlin, Johannes, 35-6, 52, 54, 78-9, 85-6, 91-4, 96, 99, 103, 121, 129-31, 134, 137, 141-3, 146-7, 160, 170, 176, 194-6, 287
Reuter family: Barbara, *see* Schwartzerdt; Elisabeth, 35-6, 77-8; Iohannes (Hans),the Elder, 32, 53, 57-8, 69-70, 76, 318; Iohannes (Hans), the Younger, 36, 78, 94
Reutlingen, 194-5
Rhetoric, 109, 125, 132, 135, 138, 170, 227, 329
Rhine River, 9, 19, 39, 68
Rhodes, isle of, 9, 172, 191, 242, 292
Riccius, Paul, 160
Rinklingen, 64, 66-7
Romandy, 24
Rome (imperial), 1, 7
Rome (city), 8, 10, 17, 106, 154, 189, 246, 291, 323
Rubianus, Johannes Crotus, 310-11
Ruit, 39, 41, 64, 319

Safavids, 322, 333
Schaller, Bartholmäus, 227-8

Schedel, Albrecht, 69-70
Scheurl, Christoph, 149, 162, 169, 177, 186
Schleupner, Dominicus, 209
Schmalkaldic League, 325
Schmalkaldic War, 330
Schmeltzle, Jacob, 69-70
Schnepf, Erhard, 102, 155
scholasticism, 110, 118, 123, 125, 176, 187, 198-9, 240
Schurf, Jerome, 161 (cf. 254)
Schurff, Augustine, 327
Schurff, Hieronymous, 254 (cf. 161)
Schwartzerdt coat of arms, 25
Schwartzerdt family: Anna (M's sister), 45; Barbara (M's aunt), 27-8; Barbara (M's mother), 32, 35-48, 52, 58, 76-8, 95, 115, 145-7, 195, 224, 307, 309, 312-14; Barbara (M's sister), 46; Elisabeth (M's paternal grandmother), 27; Georg (the Elder) (M's father), 25, 27-33, 35-48, 52-3, 58, 61, 75-6, 95; Georg (the Younger) (M's brother), 45, 71, 73, 78, 94, 313; Iohannes (Hans) (M's uncle), 27-8, 52; Margarethe (M's sister), 46; Nikolaus (Claus) (M's grandfather), 27

Schwebel, Johannes, 102, 119, 195
Seegrehna, 261, 265, 275
Seidler, Jacob, 251
"September Testament," 258, 281, 301
Setzer (Secerius), Johann, 133
Shakespeare, 125
Shalmaneser, 10
Sicily, 9, 22, 326
Silberborner, Johannes, 309, 313
Simler, Georg, 78-94, 96, 99, 120, 135, 137, 141, 146, 175
simony, 12-14
Sistine Chapel, 12, 323
Sixtus IV (1471–84), 11, 12, 17
sola scriptura, 199
Solomon, 10
Sorbil, Iohannes, 102
Sorbonne, 233, 240
Spain, 8, 16, 18-19
Spalatin, Georg, 148-9, 161-2, 164, 170-1, 232, 238, 245-6, 256-8, 268, 283, 329
Spangel, Pallas, 97-8, 103, 110-12, 115
Speyer, 33, 53, 76, 94-5; diet of, 322, 324
spiritual disciplines, 30
Sprantal, 64, 66-7
St. Peter's basilica, 96, 116-17, 151

Stadian, Francis (*aka* Franz Kircher), 121, 137
Staupitz, Johannes, 154, 171-72, 219
Stein, Wolfgang, 293
Stockholm, bloodbath, 231, 287
Stöffler, Johannes, 121-2, 135, 140
stoicism, 45
Storch, Nicholas, *see* Zwickau prophets
Strasbourg, 68, 84, 102-3
Strauss, Jacob, 310
Strigel, Victor, 246
Stübner, Marcus, *see* Zwickau prophets
Stuchs, Andreas, 46
Stuttgart, 39, 78, 129, 146, 194-6, 287, 316
Suleiman, 9-10, 19, 240, 322, 325-7
Summenhart, Konrad, 118
Sturm, Jacob, 102
Sturm, Peter, 102
Sundgau, 70
Swabia, 39
Swabian League, 194-6, 237, 294-5
Swiss Confederation, 16
Switzerland, 24, 289-90

Terence, 123, 132, 135, 139

theology (Melanchthon's), 4
Torquemada, 11
Tours, Battle of, 20
translation of New Testament into German, *see* "September Testament"
transubstantiation, 123, 193
Trent, Council of, 329-31
Trier, 282, 292-3
trivium, 107
Tübingen University, 45, 84, 94, 112, 115-43, 170, 326
Tunis, , 326
Turks, *see also* Ottoman Empire
typhus , 53-4

Ulrich, Duke, von Württemberg, 31, 65, 67, 70-4, 78, 84, 116, 145, 194-6, 275
Umayyads, 20
Unger, Iohannes, 54-8, 87
Utrecht, 297

Valois dynasty, 16-20, 23-4, 116; Henry, 18; Philip, 18
via antiqua, 105, 108, 118
via moderna, 105, 111, 118, 126, 132
Vienna, 9, 23, 324, 326
Vierdung, Iohannes, 44
Virgil, 55, 122, 132, 227

Visigoths, 17
von Amsdorf, *see* Amsdorf
von Baden, Margrave Ernst, 58
von Bora, Katharine, 322
von Dalberg, Johann, 47, 98-9, 101
von dem Busche, Hermann, 315
von Dolzig, Hans, 250
von Hutten, Ulrich, 115, 130, 216, 230, 282, 292, 294-7, 309, 311, 317
von Karldstadt, Andreas Bodenstein, *see* Karlstadt
von Löwenstein, Count (and sons), 105, 111, 113, 132-3, 136
von Mochau, Anna (wife of Karlstadt), 261-2, 275-6
von Sickingen, Conrad, 145
von Sickingen, Francis (Franz), 130, 216, 230, 282, 292-5
von Staupitz, 154, 171 *see also* Staupitz

Wartburg, 237-40, 250, 281-2
Weimar, 251, 293, 310, 328
Weingarten, 67-8
Weinsberg, 72, 103
Welschland, *see* Romandy
Wettin family, 160

Wimpfeling, Jacob, 88, 99, 101, 105–6, 135, 175
Wimpina, Konrad, 86
Windsor, Treaty of, 291
witchcraft, 11, 61–3, 67, 276
Wittenberg: city, 3, 142–78, and *passim*; Concord, 327; University, 160–1, and *passim*
Worms, 24, 31; diet of, 229–37, 240–2; Edict of, 236, 238, 297, 322, 324
Wroclaw, *see* Breslau

Württemberg, 39, 96, 102, 117–18, 194–6, 326, 331

Zerbst, 330
Zweibrücken, 102
Zwickau prophets, 261, 265–72, 274–5, 280, 286, 292
Zwilling, Gabriel, 238, 250–7, 259–63, 267, 276–8, 280, 283
Zwingli, Huldrych, 83, 103, 289–91, 324–5

Index of Biblical References

Genesis
12:1-2.......145

Exodus
20:3-5.......279, 304 n. 47
34:13.......279

Deuteronomy
4:24.......273

Joshua
1:6-7.......234-5

1 Kings
15:14.......279

2 Kings
2:9-14.......241

Psalms
103:15-16.......1
119:164.......30

Proverbs
22:6.......49

Matthew
5:39.......190
7:15-20.......272
13:57.......145, 317
16.......186
22:37.......262
23:8.......261
24:6-8.......7

Mark
12:30.......262

Luke
7:23.......262
10:27.......262
23:38.......77

John
4:24.......264

Acts
5:38.......272
25:11.......223

Romans
3:4.......173
6:5.......339
8:31.......212, 339

1 Corinthians
6:1-7.......30

2 Corinthians
12:2.......273

Galatians
6:2.......239
5:13.......207

Ephesians
6:13.......27

Hebrews
12:29.......273
13:14.......291

1 John
4:1.......267, 272
4:16.......47

Revelation
10:10.......323

www.ingramcontent.com/pod-product-compliance
Lightning Source LLC
Chambersburg PA
CBHW071146070526
44584CB00019B/2677